Burning Desires

Also by W. Park Kerr:

THE EL PASO CHILE COMPANY'S
TEXAS BORDER COOKBOOK
(1992)

THE EL PASO CHILE COMPANY S

Burning Desires

Salsa, Smoke, and Sizzle from Down by the Rio Grande

W. PARK KERR and MICHAEL McLAUGHLIN

WILLIAM MORROW AND COMPANY, INC.

NEW YORK

Library of Congress Cataloging-in-Publication Data

Kerr, W. Park.
    The El Paso Chile Company's burning desires : salsa, smoke, and
sizzle from down by the Rio Grande / by W. Park Kerr and Michael McLaughlin.

        p.   cm.
    Includes index.
    ISBN 0-688-12818-1
    1. Salsas (Cookery)   2. Cookery—Texas—El Paso Region.
3. Cookery, American—Southwestern style.   I. El Paso Chile
Company.   II. McLaughlin, M.   III. Title.
TX819.A1K47   1994
641.8'14—dc20   93-42039
                                                        CIP

Printed in the United States of America

First Edition

1   2   3   4   5   6   7   8   9   10

BOOK DESIGN BY LESLIE PIRTLE

To
Monica Lee Belle Kerr Henschel
and
Sean Michael Henschel

For tremendous sacrifice, dedication, and love,
giving new meaning to the words "family business"

CONTENTS

WITH BOUNDLESS GRATITUDE (BUT LIMITED SPACE), I WOULD LIKE to gratefully acknowledge the substantial contributions the following people have made to this book:

Elaine Corn, for the title

Linda Fields, Chantal Cookware; Nancy Ganassini, Cuisinart; Pat Tate, House of Seagram's; and Della Burns, Jim Beam Distillers, for helping to stock the kitchen and the bar

Francine Maroukian, Rick and Deanne Bayless, Steve Lange, and Mick Lynch, for sharing recipes with me

Cousin Don Seward of The Wagon Wheel Café in Lampassas, Texas, for giving me long-distance brisket lessons and for telling me about the smoke ring

Bill Adler, my agent, and Lisa Ekus, Lou Ekus, and Merrilyn Siciak, my publicists, for battling my battles and singing my praises

Lauren Lynch, for being the most cheerful and energetic kitchen assistant any author could wish for

John Werner, for introducing me to Michael McLaughlin

Michael McLaughlin, for cooking and writing in the true Southwestern spirit

Lisa Haney and Leslie Pirtle, for illustrating and designing beautiful books

A whole passel of people at William Morrow, including Al Marchioni, a publisher with one hell of a sense of humor; Skip Dye in Marketing; Scott Manning in Publicity; and all my editors—Maria Guarnaschelli, Harriet Bell, and Ann Bramson—all of whom like it as hot and smoky as I do

Martina Lorey, my wife, for designing a beautiful and practical kitchen, for not divorcing me during this book either, and for collaborating with me on my most exciting project yet, our son, Greyson Park Kerr.

why i like it hot and smoky

YOU MAY THINK YOU KNOW SOUTHWESTERN COOKING, AND YOU MIGHT FAIRLY confidently list among its main flavors chiles, cumin, garlic, oregano, and cilantro. You would surely name among its major building blocks beans and tortillas. You would be right, of course, but your list would be lacking two elements, ones that are not quite flavors and that cannot quite be thought of as building blocks but are nevertheless essential to understanding, duplicating, and celebrating the unique foods of the American Southwest.

Try this. On a late summer day, in the heart of west Texas, still hot but with the promise of fall in the air and a bumper crop of green chiles in the fields of the Mesilla Valley, lay a fat, just harvested specimen (Big Jim, Sandia, or another favorite cultivar) on a grill rack close above a hot mesquite fire. First comes the sizzle and then your nose is filled with the twin smells that will complete your list: smoke, and the heated tingle (not the taste) of chiles. Together these fiery fumes sum up for me the cooking of this intersection of Texas, Old Mexico, and New Mexico.

And just about everywhere else, I might add. No one needs to argue that grilling and smoking have found their way out of the backyard and on to the culinary main stage all across the land, a state of affairs that leaves me, a ninth-generation Texan and a man who has been grilling and smoking for many years, very happy indeed.

Now consider this: Slip the burned peel off that mesquite-roasted green chile, chop it together with a ripe tomato, a bit of onion, a minced fresh serrano, and a squeeze of lime juice and you'll then have the ultimate garnish, accompaniment, condiment, and best friend to grilled or smoked food anyone, anywhere, every stirred up—*salsa!*

I'm passionate about salsa, its forms and permutations, its colors, textures, consistency, and burn quotient. I'm also hot for barbecue sauces, marinades, rubs, glazes, mops, butters, and all the other countless spicy and savory ways a hot-from-the-grill or fragrant-from-the-smoker plate of food can get powered up. This happy mating dance between the smoky and the hot is the subject of this book, intended to be a kind of bible for salsa lovers, a friendly guide to amateur grillers and beginning smokers, and an absolutely essential addition to the bookshelf of every home cook who, like me, loves it oh-so-hot.

W. Park Kerr
El Paso, Texas

PART ONE

Light My Fire

salsas and sauces

IN THE BEGINNING, THERE WAS ONLY COOKED MEAT—A DARK TIME, AS I'M SURE you'll agree. Then there was light, or at least there was heat, and the fiery condiments that make life really worth living were born. Some credit the creator, others the Pace Picante Sauce Company of San Antonio, Texas, while I give more general thanks, since for me, the sauce (*salsa* in Spanish) is, to quote a great chef, everything. Smoky and juicy from the grill, a piece of chicken, beef, or pork is merely an edible blank canvas, waiting for the color, form, and content that a properly made sauce or salsa provides. Even though I manufacture salsas, as a perfectionist (and a man who loves to dabble in the kitchen), I can understand all too well your desire to stir up salsas, sauces, glazes, bastes, dips, and mops from scratch. That's what the following section of this book is all about.

Grilled Pico de Gallo

MAKES ABOUT 3 CUPS

Pico de gallo is the reigning fresh table condiment of El Paso. Not a soupy salsa, more a crunchy, hot, and smoky vegetable relish, it's hand-chopped with a knife rather than puréed in a blender. When made with ingredients that have been grilled over a wood chip—boosted fire, it's particularly habit-forming, and very appropriate served with tostaditas, eggs, fajitas, tacos al carbón, and indeed almost anything else that wants a little spicing up. (Several days past its prime, when the salsa's texture has softened but its flavor remains, purée it into marinades for fajitas or other foods destined for the grill.)

❧

INGREDIENTS

2 cups wood smoking chips, preferably mesquite
2 large ripe tomatoes (about 1 pound total), halved
1 medium white onion (about 8 ounces),
cut into 3 thick slices
Olive oil for grilling
6 long green chiles

¾ cup canned tomato juice
2 fresh yellow (güero) or jalapeño chiles, stemmed
and finely hand-chopped
⅓ cup finely chopped fresh cilantro
3 tablespoons fresh lime juice
¾ teaspoon salt

Light a charcoal fire and let it burn until the coals are evenly white or preheat a gas grill (medium). Wrap the wood chips partially in foil, creating a small packet that is open at the top. Set the packet on the hot coals or hot lava stones; position the grill rack about 6 inches above the heat source.

When the chips are smoking, brush the tomato halves and onion slices with a little olive oil. Place the tomato halves, onion slices, and long green chiles on the grill rack, cover, and cook,

turning once or twice, until the tomatoes are smoky and lightly colored, the onions are fairly well browned, and the chiles are lightly and evenly charred, about 8 minutes. Remove from the heat. In a closed paper bag, steam the chiles until cool. Rub off the burned peels, then remove the stems and seeds.

With a long, sharp knife, finely chop the chiles, tomatoes, and onions. In a medium bowl, combine the chopped chiles, tomatoes, and onions with the remaining ingredients. Adjust the seasoning. *Refrigerate for about 30 minutes before serving.* The texture of the salsa is best the same day it is prepared.

HOT TIP Set up your backyard grill near the garden hose. This is useful for rinsing barbecue sauce off your hands, putting out accidental brushfires, and warning the dog away from the steaks.

Evil Jungle Prince Salsa

MAKES ABOUT 4 CUPS

Somewhere in the jungles of tropical Central America (as played in the Saturday matinee movie screen in my mind) there lives the villain for whom this fiery condiment is named. All you need to know is that the habanero—or Scotch bonnet—is the hottest chile on earth. And that is why the jungle prince is called evil. Actually things don't get really devilish until you add that second habanero. Up until that point, this salsa is sweet-hot and crunchy, the perfect accompaniment to smoky grilled chicken, fish, and shrimp. So unique is the heat generated by the habanero that while you can use jalapeños instead, even a lot of jalapeños, and make a salsa every bit as hot or hotter, the dazzling effect still won't be the same.

❧

INGREDIENTS

3 large ripe tomatoes (about 1½ pounds total)
⅓ cup finely chopped white onions
¼ cup fresh orange juice
1 or 2 fresh habanero chiles, stemmed and coarsely chopped
1 tablespoon fresh lime juice
1½ teaspoons salt

⅔ cup finely diced seedless cucumber
⅔ cup finely diced red radish
⅔ cup finely diced jicama root
⅓ cup finely chopped cilantro
3 tablespoons finely chopped fresh mint

Trim and halve the tomatoes. Gently squeeze out and discard the seeds and juice. Chop the tomatoes.

In a food processor, combine the tomatoes, onions, orange juice, habaneros, lime juice, and salt and process until fairly smooth. Transfer the purée to a bowl and stir in the diced cucumber, radish, jicama, cilantro, and mint. Adjust the seasoning. *Refrigerate for at least 30 minutes before serving. The salsa can be prepared up to 1 day in advance.*

Salsa Borracho

Dried chiles rather than fresh, as well as broiled tomatoes and a generous splash of good tequila, all contribute to this brick-colored potion's almost overwhelming depth of flavor. It's good with tostaditas and drinks, maybe even better on grilled meats, burgers, and even pizza. Among salsas, this is one of the more labor-intensive, but all that toasting, roasting, and soaking can be completed well in advance: This is one fresh salsa that actually improves after a day or two in the refrigerator.

INGREDIENTS

4 large dried red New Mexico chiles
1 large ancho chile
2 cups boiling water
2 large ripe tomatoes (about 1 pound total)
¹/₃ cup finely chopped white onions
¹/₄ cup gold tequila

4 garlic cloves, peeled and coarsely chopped
3 tablespoons fresh lime juice
1 to 1¹/₂ fresh jalapeño chiles, stemmed and coarsely chopped
³/₄ teaspoon salt
¹/₃ cup finely chopped cilantro

Set a heavy skillet or griddle over medium-low heat. Place the dried red and ancho chiles on the skillet and toast them, turning once or twice, until they are flexible, fragrant, and lightly colored but not scorched, 4 to 5 minutes. Remove them from the heat and cool slightly. Stem and seed the chiles and tear them into small pieces.

In a medium heat-proof bowl, pour the boiling water over the chile pieces. Cover and let stand, stirring once or twice, until cool. Drain the chile pieces, reserving 3 tablespoons of the soaking water.

Meanwhile, position a rack in the upper third of the oven and preheat the broiler. In a shallow broiler-proof pan, broil the tomatoes, turning them once, until the peels are blackened, about 20 minutes total. Remove from the broiler and cool to room temperature. Core (do not peel) the tomatoes and coarsely chop them.

In a food processor, combine the tomatoes, their peels, and juices, the chile pieces and reserved soaking water, onions, tequila, garlic, lime juice, jalapeños, and salt and process until fairly smooth. Transfer to a bowl. *Refrigerate the salsa for at least 30 minutes, or up to 3 days.* Just before serving, stir in the cilantro and adjust the seasoning.

Two Tomato–Chipotle Salsa

For some pop historians, pumate—sun-dried tomatoes—are the symbol for every excess of the 1980s. I, on the other hand, think they just taste good, and in my kitchen they remain an indispensable pantry item as well as an utterly reliable flavor booster, even in a back-to-basics decade. The good brands are expensive, but a few pumate go a long way, as in this ruddy, new wave salsa, with its intriguing touch of fresh oregano. It works best as a condiment, not as a snack, and goes especially well with eggs, chicken, lamb, and robust fish dishes.

❧

INGREDIENTS

4 long green chiles
2 large ripe tomatoes (about 1 pound)
¼ cup finely chopped white onions
2 chipotles adobado, homemade (page 166) or commercial, with about 2 teaspoons clinging sauce
2 tablespoons fresh lime juice

2 tablespoons olive oil from sun-dried tomatoes
2 garlic cloves, peeled and coarsely chopped
¾ teaspoon salt
½ cup finely chopped olive oil–packed sun-dried tomatoes
2 tablespoons minced fresh oregano

In the open flame of a gas burner, on a preheated grill (over wood smoking chips if desired), or under a preheated broiler, roast the long green chiles, turning them often, until the peels are lightly and evenly charred. In a closed paper bag, steam the chiles until cool. Rub off the burned peels, remove the stems, ribs, and seeds, and with a knife, coarsely chop the chiles. Halve the tomatoes crosswise and gently squeeze out and discard the liquid and the seeds. Chop the tomatoes. In a food processor, combine the tomatoes, onions, chipotles with their sauce, lime juice, olive oil, garlic, and salt and process until fairly smooth.

Transfer the purée to a bowl and stir in the chopped green chiles, sun-dried tomatoes, and oregano. *Cover the salsa and refrigerate for at least 30 minutes before serving. The salsa can be prepared up to 2 days ahead.*

Thunder and Lightning Salsa

MAKES ABOUT 4 CUPS

The name says it all. This smoky pinto bean salsa is as hot as lightning. (As for the thunder, well, that depends on you and your digestive system. Practice seems to help: Eat more beans.) Serve it as a condiment on any grilled or smoked meat, especially beef or pork, or offer it as a nibble with drinks, sprinkled with grated Jack cheese and accompanied by Tostaditas (page 205) for dipping.

INGREDIENTS

1 cup dry pinto beans, picked over

1¾ teaspoons salt

4 large ripe tomatoes (about 2 pounds total)

2 large fresh jalapeño chiles, stemmed and coarsely chopped

4 garlic cloves, peeled and coarsely chopped

¼ cup fresh lime juice

1 teaspoon ground cumin, preferably from toasted seeds (page 9)

½ teaspoon liquid smoke seasoning

⅔ cup thinly sliced green onions

½ cup finely chopped fresh cilantro

In a medium bowl, generously cover the beans with cold water and let them soak for 12 hours. Drain the beans. In a medium saucepan, generously cover the beans with cold water. Over medium heat, bring the water to a boil, then lower the heat, partially cover the pan, and simmer, stirring once or twice, for 20 minutes. Add 1 teaspoon of the salt and continue to cook, stirring once or twice, until the beans are just tender, about 15 minutes. Drain and cool to room temperature.

Meanwhile, adjust the rack to about 6 inches from the heat source and preheat the broiler. In a shallow pan, broil the tomatoes, turning them once, until the peels are blackened, about 20 minutes total. Remove from the broiler and cool to room temperature. Core (do not peel) the tomatoes and coarsely chop them.

In a food processor, combine the tomatoes (including the peels and any juices), jalapeños, garlic, lime juice, cumin, the ¾ teaspoon of salt, and the liquid smoke and process until fairly smooth.

Transfer the purée to a bowl and stir in the beans, green onions, and cilantro. Adjust the seasoning. *Cover and refrigerate for 30 minutes before serving. The salsa can be prepared up to 1 day in advance.*

HOT TIP Toasted cumin has a dark, rich, and especially intriguing flavor. In a heavy dry skillet over medium-low heat, toast about ½ cup of cumin seeds, stirring often, until they are a rich brown—about 7 minutes. Transfer them to a plate or bowl, cool completely, and store airtight, grinding them as needed in a spice mill or with a mortar and pestle.

HOT MENU

Thunder and Lightning Salsa (page 8) with Grated Jack Cheese and Warm Tostaditas (page 205)

BBQ Tuna Steaks with Roasted Corn Vinaigrette (page 78)
Rosemary-Grilled New Potatoes (page 190)

Mandarin-Coconut Yogurt Freeze (page 223)
with Raspberry Sauce (page 225)

Roasted Red Pepper–Mango Salsa

MAKES ABOUT 4 1/2 CUPS

Sweet-hot and very colorful, this chunky red, gold, and green salsa is used as a condiment or dip for grilled or smoked meats and seafoods, not as a snack with tostaditas. It especially complements salmon, tuna, pork, and Skillet-Smoked Shrimp Cakes (page 82).

INGREDIENTS

2 large heavy sweet red peppers, preferably Dutch
1 large ripe tomato (about 1/2 pound)
1/3 cup finely chopped white onions
1 or 2 medium fresh jalapeño chiles, stemmed and coarsely chopped

2 tablespoons fresh lime juice
3/4 teaspoon salt
2 medium ripe mangoes (about 1 1/2 pounds total), peeled, pitted, and cut into a 1/2-inch dice
1/3 cup finely chopped cilantro

In the open flame of a gas burner, on a preheated grill (over wood smoking chips if desired), or under a preheated broiler, roast the red peppers, turning them often, until the peels are lightly and evenly charred. Transfer the peppers to a closed paper bag and let steam until cool. Rub off the burned peels, remove the stems, ribs, and seeds, and finely chop the peppers. Halve the tomato crosswise and gently squeeze out and discard the seeds and liquid. Coarsely chop the tomato.

In a food processor or blender, combine half of the chopped roasted peppers, the tomatoes, onions, jalapeños, lime juice, and salt and process until fairly smooth. Transfer the salsa to a bowl and stir in the remaining red pepper, the diced

mangoes, and cilantro. Adjust the seasoning. *Refrigerate for about 1 hour before using. The salsa can be prepared up to 1 day ahead, with some loss of texture, though its good flavor will remain.*

HOT MENU

Pineapple-Lime Agua Fresca (page 210)

Skillet-Smoked Shrimp Cakes (page 82) with Roasted Red Pepper–Mango Salsa (page 10)
Sweet Buttermilk Slaw (page 184)
Caesar Potato and Tomato Salad (page 188)

Grilled Peaches with Burnt Sugar Sauce (page 230)

Tomato-Basil Salsa

MAKES ABOUT 4 CUPS

Here is a culinary hybrid of a green chile–spiked Southwestern salsa and an Italian-inspired relish of fresh tomatoes, red wine vinegar, garlic, and fresh basil. Use it as a condiment, not as a snack; it's particularly good with plain grilled chicken, lamb, and fish, or Skillet-Smoked Shrimp Cakes (page 82). If you have any left over, toss it with hot cooked pasta, add grated Parmesan, and serve it lukewarm—wonderfully satisfying on a hot day, whether you're in El Paso or Palermo.

INGREDIENTS

4 long green chiles

3 large ripe tomatoes (about 1½ pounds total)

⅓ cup finely chopped yellow onions

¼ cup red wine vinegar

1 or 2 fresh jalapeño chiles, stemmed and coarsely chopped

3 garlic cloves, peeled and coarsely chopped

2 tablespoons olive oil

¾ teaspoon salt

⅓ cup finely chopped fresh basil

n the open flame of a gas burner, on a preheated grill (over wood smoking chips if desired), or under a preheated broiler, roast the long green chiles, turning them often, until the peels are lightly and evenly charred. In a closed paper bag or in a covered bowl, steam the chiles until cool. Rub off the burned peels, remove the stems, ribs, and seeds, and coarsely chop the chiles.

Halve the tomatoes crosswise. Gently squeeze out and discard the seeds and liquid. Cut the tomatoes into ¾-inch chunks.

In a food processor, combine two thirds of the tomato chunks, the onions, vinegar, jalapeños, garlic, olive oil, and salt and process until fairly smooth. Transfer to a bowl, stir in the remaining tomatoes, the green chiles, and the basil. *Refrigerate for at least 30 minutes before serving; adjust the seasoning before serving. The salsa is best used the day it is prepared.*

Cactus Salsa

MAKES ABOUT 4 CUPS

The El Paso Chile Company pioneered Cactus Salsa in a jar; now here is the home formula that first inspired us. Relax: The only thing sharp about this thick green salsa is the taste. Roasted green chiles, tomatillos, and cooked prickly pear cactus pad strips (nopalitos) are seasoned with jalapeños, tequila, lime juice, and cilantro to produce a deliciously fiery salsa, good on Tostaditas (page 205) or as a sauce for grilled foods, especially fish and shrimp. When cooked, fresh nopalitos make an unpleasantly slippery salsa; for this recipe bottled nopalitos actually work better.

INGREDIENTS

4 long green chiles

¾ pound (about 12 medium) fresh tomatillos, husked

2 teaspoons salt

2 cups nopalitos (cactus pad strips), drained and thoroughly rinsed

⅔ cup water

⅓ cup finely chopped white onions

2 large fresh jalapeño chiles, preferably red-ripe, stemmed and coarsely chopped

3 tablespoons gold tequila

2 tablespoons fresh lime juice

2 garlic cloves, peeled and coarsely chopped

1¼ teaspoons salt

⅓ cup finely chopped cilantro

In the open flame of a gas burner, on a preheated grill (over wood smoking chips if desired), or under a preheated broiler, roast the long green chiles, turning them often, until the peels are lightly and evenly charred. In a closed paper bag, steam the chiles until cool. Rub off the burned peels, remove the stems and seeds, and coarsely chop the chiles.

In a medium saucepan, cover the tomatillos with cold water. Stir in the 2 teaspoons salt, set over medium heat, and bring to a boil. Cook, stirring once or twice, until the tomatillos are tender, about 10 minutes. Drain and cool.

In a food processor, combine the green chiles, tomatillos, *nopalitos*, water, onions, jalapeños, tequila, lime juice, garlic, and the 1¼ teaspoons salt and process until fairly smooth. Transfer the salsa to a bowl, stir in the cilantro, and adjust the seasoning. *Refrigerate for at least 30 minutes before serving. The salsa can be prepared up to 1 day ahead.*

HOT TIP Fresh tomatillos don't turn up all that often in produce section (the bad news) but they are excellent keepers (the good news). Buy only those that are firm and free from blemishes (open a few of the papery husks if necessary to get an idea of their general condition). I select medium-large tomatillos (no more than two inches in diameter) and concentrate on those that are dark green (so the final dish has the best color). Store the tomatillos on a paper towel–lined plate in the vegetable crisper of your refrigerator. They'll stay good for at least two weeks, giving you plenty of time to decide which recipe you want to use them in. Canned tomatillos are mainly sour, slippery, and slightly tinny tasting, and I generally avoid them altogether.

HOT MENU

Cactus Salsa (page 12) with Warm Tostaditas (page 205)

Grilled Lamb Burgers (page 121) with Dark Secrets™ Mole Barbecue Sauce (page 19)
Drunken Beans (page 197)
Marinated Pepper Slaw (page 183)
Newfangled Macaroni Salad (page 180)

Strawberry-Chocolate Layer Cake with Buttermilk Fudge Frosting (page 240)

Avocado Salsa

MAKES ABOUT 3½ CUPS

A very chunky salsa, combining some of the tastiest features of fiery pico de gallo and luscious guacamole, it always vanishes quickly when I serve it with lightly salted, just-fried Tostaditas (page 205) and crunchy jicama wedges for scooping. It is also wonderful with omelets and other egg dishes and grilled lean fish.

❦

INGREDIENTS

4 long green chiles
2 large ripe tomatoes (about 1 pound total)
1 or 2 large fresh jalapeño chiles, stemmed and
    coarsely chopped
2 tablespoons fresh lime juice
2 garlic cloves, peeled and coarsely chopped

1 teaspoon salt
2 ripe California avocados, pitted, peeled, and cut
    into ¾-inch chunks
⅓ cup finely diced red onions
⅓ cup finely chopped cilantro

In the open flame of a gas burner, on a preheated grill (over wood smoking chips if desired), or under a preheated broiler, roast the long green chiles, turning them often, until the peels are lightly and evenly charred. In a closed paper bag, steam the chiles until cool. Rub off the burned peels, remove the stems, ribs, and seeds, and with a knife, finely chop the chiles.

Halve the tomatoes crosswise and gently squeeze out and discard the liquid and seeds. Coarsely chop the tomatoes. In a food processor, combine the tomatoes, jalapeños, lime juice, garlic, and salt and process until fairly smooth.

Transfer the purée to a bowl and stir in the green chiles, avocado chunks, onions, and

cilantro. *Cover and refrigerate for at least 30 minutes before serving.* This salsa is best eaten within a few hours of preparation.

HOT TIP The finest long green chiles in the world are grown in New Mexico, in the Mesilla Valley just north of El Paso. Generically called anaheim (the original hybrid of the Mexican *pasilla* was developed by the Ortega canning company of Anaheim, California), the long green has been energetically crossbred in New Mexico for a number of specific purposes—the Big Jim (some almost a foot long), for example, can be harvested, trimmed, and canned, yielding a straight, uniform chile suitable for stuffing. Long greens are workhorse chiles, contributing flavor and some heat to dozens of dishes. The actual heat levels of the numerous cultivars varies (and chiles have been known to do a little crossbreeding on their own), so taste to be certain of what you are getting. Outside the Southwest, the anaheim will probably be your only choice. Medium in size, wall-thickness, and heat, it is an ideal (if unexciting) chile. Long green chiles are blistered in an open flame (preferably on a grill over fragrant wood chips but on a gas burner will do) or under a broiler and then steamed in a paper bag, softening the flesh, loosening the peels—rub them off and then pat the chiles clean with a paper towel—and imparting a smoky flavor. Roasted, unpeeled long green chiles can be frozen, well-wrapped, for up to one year.

HOT TIP Green and aromatic cilantro is essential to Southwestern cookery. It's also quite perishable and needs special handling. Buy only cilantro sold with the roots on; it should be bright green (no brown or yellow leaves) and while it always looks rather tender and floppy, it should not be wilted. At home, fill a medium jar or a tall glass with water. Set the bunch of cilantro in the water (like cut flowers) and cover the entire operation with a plastic bag. Set it in the refrigerator and plan to use it up in no more than a day or two. Cilantro that has gotten droopy (but not off-color) can be used in recipes in which it is puréed, as can cilantro stems, fresh *or* wilted.

Guacamole Verde

MAKES ABOUT 3 1/2 CUPS

This verdant and fiery guacamole is tart, thanks to the inclusion of fresh tomatillos, and buttery-rich, due to the use of black-skinned Hass avocados. It's delicious as a dip with tostaditas (page 205) and/or raw vegetables and nearly indispensable on Grilled Lamb Burgers (page 121), Rosemary Fajitas of Lamb (page 108), Chicken Tacos al Carbón (page 92), and other grilled foods.

INGREDIENTS

3 teaspoons salt

½ pound (about 6 medium) fresh tomatillos, husked

1 cup coarsely chopped fresh cilantro (stems may be included)

5 green onions, tops included, trimmed and thinly sliced

2 fresh jalapeño chiles, stemmed and coarsely chopped

4 large ripe California avocados, pitted and peeled

Over medium heat, bring a small saucepan of water to a boil. Stir in 2 teaspoons of salt and the tomatillos and cook, stirring once or twice, until they are tender, about 10 minutes. Drain them and cool to room temperature.

In a food processor or blender, combine the tomatillos, cilantro, green onions, jalapeños, and 1 teaspoon of salt and process until fairly smooth.

In a medium bowl, coarsely mash the avocados. Stir in the tomatillo purée. Adjust the seasoning. Cover with plastic wrap, pressing the film onto the surface of the guacamole to prevent discoloration. *Store at room temperature for up to 30 minutes, or refrigerate for no more than 3 hours.*

West Texas Red

MAKES ABOUT 3 ¹/₂ CUPS

Here is my quintessential barbecue mop and table sauce, skewed to the levels of heat and sweet we prefer here on the border. When entertaining a crowd, you can multiply this formula upward as needed; leftovers keep well in the icebox or can be frozen for extended storage. Best uses to date: slathered over Smoked Beef Brisket (page 154) or Grilled Lamb Burgers (page 121) at the table and as both baste and table dip for Barbecued Tequila Shrimp with Bacon (page 177). (It's also good in and on meat loaf in place of ketchup.)

⌇x

INGREDIENTS

1 stick (4 ounces) unsalted butter
½ cup finely chopped onions
8 garlic cloves, peeled and finely chopped
¼ cup chili powder blend
2 teaspoons dried oregano, crumbled
2 teaspoons ground cumin, preferably from toasted seeds (page 9)
2 teaspoons dry mustard
2 teaspoons crushed red pepper flakes

2 teaspoons lemon pepper (page 193) or use a commercial brand
4 bay leaves
2 cups ketchup
1 cup mellow dark beer, such as Heineken
6 tablespoons fresh lime juice
5 tablespoons unsulfured molasses
2 tablespoons Worcestershire sauce
2 tablespoons soy sauce
2 teaspoons hot pepper sauce, such as Tabasco

In a medium nonreactive saucepan over low heat, melt the butter. Add the onions, garlic, chile powder, oregano, cumin, mustard, red pepper, lemon pepper, and bay leaves, cover, and cook, stirring once or twice, for 10 minutes.

Stir in the ketchup, beer, lime juice, molasses, Worcestershire sauce, soy sauce, and hot pepper sauce and bring to a boil. Lower the heat

slightly, partially cover the pan, and cook, stirring once or twice, until reduced to 3½ cups, about 30 minutes. Cool to room temperature; discard the bay leaves.

Transfer to a storage container, cover, and refrigerate. *The sauce will keep for up to 2 weeks, or it can be frozen for up to 3 months.*

Thick Poblano Table Sauce

MAKES ABOUT 2 CUPS

Deceptively cool-looking, this thick green sauce actually packs a fiery wallop. It can be enjoyed as a dip for tostaditas (page 205), but it's actually best dripped—or spooned, depending on your heat tolerance—onto grilled meats (especially pork, lamb, and chicken), seafoods, and vegetables. If you wish, add about ½ cup finely minced fresh cilantro just before serving.

INGREDIENTS

4 large fresh poblano chiles
4 tomatillos, husked
⅓ cup chopped white onions
⅓ cup canned chicken broth
2 fresh jalapeño chiles, stemmed and coarsely chopped
2 garlic cloves, peeled and coarsely chopped

1 teaspoon dried oregano, crumbled
¾ teaspoon salt
½ teaspoon ground cumin, preferably from toasted seeds (page 9)
2 tablespoons olive oil

In the open flame of a gas burner, on a preheated grill (over wood smoking chips if desired), or under a preheated broiler, roast the poblanos, turning them often, until the peels are lightly and evenly charred. In a closed paper bag, steam the chiles until cool. Rub off the burned peels, remove the stems, ribs, and seeds, and chop the chiles.

In a blender or food processor, combine the poblanos, tomatillos, onions, chicken broth, jalapeños, garlic, oregano, salt, and cumin and process until fairly smooth.

In a medium saucepan over medium heat, warm the olive oil. When it is hot, add the poblano purée (it may spatter) and bring to a boil. Lower the heat slightly and simmer, uncovered, stirring once or twice, until thick, about 10 minutes. Cool to room temperature. *The sauce can be prepared up to 3 days ahead. Cover and refrigerate, returning it to room temperature and adjusting the seasoning before using.*

Dark Secrets™ Mole Barbecue Sauce

MAKES ABOUT 3 CUPS

Mole poblano, the great and complex Mexican sauce of chiles (and many other ingredients) flavored with just a hint of chocolate, and traditionally served over turkey, is a lot of work to make, hence the popularity of commercial mole pastes, which come in jars. For many Southwesterners these rather one-dimensional pastes represent how mole should taste, and while I regret that more people aren't familiar with the genuine article from scratch, I do admire the convenience of commercial mole. I especially like what it does as one of the several dark and secret ingredients in this potent barbecue sauce. Good (as a table sauce, but not used over direct heat) with various cuts of grilled chicken and beef, this is spectacular on grilled or smoked spareribs and sublime on Chopped Smoked Pork on a Bun (page 161).

INGREDIENTS

2 tablespoons olive oil

⅓ cup finely chopped yellow onions

3 garlic cloves, peeled and finely chopped

1 tablespoon pure, unblended chili powder, preferably from Chimayo, New Mexico

1 teaspoon dried thyme, crumbled

1 teaspoon crushed red pepper flakes

¾ teaspoon ground cumin, preferably from toasted seeds (page 9)

1 cup ketchup

1 cup canned beef broth

⅓ cup finely chopped fresh cilantro

¼ cup commercial honey mustard

¼ cup unsulfured molasses

3 tablespoons sherry vinegar

¼ teaspoon salt

⅓ cup commercial mole poblano paste, such as Rogelio Bueneo or Doña Maria

n a medium saucepan over low heat, warm the olive oil. Add the onions, garlic, chili powder, thyme, red pepper, and cumin and cook, covered, stirring once or twice, for 10 minutes.

Stir in the ketchup, beef broth, cilantro, honey mustard, molasses, vinegar, and salt and bring to a simmer. Cook, uncovered, stirring occasionally, for 15 minutes. Remove the pan from the heat, add the mole paste, and stir until smooth. Cool to room temperature before using. *The sauce can be prepared up to 1 week ahead. Cover and refrigerate, returning it to room temperature before using.*

Oink Ointment™

MAKES ABOUT 3 1/2 CUPS

A salve to soothe scorched pig, particularly pork shoulder from the smoker or ribs from the grill. The generous measure of Dr Pepper in this thin mustardy basting-and-dipping sauce is exactly the right white-trash touch without which pork barbecue, however skillfully done, won't taste authentic. When it's completed, transfer the ointment to a glass Dr Pepper bottle and let it mellow in a shady spot on the back porch (or in the icebox) for 24 hours before using.

INGREDIENTS

1 cup Dijon mustard	½ cup ketchup
1 tablespoon Colman's mustard powder	½ cup frozen apple juice concentrate, thawed
1 tablespoon Hungarian sweet paprika	⅓ cup cider vinegar
1 teaspoon onion powder	1 tablespoon packed light brown sugar
¼ teaspoon garlic powder	1 teaspoon freshly ground black pepper
1 cup flat Dr Pepper	

In a medium nonreactive saucepan, whisk together the mustard, mustard powder, paprika, onion powder, and garlic powder. Whisk in the Dr Pepper, ketchup, apple juice concentrate, vinegar, brown sugar, and pepper. Set over medium heat and bring to a simmer. Cook, stirring often, for 5 minutes.

Remove from the heat and cool to room temperature. *Transfer to a storage container and let stand in a cool place or the refrigerator for 24 hours before using. Unused ointment can be refrigerated for up to 2 weeks.*

Peach of the Old South Barbecue Sauce

MAKES 4 CUPS

This sweet and tangy sauce, spiked with mustard and mellow Southern Comfort and nubbly with bits of tender peach, was designed for using on spareribs (follow the general formula on page 105, omitting the pineapple glaze, basting the ribs with half the peach sauce, and passing the remainder at the table for dipping), but it's also good on chicken and shellfish like shrimp or scallops. The recipe makes what looks like a hell of a lot of sauce, but I rarely have any left over.

INGREDIENTS

1 28-ounce can crushed tomatoes with added purée
½ cup chunky peach preserves
½ cup Dijon mustard
½ cup Southern Comfort

⅓ cup fresh lemon juice
¼ cup packed light brown sugar
2 tablespoons hot pepper sauce, such as Tabasco
1 teaspoon salt

In a medium nonreactive saucepan over medium heat, stir together all the ingredients. Bring to a boil, then lower the heat, partially cover the pan, and simmer, stirring occasionally, until reduced to 4 cups, about 35 minutes. Cool to room temperature.

Transfer to a storage container, cover, and refrigerate. Keeps for up to 1 month.

Mick's Ja-Makin'-Me-Crazy Jerk Marinade and Sauce

MAKES ABOUT 5 CUPS

Inspired by the Jamaican method of marinating and roasting or grilling meats known as jerk, this sauce is dark and fiery. It's loaded with rum and crushed red chiles and generously seasoned with sweet spices, among them allspice (pimienta in Jamaica), without which the authentic island flavor would be missing. Use the sauce to marinate chicken, beef, or pork—especially spareribs or country-style ribs—before grilling, and serve plenty more at the table for dipping.

INGREDIENTS

1½ cups finely chopped yellow onions

1½ cups canned crushed tomatoes with added purée

1 cup Meyers's dark rum

1 cup fresh lime juice

1 cup tomato juice

1 cup molasses

1 cup dark corn syrup

6 garlic cloves, peeled and finely chopped

4 teaspoons crushed red pepper flakes

1½ teaspoons ground cinnamon

1¼ teaspoons ground turmeric

¾ teaspoon ground allspice

½ teaspoon salt

In a medium nonreactive saucepan over medium heat, combine the onions, tomatoes, rum, lime juice, tomato juice, molasses, corn syrup, garlic, red pepper, cinnamon, turmeric, allspice, and salt. Bring to a boil, then lower the heat slightly and simmer, uncovered, stirring occasionally, until the sauce is reduced to 5 cups, about 35 minutes.

Cool to room temperature, and in a food processor, purée the sauce until smooth. *Transfer to a storage container, cover, and refrigerate. Keeps indefinitely.*

Sweet and Hot Red Chile Mustard

This nubbly, burnt orange mustard is perfectly balanced between hot and sweet, and gets a marvelous depth of flavor from puréed New Mexico red chiles. Store it in the refrigerator for up to two weeks and use it on anything that a sweet mustard is good on—smoked meats or seafood, sharp cheeses, hamburgers, and other sandwiches of all kinds. I also like to whisk it into a vinaigrette for spinach salad and often include a spoonful or two in marinades, especially for pork, chicken, and seafood.

⌒∞

INGREDIENTS

¾ cup sherry vinegar

1 cup (about 3 ounces) Colman's mustard powder

2 tablespoons whole yellow mustard seeds

¾ cup Dried Red New Mexico Chile Purée (page 44)

¾ cup sugar

3 large eggs, well-beaten

¼ cup minced yellow onions

2 garlic cloves, peeled and crushed through a press

2 tablespoons fresh lime juice

¾ teaspoon salt

¾ teaspoon dried oregano, crumbled

In a small bowl, gradually whisk the vinegar into the mustard powder. Stir in the mustard seed. Cover and let stand at room temperature overnight.

In the top of a doubler boiler set over medium heat, whisk together the mustard mixture, red chile purée, sugar, eggs, onions, garlic, lime juice, salt, and oregano. Cook, stirring occasionally, until the mustard begins to thicken, about 45 minutes. Continue to cook, stirring often, until very thick, another 20 to 30 minutes.

Transfer to a storage container and cool to room temperature. *Cover and refrigerate; return to room temperature before using. Keeps for up to 10 days.*

Christmas Ketchup

MAKES ABOUT 2¹/₂ CUPS

Long before there was pretty much only tomato ketchup, there were various savory sweet-and-sour condiments that went by that name. Here's a wintertime favorite of mine, utilizing cranberries and fresh pomegranate juice. Though pomegranate trees grace many El Paso yards (and are beautifully ornamental), when I need a generous quantity of fresh juice I prefer to buy the larger fruits that are available in the produce sections of many supermarkets, beginning in late fall. Serve this smooth, thick, and dark purple sauce with Smoked Wild Turkey (page 150), Smoked Loin of Venison (page 165), or Smoked Pork Loin (page 160). It's also great with grilled sausages, on a burger, or as a dip for crisp, hot French fries.

INGREDIENTS

1 12-ounce bag fresh cranberries, picked over and rinsed
1 large heavy sweet red pepper, preferably Dutch, stemmed, seeded, and finely chopped
1²/₃ cups sugar
1 cup fresh pomegranate juice
1 cup red wine vinegar

1 teaspoon salt
¼ teaspoon ground cinnamon
¼ teaspoon ground allspice
¼ teaspoon ground ginger
¼ teaspoon cayenne pepper

In a medium nonreactive saucepan, combine the cranberries, red pepper, sugar, pomegranate juice, vinegar, salt, cinnamon, allspice, ginger, and cayenne pepper. Set over medium heat and bring to a brisk simmer. Cook, stirring occasionally, until most of the cranberries have burst and the liquid has thickened slightly, about 20 minutes.

Remove from the heat and cool slightly, then force the mixture through the medium blade of a food mill set over a bowl. Transfer to a storage container and cool to room temperature. Cover and refrigerate for at least 24 hours to mellow the flavors. *The ketchup can be prepared up to 2 weeks in advance. Return it to room temperature and stir it well before using.*

HOT TIP Pomegranates are mostly seeds, each enclosed in a tiny sac of tart, crimson juice. To extract the most juice possible, buy large fruits. Roll them gently on a flat surface with the palm of your hand until they're soft and rather squelchy-sounding. Hold the fruits over a strainer set over a bowl and one at a time carefully cut each fruit in half horizontally—there will be plenty of juice. Squeeze the seeds out of each half into the strainer. With a wooden spoon, mash the seeds into (but not through) the strainer, to burst the remaining juice sacs. Discard the seeds. Two or three large pomegranates (about 2½ pounds total) will be needed to produce 1 cup juice.

Spicy Peanut Butter Dipping Sauce

MAKES ABOUT 2 CUPS

This smooth and fiery peanut butter sauce will remind you of Southeastern Asian dipping sauces for the skewered, grilled foods collectively known as saté. Pickled jalapeños and a touch of cumin give it border character; try it at the table on spareribs, grilled shrimp, thinly sliced grilled flank steak, or pork kebabs.

INGREDIENTS

¾ cup smooth supermarket (not "natural") peanut butter
⅓ cup minced pickled jalapeño chiles
1 tablespoon unsulfured molasses

1 tablespoon fresh lime juice
½ teaspoon soy sauce
1 cup canned beef or chicken broth

In a small saucepan, stir together the peanut butter, jalapeños, molasses, lime juice, and soy sauce. Set over low heat. Gradually whisk in the beef broth. Heat, stirring often, until the sauce is smooth; do not boil.

Transfer the sauce to a serving dish, cool to room temperature, and use immediately. *Or cover and refrigerate; return to room temperature before using. The sauce can be prepared up to a week in advance.*

Pesto

I know this basil, garlic, and cheese sauce is Italian, but it has a flavor intensity similar to and a wonderful affinity for our local Southwestern ingredients, and when I'm feeling innovative, I often combine it with them. (Perhaps the pine nuts, another essential pesto ingredient, which grow abundantly in the Southwest as well, account for at least some of the success of this culinary hybridization.) Here is my basic formula, followed by two friskier variations.

❧

INGREDIENTS

¾ cup pine nuts

2 cups lightly packed clean, dry basil leaves and tender stems

6 garlic cloves, peeled and coarsely chopped

1 cup olive oil

¾ cup grated Parmesan cheese, preferably Parmigiano-Reggiano

½ cup grated Romano cheese, preferably pecorino Romano

½ teaspoon salt

½ teaspoon freshly ground black pepper

In a medium skillet over medium heat, toast the pine nuts, stirring them often, until they are lightly browned, 5 to 7 minutes. Remove them immediately from the skillet and cool to room temperature.

In a food processor, combine the pine nuts, basil, and garlic and process, scraping down the sides of the work bowl once or twice, until fairly smooth. With the motor running, gradually add the olive oil through the feed tube; the mixture will thicken. Transfer the mixture to a bowl and stir in the Parmesan, Romano, salt, and pepper.

Tightly cover the pesto and refrigerate for up to 3 days. The pesto can also be frozen for up to 3 months; add the cheeses to the pesto only after it is defrosted.

Chipotle Pesto Mince 2 or 3 canned chipotles adobado, homemade (page 166) or commercial. Stir them, along with 2 or 3 teaspoons of their sauce, into 1¼ cups of the basic pesto.

Green Chile Pesto In the open flame of a gas burner, on a preheated grill (over wood smoking chips if desired), or under a preheated broiler, roast 3 large long green chiles or 2 medium poblanos, turning them often, until the peels are lightly and evenly charred. Steam the chiles in a closed paper bag until cool. Rub off the charred peels, remove the stems and seeds, and coarsely chop the chiles. In a food processor or blender, combine the chopped chiles with 1¼ cups basic pesto and process until fairly smooth.

Apricot-Piñon Chutney

MAKES 3 ¹/₂ CUPS

If you think of the Southwest as irredeemably dry, dusty, and unproductive, the number of nut and fruit tree orchards—among other agricultural wonders—that dot the region would astonish you. Chiles (of course), apples, pecans, and especially apricots are among the many products that are locally grown. This chutney celebrates dried apricots, along with another Southwestern resource, pine nuts, in a chunky, sweet-tart relish that perfectly complements smoked meats like Smoked Fresh Ham (page 158), Smoked Pork Loin (page 160), or Smoked Wild Turkey (page 150).

INGREDIENTS

¹/₃ cup pine nuts

1 pound dried apricots, quartered

¹/₂ cup dark raisins

4 cups boiling water

²/₃ cup white wine vinegar

²/₃ cup sugar

2 small dried red chiles, such as
de árbol or japonés

n a medium skillet over medium heat, toast the pine nuts, stirring them often, until they are lightly brown, 5 to 7 minutes. Remove them immediately from the skillet and cool to room temperature.

In a medium heat-proof bowl, combine the apricots, raisins, and boiling water. Cover and let stand, stirring once or twice, for 10 minutes. Drain the fruit, reserving 1 cup of the soaking water.

In a medium heavy nonreactive saucepan over medium heat, combine the soaked fruit, reserved water, vinegar, sugar, and chiles. Bring to a simmer, partially cover, and cook the chutney, stirring often, until it is thick and the fruit is just tender, about 30 minutes. Remove it from the heat, cool to room temperature, and stir in the pine nuts.

Transfer to a storage container and refrigerate for at least 24 hours to mellow the flavor. The chutney can be prepared up to 1 month ahead. If the chutney is to be prepared more than 24 hours in advance, reserve the pine nuts and add them just before serving.

quick-fix:
almost no-cook sauces
for the grill

i am, I admit it, an impatient man. My mother claims never to have read (much less heeded) Benjamin Spock's advice that children should be fed upon demand, and so I have no explanation for that constant, urgent inner voice saying, "Feed me, *now*, damnit!" It is, nevertheless, there, and won't be denied. When the voice is particularly insistent, I head for the grill, and rather than slow things down by simmering up a time-consuming sauce, glaze, or baste from scratch, I turn to the following easy stir-togethers, a modest repertoire of quick and zesty embellishments that mix up in the twinkling of a hungry eye.

Fast and Furious Ketchup

MAKES 1 CUP

This hot and chunky ketchup is good wherever the tamer sort is good—burgers, French fries, hot dogs, onion rings, meat loaf, and on and on.

INGREDIENTS

½ cup thick tomato ketchup
½ cup thick tomato-based commercial medium or hot salsa

i n a small bowl, stir together the ketchup and salsa. Use immediately, or cover and refrigerate; keeps indefinitely.

Chili Ketchup Stir I tablespoon chili powder blend into the ketchup. *Let stand 30 minutes before using.*

Hot and Hasty Barbecue Sauce

MAKES 1 CUP

Use this red-hot concoction as a table sauce for hamburgers, sausages, French fries, beef brisket, or pork spareribs.

❧

INGREDIENTS

½ cup hot, thick and smoky, tomato-based commercial barbecue sauce
½ cup thick tomato-based commercial medium or hot salsa

In a small bowl, stir together the barbecue sauce and salsa and use immediately. *Or cover and refrigerate; keeps indefinitely.*

Pineapple-Mustard Glaze

MAKES ABOUT 2 CUPS

The intense pineapple flavor of this tropical glaze is deliciously apparent no matter which grilled food you choose to brush it on. It goes particularly well with spareribs (page 105) but chicken, pork chops, pork kebabs, salmon, shrimp, or scallops are also successful partners. (For a delicious, completely non-Southwestern variation, I sometimes add a tablespoon or so of grated fresh ginger and a splash of dark Oriental sesame oil.)

❧

INGREDIENTS

1 12-ounce can frozen pineapple juice concentrate, thawed
2 tablespoons Dijon mustard

1 tablespoon soy sauce
2½ teaspoons hot pepper sauce, such as Tabasco

In a small bowl, whisk together the pineapple juice concentrate, mustard, soy sauce, and hot pepper sauce and use immediately. *Or cover and refrigerate; keeps up to 1 week.*

Moonshine Mop

MAKES ABOUT 1³/₄ CUPS

If a man named Jack, who appears to know what he's doing, gives you a mason jar of homemade whiskey, by all means accept it, just be careful how you use it. Memories of a bad morning-after in Philadelphia (apparently a center for clandestine distilling) drove me to find an alternative use for what had mistakenly been billed as a sipping whiskey. The result was this mop. Meant to be slathered over foods as they smoke (where it forms a flavorful crust and helps to retain moisture), it's also good brushed on chicken or ribs near the end of their grilling time. Or, it can be served as a table sauce, though guests should be warned—it's potent!

∾x

INGREDIENTS

1 cup hot, thick, and smoky tomato-based commercial barbecue sauce

1 cup ketchup

½ cup bourbon

¼ cup cider vinegar

1 tablespoon hot pepper sauce, such as Tabasco

n a storage container, stir together the barbecue sauce, ketchup, bourbon, vinegar, and hot pepper sauce. *Cover and refrigerate; keeps indefinitely.*

Orange Barbecue Glaze

MAKES ABOUT 1 CUP

This quick stir-together is vastly tastier than the sum of its simple parts sounds, and is particularly good on grilled spareribs or the pork tenderloin sandwiches on page 126, as well as on chicken and shellfish, especially shrimp.

INGREDIENTS

½ cup hot, thick, and smoky tomato-based commercial barbecue sauce

½ cup sweet orange marmalade

1 tablespoon hot pepper sauce, such as Tabasco

n a small bowl, stir together the barbecue sauce, marmalade, and hot pepper sauce and use immediately. *Or cover and refrigerate; keeps indefinitely.*

Apricot–Double Mustard Glaze

MAKES ABOUT 1½ CUPS

Fruity and mustardy, this glaze is particularly good on chicken or turkey, as well being highly complementary to pork and shellfish grills. Peach preserves or orange marmalade can replace the apricot jam with equally tasty results.

INGREDIENTS

1 cup apricot jam
¼ cup Dijon mustard
¼ cup grainy mustard
1 tablespoon packed light brown sugar

1 tablespoon fresh lemon juice
1 tablespoon soy sauce
½ teaspoon freshly ground black pepper

n a small saucepan over low heat, combine the apricot jam, both mustards, brown sugar, lemon juice, soy sauce, and pepper. Heat, stirring often, until smooth. Transfer to a storage container, cool to room temperature, and use immediately. *Or refrigerate; keeps indefinitely.*

Rio Bravo Baste and Table Sauce

MAKES ABOUT 2 1/2 CUPS

Canned enchilada sauce isn't much use in enchilada making (for that the sauce must be made from scratch), but for adding the sharp note of red chiles to a sweet and smoky basting and dipping sauce, it's ideal. This is especially good on pork, but chicken, lamb, and beef all run close seconds.

INGREDIENTS

1 10-ounce can hot enchilada sauce

1 1/4 cups hot, thick, and smoky tomato-based commercial barbecue sauce

In a bowl, stir together the enchilada sauce and barbecue sauce. *Transfer to a storage* container, cover, and refrigerate. Keeps for up to 1 week.

Six Strange Friends

MAKES ABOUT 1 CUP

Unusual flavors are at work in this intriguing sweet, spicy, and slightly salty sauce. Brush it over chicken, pork, or shrimp near the end of the grilling time, or pass it as a table sauce.

INGREDIENTS

1/2 cup hoisin sauce (available in specialty food stores and some supermarkets)

1/4 cup apple butter

1 tablespoon maple syrup

1 tablespoon commercial horseradish

1 1/2 teaspoons soy sauce

1 1/2 teaspoons Chinese hot oil (available in specialty food stores and some supermarkets)

In a bowl, stir together the hoisin sauce, apple butter, maple syrup, horseradish, soy sauce, and hot oil. *Transfer to a storage container, cover, and refrigerate. Keeps indefinitely.*

Sweet and Smoky Glaze

MAKES 1 CUP

This is fairly fiery, with a flavor that reminds me of Thai cooking, and it grills up into a beautifully shiny glaze flecked with green and red. It's best on chicken, shrimp, pork, and rich fish like salmon or tuna, but lamb and beef will benefit from a generous application as well.

INGREDIENTS

½ cup minced fresh cilantro

⅓ cup orange marmalade

⅓ cup frozen orange juice concentrate, thawed

¼ cup Red-As-Rubies Pepper Jelly (page 62) or commercial hot pepper jelly

¼ cup minced chipotles adobado, homemade (page 166) or commercial

2 tablespoons Oriental sesame oil, from roasted seeds

1 tablespoon fresh lime juice

In a small nonreactive saucepan over low heat, stir together the cilantro, marmalade, orange juice concentrate, hot pepper jelly, chipotles, sesame oil, and lime juice. Heat, stirring often, until the marmalade and jelly have melted and the sauce is fairly smooth. Cool to room temperature before using. *The sauce can be refrigerated, covered, for up to 1 week. Rewarm until smooth if necessary before using.*

Peppery Apple Sauce for Basting and Dipping

MAKES ABOUT 2¹/₄ CUPS

Sweet, hot, and tart, this crimson, apple-flavored sauce is a natural baste for spareribs, shrimp, turkey, and chicken. Brush some over the foods as they near the end of their grilling time; warm the remainder slightly and pass it at the table for dipping and drizzling.

∾

INGREDIENTS

1 cup frozen apple juice concentrate, thawed

²/₃ cup ketchup

¹/₃ cup hot, thick, and smoky tomato-based commercial barbecue sauce

2 tablespoons fresh lemon juice

1 tablespoon soy sauce

1 teaspoon freshly ground black pepper

1 teaspoon hot pepper sauce, such as Tabasco

1 teaspoon natural liquid smoke flavoring

In a bowl, whisk together the apple juice concentrate, ketchup, barbecue sauce, lemon juice, soy sauce, pepper, hot pepper sauce, and liquid smoke. *Transfer to a storage container, cover, and refrigerate. The sauce can be prepared up to 1 week in advance.*

Three Red Fruits Glaze

MAKES ABOUT 1 ½ CUPS

This glistening glaze is hot, sweet, and tomato-y—perfect for slathering over chicken, turkey, shrimp, or spicy pork sausages (page 106) as they near the end of their time on the grill.

INGREDIENTS

½ cup crab apple jelly

½ cup Red-As-Rubies Pepper Jelly (page 62) or commercial hot pepper jelly

½ cup canned crushed tomatoes with added purée

In a small saucepan over low heat, combine the crab apple jelly, hot pepper jelly, and tomatoes. Heat, stirring often, until smooth.

Cool slightly before using. *Keeps, refrigerated, indefinitely; reliquefy over low heat if necessary before using.*

Curried Marmalade-Mustard Glaze

MAKES 2 CUPS

This sweet-hot, pungent mixture grills into a shiny golden glaze that is particularly good on shrimp, chicken (page 87), or almost any cut of pork.

❧

INGREDIENTS

1 cup Dijon mustard

½ cup orange marmalade

½ cup Red-As-Rubies Pepper Jelly (page 62) or commercial hot pepper jelly

¼ cup honey

1 tablespoon curry powder

1 tablespoon fresh lemon juice

In a small heavy nonreactive saucepan, combine the mustard, marmalade, hot pepper jelly, honey, curry powder, and lemon juice. Set the pan over low heat and bring to a simmer.

Cook, stirring constantly, for 5 minutes. Cool to room temperature, transfer to a container, and cover. *The glaze can be refrigerated for up to 2 weeks. Return it to room temperature before using.*

Barbecue Mustard

MAKES ABOUT 1 CUP

This quickly-mixed-up and altogether delicious little sauce is always in my refrigerator, waiting to be lavishly spread on burgers, grilled chicken, or spicy pork sausages like those on page 106. It also makes a fine dip for grilled shrimp or vegetables and is an excellent addition to a towering (ungrilled) ham and Swiss cheese sandwich.

INGREDIENTS

½ cup hot, thick, and smoky tomato-based commercial barbecue sauce

⅓ cup Dijon mustard

2 teaspoons packed light brown sugar

2 teaspoons adobo from homemade (page 166) or commercial chipotles adobado

In a small bowl, stir together the barbecue sauce, mustard, brown sugar, and adobo.

Transfer to a storage container and refrigerate until using. *Keeps indefinitely.*

spice mixtures, marinades, dressings, and butters

I F FINESSE WERE EASY TO COME BY, IT WOULD BE CALLED SOMETHING ELSE— dumb luck, probably. You may grill and smoke for years, getting the timing, the fuel, and the other basics honed to a fare-thee-well and still fail to approach real glory. Such splendor is in the details, and when it comes to food, "details" translates into three simple words: flavor, flavor, flavor. Without this there is only okay, which is fine for some humdrum people, but not, I think, for you or me. The point I'm getting at here is, more is more. Even a terrific, *homemade* table salsa or sauce can use a little assistance. Spice mixtures rubbed into the meat or seafood before it hits the heat, marinades that flavor and tenderize, zesty butters that melt unctuously over the finished food, and tangy dressings that aid and abet rubs, marinades, and plain old smoke, provide, fore and aft, the layering of tastes that transforms your grilled or smoked food into truly sublime fare. Consider, to begin, the following.

Hot and Heavy Rub

MAKES ENOUGH DRY RUB FOR ABOUT 3 POUNDS OF MEAT, CHICKEN, OR ROBUST FISH

Rubs possibly contribute deep, inner flavor to smoked foods (they are definitely part of the kind of messing around in the kitchen guys love), but the crusts they form really do help seal in juices, and they taste good too. More fundamental than this it doesn't get, but I confess that when confronted by a well-filled spice rack, I'm likely to triple this ingredient list. A little of this and a lot of that added to a rub always make me feel better, whether they do the barbecue any good or not.

❧

INGREDIENTS

¼ cup packed light brown sugar
1 tablespoon kosher salt

1 tablespoon freshly ground black pepper

In a small bowl, thoroughly mix together the sugar, salt, and pepper. Pat the rub thickly over the meat or fish you are going to smoke. *Cover and let stand at room temperature for at least 1 hour or refrigerate for up to 24 hours.*

Chimayo Chile Rub When mixing together the Hot and Heavy Rub, add 2 tablespoons pure, unblended chili powder from Chimayo, New Mexico.

Rib Rub

This spicy and deeply flavorful rub, especially when paired with the barbecue sauce I call West Texas Red (page 17), is the best friend a rack of ribs (or a brisket of beef) can have. Mix up a big batch of this and keep it on hand.

INGREDIENTS

1 tablespoon ground cumin, preferably from toasted seeds (page 9)

1 tablespoon chili powder blend

1 tablespoon sugar

1 tablespoon kosher salt

1 tablespoon freshly ground black pepper

1 tablespoon dried oregano, crumbled

2 teaspoons garlic powder

In a small bowl, stir together the cumin, chili powder, sugar, salt, pepper, oregano, and garlic powder. Pat the rub thickly over the meat you are going to smoke, using it all. *Cover and let stand at room temperature for at least 1 hour or refrigerate for up to 24 hours.*

Fresh Herb–Cumin Rub

MAKES ENOUGH RUB FOR ABOUT 5 POUNDS OF MEAT OR POULTRY

This robust mixture is particularly good with pork (try spareribs destined for the smoker) or chicken, especially chicken to be grilled over indirect heat or (bite your tongue!) baked in the oven.

INGREDIENTS

1 cup loosely packed mixed fresh strong herbs, such as oregano and thyme

2 tablespoons ground cumin, preferably from toasted seeds (page 9)

3 tablespoons olive oil

1 teaspoon salt

1 teaspoon freshly ground black pepper

In a mini food processor, combine the herbs, cumin, olive oil, salt, and pepper and process to form a rough paste. *Spread the rub over the meat you are going to cook, cover, and let stand at room temperature for 1 hour or in the refrigerator overnight.*

Red Chile Paint

MAKES ABOUT 1 1/2 CUPS

This thick crimson paste is a potent all-purpose flavor maker. I rub it onto meats and seafood before smoking, whisk it into marinades, use it to boost anemic sauces, flavor mayonnaise with it, and spread it directly onto foods for the grill, where it cooks into a sweetly fiery crust.

INGREDIENTS

1 cup Dried New Mexico Red Chile Purée (page 44)

2 tablespoons honey

1 tablespoon Dijon mustard

2 garlic cloves, peeled and crushed through a press

1/2 teaspoon dried oregano, crumbled

1/2 teaspoon ground cumin, preferably from toasted seeds (page 9)

In a small bowl, stir together the red chile purée, honey, mustard, garlic, oregano, and cumin and use immediately. *Or cover and refrigerate.*

The paint can be prepared up to 3 days ahead or frozen for up to 2 months.

Dried Red New Mexico Chile Purée

MAKES ABOUT 2 CUPS

This is not a recipe, it's more like the general technique for extracting the rich flavor from dried red chile pods. The best of these come from Hatch, New Mexico, just up the road from El Paso, as well as from other growing areas like Chimayo and Dixon farther north. The ruddy purée that results contains the very essence of the chiles and is used in all sorts of ways—in stews, chili, butters, mayonnaise, marinades, and wherever that unique regional flavor is wanted. For extra taste—a chile symphony rather than a simple melody—replace one or two of the red chiles with anchos; for a hotter purée, add two dried chiles de árbol or chipotles.

INGREDIENTS

6 cups boiling water, plus 1 cup hot tap water
¼ pound (12 large) mild dried red New Mexico chile pods, stemmed, seeded, and torn into small pieces

In a medium heat-proof bowl, combine the 6 cups boiling water with the pieces of chile. Cover and let stand, stirring once or twice, until cool. Drain, discarding the chile-soaking water. In a food processor, combine the soaked chile pieces with the hot tap water and process, stopping several times to scrape down the sides of the work bowl, until smooth.

Transfer the purée to a sieve set over a bowl. With a rubber scraper, force the purée through the sieve into the bowl; discard any tough peels or seeds that remain.

Transfer the purée to a storage container and refrigerate for up to 3 days or freeze for up to 1 month.

Chipotle Marinade

A bottle of Italian salad dressing is a convenient marinade for steak and other foods to be grilled. Only a little more work, but immeasurably tastier, is this vinaigrettelike mixture, spiked with hot and smoky chipotle chiles. Use it on beef, lamb, pork, or chicken.

INGREDIENTS

⅓ cup red wine vinegar
1 tablespoon dried oregano, crumbled
2 canned chipotles adobado, homemade (page 166) or commercial, with clinging sauce

2 garlic cloves, peeled and coarsely chopped
1 teaspoon packed dark brown sugar
½ teaspoon freshly ground black pepper
½ cup olive oil

In a blender or small food processor, combine the vinegar, oregano, chipotles with sauce, garlic, brown sugar, and pepper; process until fairly smooth. With the motor running, add the olive oil through the feed tube in a quick, steady stream; the marinade will thicken slightly. *The marinade can be prepared several days in advance. Transfer to a storage container, cover, and refrigerate; return to room temperature before using.*

Brave Bull Marinade and Mop

MAKES ABOUT $^2/_3$ CUP, ENOUGH TO MARINATE
3 POUNDS OF MEAT OR POULTRY

The Brave Bull, a potent after-dinner drink I sometimes indulge in, combines good tequila and the velvety Mexican coffee liqueur Kahlúa. One evening (after perhaps one Brave Bull too many) it occurred to me those same ingredients might well provide the basis for a tasty grilling marinade and mop. Fortunately I was not too marinated to remember this notion the next day and I was right. It's especially good on pork and chicken.

❧

INGREDIENTS

⅓ cup gold tequila

⅓ cup Kahlúa

3 garlic cloves, peeled and crushed through a press

¾ teaspoon dried thyme, crumbled

¾ teaspoon crushed red pepper flakes

 In a small bowl, combine the tequila, Kahlúa, garlic, thyme, and crushed red pepper flakes and mix thoroughly.

In a nonreactive dish, pour this over the food you are going to marinate. Marinate for at least 1 hour at room temperature or for up to 4 hours refrigerated.

HOT TIP Take a few minutes to clean the grill immediately after you use it, while it's still hot, especially if you've used a sweet glaze or baste. You'll save fuel in the long run, and the next time you head for the grill, you won't have to waste time heating and scraping it.

Tequila Bloodymarynade

MAKES ABOUT 1 1/2 CUPS, ENOUGH TO MARINATE UP TO
4 POUNDS OF MEAT, POULTRY, OR SEAFOOD

*This excellent all-purpose marinade has proven particularly successful on chicken and turkey (especially dark meat),
beef, and lamb. Vodka can be substituted for the tequila.*

INGREDIENTS

1 cup tomato juice

1/3 cup thick, tomato-based commercial hot salsa

3 tablespoons gold tequila

2 tablespoons fresh lime juice

2 tablespoons olive oil

1 tablespoon Worcestershire sauce

In a small food processor or blender, combine the tomato juice, salsa, tequila, lime juice, olive oil, and Worcestershire sauce. Process until smooth.

In a nonreactive dish, pour this over the food you are going to marinate, cover, and let stand at room temperature, turning occasionally. Fish and shellfish should marinate for no more than 30 minutes; poultry light meat for no more than 1 hour. Poultry dark meat and red meats can marinate for up to 4 hours or overnight in the refrigerator.

HOT TIP Alcohol in a marinade serves several crucial functions, adding flavor, helping the marinade penetrate, and assisting the acids in tenderizing the meat, poultry, or seafood in question. Residual or added sugars in the liquor help the meat brown, forming an attractive crust, and as the marinade drips onto the heat source of the grill, it is vaporized, coating the meat with even more savor. There's also an appetite-arousing psychological effect, depending on the liquor chosen: For example, white wine sounds elegant, red wine seems robust, tequila says Southwestern, while bourbon shouts out hearty and down-home. Alcohol in marinades can be replaced, if desired, by other appropriate flavor makers such as coffee, fruit juices, or stock.

Roasted Garlic Rosemarynade

MAKES ABOUT 1 ¹/₂ CUPS, ENOUGH TO MARINATE UP TO
4 POUNDS OF MEAT, POULTRY, OR SEAFOOD

This thick, garlicky marinade is good with so many things—lamb, chicken, shrimp, flank steak, pork chops—I find myself making it at least once a week during grilling season. Because of the oil it contains, foods marinated in this should be cooked over low or indirect heat in order to control flare-ups.

INGREDIENTS

1 cup olive oil	3 tablespoons minced fresh rosemary
8 whole unpeeled garlic cloves	½ teaspoon freshly ground black pepper
⅓ cup white wine vinegar	

Position a rack in the middle of the oven and preheat the oven to 375°F.

In a small ovenproof dish, combine ¼ cup of the olive oil and the garlic cloves and bake, stirring them once or twice, until they are golden and very tender, about 20 minutes. Cool to room temperature. Squeeze the softened cooked garlic out of the peels; reserve the garlic-flavored oil.

In a small food processor, combine the soft garlic, garlic oil, the remaining ¾ cup olive oil, the vinegar, rosemary, and pepper. Process until thick and fairly smooth.

In a shallow nonreactive dish, pour this over the food you are going to marinate, cover, and let stand at room temperature, turning occasionally. Fish and shellfish should marinate for no more than 30 minutes; poultry light meat for no more than 1 hour. Poultry dark meat and red meats can marinate for up to 4 hours or overnight in the refrigerator.

Salsa Dressing

MAKES 1 1/2 CUPS

This creamy orange dressing was originally intended for Chicken Fajitas Salad (page 136), but it's just as good on plain green salads, as a dip for grilled shrimp, or as a sauce for grilled vegetables or fish, especially leaner varieties like snapper or swordfish. For proper punch, begin with a very thick, very spicy salsa.

INGREDIENTS

⅓ cup thick, tomato-based bottled hot salsa

2 tablespoons fresh lime juice

1 large egg yolk, at room temperature

1 tablespoon Dijon mustard

½ teaspoon salt

1 cup corn oil

n a medium bowl, whisk together the salsa, lime juice, egg yolk, mustard, and salt. Continue to whisk while gradually adding the corn oil; the dressing will thicken. Adjust the seasoning. *The dressing can be prepared 1 or 2 hours in advance; cover and refrigerate. Return to room temperature before stirring or serving it.*

Pesto Ranch Dressing

MAKES ABOUT 1³/₄ CUPS

The tart taste of buttermilk—which American palates now understand as "ranch" flavor—is perfectly compatible with pesto, whether it's my homemade, green chile–spiked version (page 26) or store-bought. Use the dressing on a big old cool white platter of sliced beefsteak tomatoes (page 185) or on any grilled or fresh-from-the-garden vegetables. It's also nice as a dip for grilled shrimp and as a dressing for chicken or pasta salad.

INGREDIENTS

1 cup mayonnaise

¹/₃ cup pesto, preferably Green Chile Pesto (page 26)

¹/₄ cup cultured buttermilk

1 tablespoon fresh lemon juice

n a medium bowl, stir together the mayonnaise, pesto, buttermilk, and lemon juice. *Cover and refrigerate; return to room temperature* before using. The dressing can be prepared up to 3 days ahead.

HOT MENU

Chilled White Wine
Cherry Tomatoes Dipped into Pesto Ranch Dressing (above)

Fiery Lemon Chicken (page 86)
Rosemary-Grilled New Potatoes (page 190)
Grill-Toasted Garlic Bread (page 200)

Mandarin-Coconut Yogurt Freeze (page 223) with Quick Mocha Sauce (page 239)

Great Caesar Dressing

As you read this book it will become obvious to you that this dressing is a mainstay in my kitchen. I make a batch at least once a week, and in addition to tossing it with grilled shrimp, romaine lettuce and homemade croutons in a more-or-less classic Caesar salad (page 133), I use it as a marinade and baste for seafood and chicken I plan to grill. (It also makes a great dressing for a potato salad, page 188.) I discovered it in Michael's book Cooking for the Weekend *and have adapted it slightly.*

INGREDIENTS

¼ cup fresh lime juice

¼ cup grated Parmigiano-Reggiano or pecorino Romano cheese

1 large egg, at room temperature

1 large egg yolk, at room temperature

4 to 6 oil-packed anchovy fillets, coarsely chopped

3 garlic cloves, peeled and coarsely chopped

1 tablespoon Worcestershire sauce

1 tablespoon Dijon mustard

½ teaspoon salt

1 teaspoon freshly ground black pepper

1 cup corn oil

1 cup olive oil

n a food processor, combine the lime juice, cheese, egg, egg yolk, anchovies, garlic, Worcestershire sauce, mustard, salt, and pepper; process until smooth. With the motor running, add the oils through the feed tube in a fairly quick, steady stream; the dressing will thicken. *Transfer to a storage container, cover, and refrigerate. The* dressing can be prepared up to 3 days ahead. Return to room temperature before using.

Red Chile Caesar Dressing Add ⅓ cup Dried Red New Mexico Chile Purée (page 44) to the food processor with the first batch of ingredients, then complete as above.

Roasted Garlic Mayonnaise

Roasting garlic mellows its bite, producing a rich, nutty quality that makes this fresh mayonnaise addictive. Slather the golden stuff onto Grilled Lamb Burgers (page 121) or Grilled Swordfish Club Sandwiches (page 130), or offer it as a dip for Rosemary-Grilled New Potatoes (page 190) or plain boiled or grilled shrimp.

INGREDIENTS

12 large unpeeled garlic cloves
1¼ cups olive oil
2 large egg yolks, at room temperature
2 tablespoons fresh lemon juice, plus up to 1 additional tablespoon to taste

1 tablespoon Dijon mustard
¼ teaspoon salt
½ teaspoon freshly ground black pepper

Position a rack in the middle of the oven and preheat the oven to 375°F.

In a small ovenproof dish, combine the garlic cloves and 3 tablespoons of the olive oil. Bake, stirring them once or twice, until they are tender and lightly colored, about 20 minutes. Cool to room temperature. Peel and mince the garlic; reserve the oil.

In a medium bowl, whisk together the garlic, egg yolks, 1 tablespoon of the lemon juice, the mustard, salt, and pepper. Slowly whisk in the garlic oil and remaining olive oil; the mayonnaise will thicken.

Adjust the seasoning, adding up to 1 more tablespoon lemon juice to taste. *Transfer to a storage container, cover, and refrigerate. The mayonnaise can be prepared up to 3 days ahead.*

Rosemary Mayonnaise

MAKES ABOUT 2 CUPS

Fragrant, resinous rosemary insinuates itself into my cooking more and more every day. It grows well here in the desert Southwest and is often seen as ornamental ·hedges, fragrant and neatly trimmed, along the sidewalks of college campuses, for example. Nurtured in pots it becomes green and lush or, when a little stressed by heat and drought, grows into a kind of gnarled Texas bonsai. Handfuls of rosemary get thrown onto the fire to produce a flavorful smoke when I'm grilling seafood or vegetables. Of course I use it with chicken and lamb (on and off the grill) as well as in tomato dishes. This silky mayonnaise adds the herb's distinctive taste to sandwiches and hors d'oeuvres.

INGREDIENTS

1 large egg, at room temperature
1 large egg yolk, at room temperature
3 tablespoons fresh lemon juice
1½ tablespoons minced fresh rosemary
1 tablespoon Dijon mustard
½ teaspoon salt, plus additional salt to taste
½ teaspoon freshly ground black pepper, plus additional pepper to taste
1 cup olive oil
½ cup corn oil

In a food processor, combine the egg, egg yolk, I tablespoon of the lemon juice, the rosemary, mustard, salt, and pepper and process until fairly smooth. With the motor running, gradually add the oils through the feed tube; the mayonnaise will thicken. Adjust the seasoning, adding more lemon juice (the mayonnaise should be tart), salt, and pepper to taste.

Transfer to a storage container, cover, and refrigerate for at least 2 hours to develop the flavors before using. The mayonnaise can be prepared up to 3 days in advance.

Black Olive, Lemon,
and Cilantro Butter

MAKES ABOUT ³/₄ CUP

Olives are not very Southwestern (for a long time the Spaniards despaired of ever getting them to grow here), but the same robust quality that makes other essentially Mediterranean ingredients (basil, sun-dried tomatoes, balsamic vinegar) go so well with Southwestern food is also at work in this flavorful olive butter. Melt it over just-grilled meats or fish, especially tuna and lamb.

INGREDIENTS

6 tablespoons (3 ounces) unsalted butter, softened
2 tablespoons finely chopped fresh cilantro
1½ teaspoons minced lemon zest (colored peel)

¼ teaspoon freshly ground black pepper
2 tablespoons minced pitted imported black olives, such as Kalamata

In a medium bowl, mash together the butter, cilantro, lemon zest, and pepper. Stir in the olives (do not overmix or the butter will turn an unattractive purple). *Transfer to a storage container* and cover. *The butter can be refrigerated for up to 3 days or frozen for up to 2 months. Soften to room temperature before using.*

Chipotle-Lime Butter

MAKES ABOUT ¹/₂ CUP

Orange and quite picante, this compound butter is great on beefsteaks, lamb chops, or chicken, but its main use as far as I'm concerned is melting over the tender, smoky flesh of just-grilled lobsters. (See the taco recipe on page 81 for the how-to of the actual grilling.) Set the lobsters, cut side up, on plates, spread the softened butter over the visible lobster meat, and serve immediately. (Provide plenty of napkins and maybe even bibs—this is a messy treat.)

❧

INGREDIENTS

6 tablespoons (3 ounces) unsalted butter, softened
1½ tablespoons minced chipotles adobado, homemade (page 166) or commercial

1½ teaspoons finely chopped fresh lime zest (colored peel)
Pinch of salt

n a medium bowl, mash together the butter, chipotles, lime zest, and salt. *Transfer to a storage container and cover. The butter can be* refrigerated for up to 3 days or frozen for up to 2 months. Soften to room temperature before using.

Roquefort Butter

This rich and tangy spread was intended to be used with grilled new potatoes (page 189) and, indeed, it's delicious that way, but I've learned it's also wonderful on steak or in place of garlic butter on thick, smoky slices of grilled bread. Nowadays, there's always some in my freezer, just in case.

INGREDIENTS

1½ sticks (6 ounces) unsalted butter, at room temperature
½ pound Roquefort cheese, crumbled

¾ teaspoon Worcestershire sauce
¾ teaspoon freshly ground black pepper

In a medium bowl, cream the butter until smooth. Fold in the Roquefort, Worcestershire sauce, and pepper; some chunks of Roquefort should remain. *Transfer to a storage* container and cover. The butter can be prepared ahead and refrigerated for up to 3 days or frozen for up to 2 months. Soften to room temperature before serving.

Roasted Garlic–Green and Red Chile Butter

MAKES ABOUT ²/₃ CUP

Let this savory, terra-cotta-colored butter melt over grilled beef or lamb and seafood such as shrimp, lobster, or salmon. It's also good on grilled bread (page 200) in place of conventional garlic butter.

❧

INGREDIENTS

1 large fresh poblano chile or 2 long green anaheim-type chiles
6 large whole unpeeled garlic cloves
2 tablespoons olive oil

½ stick (2 ounces) unsalted butter, at room temperature
1 teaspoon pure, unblended red chili powder, preferably from Chimayo, New Mexico

In the open flame of a gas burner, on a preheated grill (over wood smoking chips if desired), or under a preheated broiler, roast the poblano, turning it often, until the peel is lightly and evenly charred. In a closed paper bag, steam the chile until cool. Rub off the burned peel, remove the stem and seeds, and finely chop the chile.

Preheat the oven to 375°F. In a small ovenproof dish, combine the garlic cloves and olive oil.

Bake, stirring them once or twice, until they are soft, tender, and lightly colored, about 20 minutes. Cool to room temperature. Peel the cloves; reserve the garlic-flavored oil.

In a medium bowl, mash together the butter, chopped poblano, garlic, garlic oil, and chili powder. *Transfer to a storage container and cover. The butter can be refrigerated for up to 3 days or frozen for up to 2 months. Soften to room temperature before using.*

pickles and preserves

I can foods for a living—I'm not, pioneer-style, rushing to put up the summer's fleeting harvest in order to keep my family fed during the coming winter. To be honest, hired help and industrial machinery make it painless. Is it perhaps then a little improbable of me to suggest that a modern cook would find any satisfaction at all in the sweaty business of cooking, sterilizing, and sealing up jars of this or that at home when supermarkets full of canned goods are around every corner? And yet... there is a charm to the process, I admit it—the shock of hot vinegar, a sharp blow to the sense of smell; the lesson of patience, since most of this food will not be eaten this day or the next; the pride of ownership as jars or bottles are lined up, glowing with tantalizing color on the kitchen counter. Easy condiments, these, no pressure canning or other risky business, and each meant to make your grilled or smoked foods sparkle with extra flavor.

Salsa Vinegar

MAKES 3 CUPS

Flavored vinegars are among the simplest and most satisfying kitchen "canning" chores. Select a tall, elegant bottle and tie it up with raffia and a garnish of dried chiles when you've finished and you have a very useful, very beautiful gift. Splash this salsa-flavored vinegar onto grilled foods (especially during diet season), use it in salad dressings and marinades, or add it to salsa in place of the more traditional lime juice.

INGREDIENTS

3 or 4 large jalapeño chiles, preferably red, quartered lengthwise
3 thin green onions, well washed, with the green tops trimmed to fit the bottle you are using

12 large sprigs fresh cilantro
2 garlic cloves, peeled and halved lengthwise
About 3 cups good-quality white wine vinegar

Stuff the jalapeños, green onions, cilantro, and garlic into a tall, preferably decorative, I-quart bottle, using the thin handle of a wooden spoon if necessary. Fill the bottle with the vinegar (it should completely cover the other ingredients). *Seal the bottle and let it stand in a cool, dark place for at least 2 weeks before using.*

Serrano-Rosemary Vinegar

This second vinegar is equally fiery, equally beautiful to look at, and very robust. Because of its heartier nature, I use it in marinades, sauces, and dressings for red meats, especially lamb and beef. Its red-and-green color scheme makes it a perfect Christmas gift.

INGREDIENTS

8 large sprigs fresh rosemary, washed and patted dry
6 to 8 red-ripe serrano chiles, partially split (leave them joined at the stem end)
About 3 cups good-quality red wine vinegar

Stuff the rosemary and chiles into a tall, preferably decorative, I-quart bottle, using the thin handle of a wooden spoon if necessary. Fill the bottle with the vinegar (it should completely cover the other ingredients). *Seal the bottle and let it stand in a cool, dark place for at least 2 weeks before using.*

Red-As-Rubies Pepper Jelly

MAKES 6 PINTS

Among jellies, none is easier to make than this, which is actually a spicy, savory condiment. Enjoyed not only in Texas but throughout the South, pepper jelly is traditionally spooned over a block of cream cheese and the two together are then spread onto crackers, as a kind of low-tech hors d'oeuvre. Creative types dollop it alongside slices of smoked meat (turkey or brisket), melt and brush it over a big ham to glaze it as it bakes, or stir it into marinades for foods to be grilled. My variation uses only red chiles— jalapeños and poblanos—for the reddest color and deepest flavor, but red bell peppers and green jalapeños can be substituted—you'll just have a jelly that is more greenish-brown than red.

INGREDIENTS

4 large red poblano chiles (see the Note)
12 red jalapeño chiles (see the Note), stemmed
   and coarsely chopped
11 cups sugar

2 cups red wine vinegar
¼ cup fresh lemon juice
4 3-ounce packets liquid pectin

In the open flame of a gas burner, on a preheated grill (over wood smoking chips if desired), or under a preheated broiler, roast the poblanos, turning them often, until the peels are evenly charred. In a closed paper bag, steam the chiles until cool. Rub off the burned peels, remove the stems, ribs, and seeds, and coarsely chop the chiles.

Fill a large pot with water, set it over high heat, and bring it to a boil. Lower six I-pint canning jars into the water and boil them for 10 minutes. Remove the pot from the heat and hold the jars in the hot water. Bring a medium pan of water to a boil. In a large bowl, cover 6 *new* jar lids with the boiling water and hold until ready to use.

In a food processor, combine the poblanos and the jalapeños and process with short bursts of power until finely chopped.

In a nonreactive 4½- to 5-quart pan over medium heat, combine the chopped chiles, sugar, vinegar, and lemon juice. Bring to a boil, skimming any scum that foams to the top.

When the mixture reaches a hard boil that cannot be stirred down, cook undisturbed for 5 minutes.

Remove from the heat and let stand for 5 minutes. Stir in the liquid pectin. One at a time, remove the jars from the hot water, drain them, and fill each with the hot jelly mixture, leaving ½ inch of headspace. With a clean, damp cloth, wipe the rims of the jars, cover them with the lids, and firmly screw the rings in place.

Place a metal canning rack in the bottom of the large pot of hot water, set the pot over high heat, and return the water to a boil. Working in batches if necessary, place the jars of jelly without crowding on the rack in the pot; the boiling water should completely cover the jars. Boil for 5 minutes (timing from when the water returns to a full boil), then transfer the jars to a rack and cool to room temperature.

The lids on the jars should pop audibly as they cool to indicate they have sealed. Wait 4 hours, then test them by pressing on the center of each lid with a finger. The lids that sealed will be inverted and will not pop back and these jars can be stored at room temperature. Jars with lids that did not seal should be refrigerated immediately.

Let the jelly stand for at least 1 month to mellow the flavor. Store unopened jars away from heat and light and try to use up within 1 year.

NOTE: Poblanos and jalapeños that have begun to blush red before they are picked will eventually do so completely (those that haven't, won't). Store them at room temperature, uncovered, in a single layer on several thickness of paper towels, for 2 or 3 days, watching them carefully, refrigerating those that turn fully red, and standing by to make your jelly more or less immediately when all are red, since they will then quickly spoil. I think the ruby-red results are worth the extra fuss.

Steve Lange's Jalapeños en Escabeche

MAKES 9 PINTS

From a friend in Tucson, who puts up a batch of these several times a year, comes what I believe to be the best and most beautiful recipe ever for home-pickled peppers. (The pink peppercorns and the bay leaves were my additions to what remains an ongoing quest for perfection.) My wife, Martina, eats these the way other people eat peanuts; two recipients of gift jars from my last batch report, respectively, that the baby carrots and the pearl onions were nearly addictive.

INGREDIENTS

1½ pounds (about 75) small-to-medium firm, fresh jalapeño chiles, preferably red-ripe (see the Note, page 63)

3 cups good-quality white wine vinegar, of at least 5 percent acidity

3 cups water

¾ teaspoon salt

1 8-ounce basket pearl onions (about 18 small onions)

1 small head (about 1 pound) cauliflower, trimmed and separated into small florets

1 pound peeled baby carrots (available in produce stores and some supermarkets) or 1 pound regular carrots, peeled and cut diagonally into ½-inch slices

27 large sprigs fresh oregano, marjoram, or rosemary

18 whole garlic cloves, peeled

18 dried red chiles, such as de árbol, *preferably with stems attached*

18 bay leaves

3 tablespoons dried pink peppercorns

In a dry skillet over medium-high heat, working in batches if necessary, sear the jalapeños, turning them often, until the skins are partially blackened, blistered, and split, about 7 minutes. Do not overcook or allow them to soften. Remove them from the skillet and cool.

Fill a large pot with water, set it over high heat, and bring the water to a boil. Lower nine 1-pint widemouthed canning jars into the water and boil them for 10 minutes. Remove the pot from the heat and hold the jars in the hot water. Bring a medium pan of water to a boil. In a large bowl, cover 9 *new* jar lids with the boiling water and hold until ready to use.

In a medium nonreactive saucepan, combine the vinegar, water, and salt. Set over medium heat and bring to a boil. Lower the heat, cover the pan, and keep the brine hot.

Meanwhile, remove the jars from the pot of hot water and tightly pack them with the jalapeños, onions, cauliflower, carrots, oregano, garlic, dried chiles, and bay leaves, leaving ½ inch of headspace. (For maximum visual appeal in the finished product, the oregano, dried chiles, and bay leaves should be up against the sides of the jars.) Add I teaspoon of pink peppercorns to each jar.

Pour the hot vinegar mixture into the jars, covering the contents of each completely and leaving ½ inch of headspace. (You might not use all of the vinegar mixture.)

With a clean, damp cloth, wipe the rims of the jars, cover them with the lids, and firmly screw the rings in place.

Place a metal rack in the bottom of the large pot of hot water, set the pot over high heat, and return the water to a boil. Working in batches if necessary, place the jars of chiles without crowding on the rack in the pot; the boiling water should completely cover the jars. Boil for 15 minutes (timing from when the water returns to a full boil), then transfer the jars to a rack and cool to room temperature.

The lids on the jars should pop audibly as they cool to indicate they have sealed. Wait 4 hours, then test them by pressing on the center of each lid with a finger. The lids that have sealed will be inverted and will not pop back and these jars can be stored at room temperature. Jars with lids that did not seal should be refrigerated immediately.

Let the jalapeños stand for 1 month to mellow the flavor. Store the unopened jars away from heat and light and try to use them up within 1 year.

Chile Chowchow

MAKES 3 PINTS

The sweet, mustardy cabbage and green tomato relish known as chowchow (a cousin if not a sibling of the relish called piccalilli) is only improved by the addition of roasted poblano chiles and fresh jalapeños. Chowchow is great, chutney style, alongside smoked or grilled beef or pork, and it's wonderful on a big sandwich of either of them.

❧

INGREDIENTS

4 large poblano chiles

3 large heavy sweet red peppers, preferably Dutch

4 cups finely chopped white cabbage

3 cups finely chopped yellow onions

3 large green tomatoes (about 1½ pounds), cored, juiced, and chopped (2 cups)

4 medium fresh jalapeño chiles, stemmed and finely chopped

2 tablespoons salt

1¼ cups sugar

1 tablespoon mustard powder, preferably Colman's

1 tablespoon whole yellow mustard seeds

2 teaspoons pickling spices, tied in a cheesecloth bag

¾ teaspoon ground celery seed

¼ teaspoon ground turmeric

¼ teaspoon ground ginger

¼ teaspoon ground coriander

2½ cups apple cider vinegar

In the open flame of a gas burner, on a preheated grill (over wood smoking chips if desired), or under a preheated broiler, roast the poblanos and sweet peppers, turning them often, until the peels are lightly and evenly charred. In a closed paper bag, steam the chiles and peppers until cool. Rub off the burned peels, remove the stems and seeds, and finely chop the chiles and peppers.

In a large bowl, combine the chopped chiles and peppers, cabbage, onions, tomatoes, jalapeños, and salt. Cover and refrigerate overnight, stirring once or twice.

In a large strainer set over a bowl, drain the chopped vegetables and chiles thoroughly. Fill a large pot with water, set it over high heat, and bring the water to a boil. Lower three I-pint canning jars into the water and boil them for 10 minutes. Remove the pot from the heat and hold the jars in the hot water. Bring a medium pan of water to a boil. In a large bowl, cover 3 *new* jar lids with the boiling water and hold until ready to use.

In a medium heavy nonreactive saucepan, stir together the sugar, mustard powder, mustard seed, pickling spice bag, celery seed, turmeric, ginger, and coriander. Gradually stir in the vinegar. Set the pan over medium heat and bring to a simmer. Partially cover and cook, stirring once or twice, for 20 minutes.

Add the chopped vegetables and chiles and continue to cook, partially covered, stirring often as the mixture thickens, for 10 minutes. Discard the pickling spice bag. Remove the sterilized jars from the hot water and drain them. Fill the jars with the chowchow, leaving ½ inch of headspace. Wipe the rims of the jars with a clean, damp cloth. Remove the lids from the hot water and cover the jars. Firmly screw the rings in place.

Place a metal rack in the bottom of the large pot of hot water, set the pot over high heat, and return the water to a boil. Set the jars of chowchow on the rack in the pot; the boiling water should completely cover the jars. Boil for 15 minutes (timing from when the water returns to a full boil), then transfer the jars to a rack and cool to room temperature.

The lids on the processed jars should pop audibly as they cool to indicate they have sealed. Wait 4 hours, then test them by pressing on the center of each lid with a finger. The lids that have sealed will be inverted and will not pop back and these jars can be stored at room temperature. Jars with lids that did not seal should be refrigerated immediately.

Let the sealed jars stand for 1 month to mellow the flavor of the chowchow. Store unopened jars away from heat and light and try to use up within 1 year.

Peppery Pickled Peaches

MAKES 4 QUARTS

*Golden pickled peaches are like Texas sunshine trapped in a jar. Put up in summer, they really reach their flavor
peak around the winter holidays, where they make the perfect sweet-and-sour accompaniment to such festive fare
as Smoked Fresh Ham (page 158), Smoked Wild Turkey (page 150), or Smoked Loin of Venison
(page 165). Select the smallest firm, ripe peaches you can find—you'll still only be able to fit four
in a quart jar—and though it can be annoying, for the best appearance they must be peeled:
Properly prepared pickled peaches should be as spectacular to look at as they are to taste.*

INGREDIENTS

4 pounds (16 small) ripe but firm peaches
64 whole cloves
7 cups (3½ pounds) sugar
6 cups cider vinegar

4 4-inch pieces of cinnamon stick
12 small dried red chiles, such as de árbol or japonés
32 whole allspice berries

With a knife, cut a shallow X in the tip end
of each peach. Over medium heat, bring a
large pan of water to a boil. Working in batches
if necessary, lower the peaches into the water.
Turn the peaches in the hot water once or twice.
After 30 seconds, with a slotted spoon, transfer
the peaches to a large bowl of cold water. When
the peaches are cool enough to handle, peel
them. (Depending on the peach variety, the peels
may slip off easily or they may need to be
pulled off in strips.) Drain the peeled peaches
and pat them dry. Stick 4 whole cloves into each
peach.

Fill a large pot with water, set it over high heat,
and bring it to a boil. Lower four I-quart
canning jars into the water and boil them for 10
minutes. Remove the pot from the heat and
hold the jars in the hot water. Bring a medium
pan of water to a boil. In a large bowl, cover 4
new jar lids with the boiling water and hold until
ready to use.

In a 3½- to 4-quart nonreactive pan, stir
together the sugar and vinegar. Set over medium
heat. Add the pieces of cinnamon stick and
dried chiles and bring just to a simmer, stirring

to dissolve the sugar. Add 8 of the peaches to the simmering syrup. Cook the peaches, turning them once or twice, for 4 minutes. Remove two jars from the hot water and drain them. With a slotted spoon transfer the peaches to the jars, packing 4 peaches into each. Repeat with the remaining peaches.

Drop 8 allspice berries into each jar. With tongs transfer a cinnamon piece and 3 chiles from the syrup into each jar. With a ladle, fill each jar with hot syrup (you may not use it all), leaving no more than ½ inch of headspace. With a clean, damp cloth, wipe the rims of the jars, cover them with the lids, and firmly screw the rings in place.

Place a metal canning rack in the bottom of the large pot of hot water, set the pot over high heat, and return the water to a boil. Working in batches if necessary, place the jars of peaches without crowding on the rack in the pot; the boiling water should completely cover the jars. Boil for 15 minutes (timing from when the water returns to a full boil), then transfer the jars to a rack and cool to room temperature.

The lids on the jars should pop audibly as they cool to indicate they have sealed. Wait 4 hours, then test them by pressing on the center of each lid with a finger. The lids that have sealed will be inverted and will not pop back and these jars can be stored at room temperature. Jars with lids that did not seal should be refrigerated immediately.

Let the peaches stand for at least 1 month (4 is better) to mellow the flavors. Store unopened jars away from heat and light and try to use up the peaches within 1 year.

PART TWO

Smoke Signals

cooking over an open flame

PLAYING WITH FIRE CAN BE FUN, AND EATING THE FOOD COOKED OVER THAT fire utter bliss. There can be no doubt of the primitive appeal of grilled meat, an ancient longing, perhaps the very instinct that moved us from strictly gatherers to *hunter-* gatherers on our climb out of the cave. The charcoal briquette, it seems, was invented shortly thereafter. Twentieth-century pioneers of outdoor cookery saw this as man's work (influenced, no doubt, by too many Hollywood trail drive movies), and some shockingly misogynistic words have been written on the subject. I disagree: It's not who's doing the grilling, but how good he or she is at it, that leads to the crisp, succulent, fragrant, smoky divinity that is great grilled food. It's a knack, not a trait, and even a Neanderthal can learn how.

how to grill:
one man's guide

if a thing can be learned, it can be botched. When it comes to great grilling, experience is the best teacher. By all means take my humble expert's advice, then head for the yard and the grill and see what happens. LESSON ONE: Practice on cheap food.

LESSON TWO: There's a lot of equipment out there, and what you grill on may not be what I grill on. Hence, LESSON THREE: All advice is guaranteed to be general.

Americans have grilled for decades now, theoretically ever since the post–World War II building boom, when many newly erected suburban houses came with gas grills (also bad Victorian-style gas lamps) by way of sales incentives. Prosperity meant leisure and leisure meant spending less time in the kitchen, even if that meant preparing dinner in the yard. Before that, cooking over an open flame was a manly, outdoorish thing, done by a few, and before *that* (pre-gas, -electric, or -wood-burning stove), it was simply all there was, and was pretty much done by anyone who wanted to eat something cooked, as opposed to raw. Thus grilling is not new, but why we're grilling and what we're grilling and how good we've become at it is.

When I was given my first propane-fired grill, I was semi-appalled. As a Texan, used to the fragrance and flavor created by a real wood or natural charcoal fire, I was certain such a sterile cooking appliance would make tasteless food. I was wrong, I'm a convert, and I now cook anything and everything over propane and love every bite (LESSON FOUR).

It takes time—a gas grill needs to be seasoned, like any piece of good cookware—and know-how. I choose grills with lava stones or permanent briquettes (hate those new "flavor bar" grills) because they acquire, after only a short time, a flavorful patina of their own. I also use unsoaked hardwood grill-smoking chips, wrapped into a partially closed foil packet or tucked into a small, clean tuna fish can (lid still attached), either of which lets a slow flow of savory smoke bathe the foods as they grill over time. For quick-grilling foods I prefer to soak the chips in water, or another flavorful liquid, drain them, and scatter them right on the grill stones, where they instantly begin to give off flavor and aroma. Stay creative, too, and consider throwing fresh herbs, citrus peels, garlic cloves, onions, or spices onto the heat source—they all contribute. Most of my grilling is thus done covered, allowing for greater penetration of the smoke flavor as well as letting me more consistently control the temperature.

Speaking of which, beginners nearly always grill too hot and too close to the fire, there being some notion that this is supposed to be a quick process. Be patient (LESSON FIVE). I rarely turn my thermostatically controlled propane grill above medium high and always set the grill rack at least six inches above the heat source (LESSONS FIVE A AND FIVE B). Foods burn quickly, so never leave a grill unwatched for more than a few minutes (LESSON SIX) and don't hesitate to adjust the temperature, the height of the grill, or the placement of the food (all propane grills seem to have cool spots—know where yours are and use them) to maintain control. Begin brushing food with sweetened barbecue sauces and glazes near the end of the grilling time, otherwise the sugars burn.

Other advice (LESSONS EIGHT THROUGH WHATEVER): It's easier to cook a small amount of food on a large grill than the reverse—so buy a big one. There's nothing wrong with charcoal if you know what you're doing, it just takes a little more time to get started and a little more watching during cooking (plus I always seem to burn myself). Never use charcoal lighter fluid, which makes for a nasty, lingering flavor, like an oil refinery fire; seek out an electric or a chimney-type fire starter instead; and try to use natural charcoal (it looks like chunks of burned wood) rather than briquettes, which include glues and petroleum products.

Always clean the grill rack thoroughly to prevent off flavors and stuck foods. Unmarinated lean meats and seafood will be less likely to stick if you brush the grill rack lightly with oil just before the food goes on. Use a pad of paper towels dipped into olive or vegetable oil. Or lightly coat the rack with nonstick spray and then set it in place (never spray an aerosol can directly into an open flame). Buy two propane tanks and keep the spare filled at all times. Gauges are inaccurate and you'll never be exactly sure you won't run out of gas halfway through a great steak. Go to a restaurant supply house and buy several pairs of long spring-loaded tongs, a big pastry brush for sauces, and an offset (bent-handled) wide spatula for moving foods without grilling knuckles. I find kitchen mitts too cumbersome to use, but you may not. Consider buying a large stand umbrella that will cover your grill: Sooner or later, rain happens.

Finally, be adventurous. You may choose to start out grilling hamburgers because I've told you to practice on cheap foods, or because that's all your kids will eat, but the possibilities are so extraordinary, as I hope this section illustrates, that it would be a shame not to experience at least some of them.

Mixed Grill of Skewered Shrimp, Mushrooms, and Hot Sausages

SERVES 8

Fiery andouille (a smoked Cajun pork sausage), sweet shrimp, and woodsy mushrooms, basted with a fragrant herbal oil, combine to create a colorful and very tasty mixed skewer of great eating. Serve these with Rosemary-Grilled New Potatoes (page 190) and Marinated Pepper Slaw (page 183).

INGREDIENTS

¾ cup olive oil

2 tablespoons packed fresh thyme leaves

2 garlic cloves, peeled and coarsely chopped

¾ teaspoon crushed red pepper flakes

2 pounds (24) very large shrimp, peeled and deveined

About 1½ pounds andouille or other spicy smoked and fully cooked sausage

32 medium cultivated brown (cremini) or white mushrooms, stems trimmed flush with the caps

2 cups mesquite or hickory wood smoking chips

*i*n a small food processor or blender, combine the olive oil, thyme, garlic, and red pepper and process until green and fairly smooth. In a medium bowl, combine the shrimp and the seasoned oil and let stand at room temperature, covered, stirring once or twice, for 1 hour.

Cut the andouille crosswise into slices as thick as the shrimp at their thickest.

Remove the shrimp; reserve the marinade. Slide a mushroom horizontally onto a 12-inch skewer, preferably of flat metal. Hold a slice of andouille in the curve of a shrimp and slide them together onto the skewer next to the mushroom. Thread a second mushroom onto the skewer, follow with a second shrimp and andouille slice, and repeat until the skewer holds 4 mushrooms and 3 shrimp and 3 andouille slices. Repeat with the remaining ingredients to make 8 filled skewers.

Light a charcoal fire and let it burn until the coals are evenly white or preheat a gas grill (medium). Wrap the wood chips partially in foil, creating a small packet that is open at the top. Set the packet on the hot coals or hot lava stones; position the grill rack about 6 inches above the heat source.

When the wood chips are smoking, brush the mushrooms and andouille slices with the remaining seasoned oil. Place the skewers on the grill rack. Cover and cook, rearranging the position of the skewers on the grill to create attractive markings, and turning them once, until the shrimp are just cooked through, the andouille is browned, and the mushrooms are tender and juicy, about 8 minutes total. Remove from the heat, slide the food from the skewers if desired, and serve immediately.

BBQ Tuna Steaks with Roasted Corn Vinaigrette

SERVES 4

This is a vivid and elegant dish, and since fresh tuna is a luxury in these parts, I reserve this one for special occasions. Thick tuna steaks are marinated in a spicy barbecue sauce, grilled medium rare over smoky wood, and napped with a light vinaigrette dressing which is chock-full of colorful vegetables.

INGREDIENTS

1 ear supersweet or sugar-enhanced corn
2 to 3 cups wood smoking chips, preferably mesquite
1 heavy sweet red pepper, preferably Dutch
4 1¼-inch-thick tuna steaks (about 3 pounds total)
1 cup West Texas Red (page 17) or another thin, spicy, tomato-based barbecue sauce
Salt to taste

Freshly ground black pepper to taste plus ¼ teaspoon pepper
1 large egg yolk, at room temperature
1½ tablespoons seasoned Oriental rice wine vinegar
½ teaspoon Dijon mustard
½ cup corn oil
1 tablespoon thinly sliced green onions

Carefully open the husk of the corn without detaching it from the ear and remove the silk. Close up the husk and in a bowl, soak the corn in cold water to cover for 30 minutes.

Position a rack in the middle of the oven and preheat the oven to 400°F Place the ear of corn on the rack and roast, turning it once or twice, until the husk is lightly browned and the corn kernels are tender and fragrant, about 40 minutes. Remove from the oven and cool to room temperature. Remove the husk and with a long, sharp knife, cut the kernels off the ear.

Measure out ½ cup corn, reserving the remainder for another use.

In the open flame of a gas burner, on a preheated grill (over some of the wood smoking chips if desired), or under a preheated broiler, roast the red pepper, turning it often, until the peel is evenly charred. In a closed paper bag, steam the pepper until cool. Rub off the burned peel, remove the stem, ribs, and seeds, and finely dice enough of the pepper to yield 2 tablespoons. Reserve the remainder for another use.

In a shallow dish just large enough to hold them, coat the tuna steaks with the barbecue sauce. Cover and let them stand at room temperature, turning them once or twice, for I hour.

Light a charcoal fire and let it burn until the coals are evenly white or preheat a gas grill (medium). Wrap the wood chips partially in foil, creating a small packet that is open at the top. Set the packet on the hot coals or hot lava stones; position the grill rack about 6 inches above the heat source.

When the wood chips are smoking heavily, place the tuna steaks on the grill. Cover and cook for 4 minutes. Turn the tuna steaks, cover, and cook until they are attractively marked by the grill and browned on their edges, about 3 minutes for medium rare. Transfer the tuna steaks to warmed plates and season them lightly with salt and pepper to taste.

Meanwhile, in a small bowl, whisk together the egg yolk, vinegar, mustard, and the ¼ teaspoon pepper. Slowly whisk in the corn oil; the dressing will thicken. Stir in the roasted corn, roasted red pepper, and the green onions and adjust the seasoning.

Spoon the vinaigrette over and around the hot tuna steaks, dividing it evenly and using it all. Serve immediately.

HOT TIP The old advice for cooking corn— wait until the water boils before you go pick the ears straight from the field—no longer applies. Specially developed corn hybrids, labeled sugar-enhanced or supersweet, are increasingly available; in both the conversion of the corn's natural sugars to starch is slowed, making for just-picked-tasting ears up to two weeks after harvest. Experts slightly favor the sugar-enhanced ears, which nicely balance corn flavor and sweetness, over the supersweets, which can be cloying. Seeds for either type of corn offered in catalogs will be identified; farmers at roadside stands should be able to tell you what you are buying. In supermarkets, you're on your own, but the hybrids are so popular, they're even turning up on the produce aisle.

HOT TIP To promote even cooking, items for the grill should be as even in size and especially in thickness as possible. All tuna steaks, for example, should be the same thickness; Chicken breasts should be pounded to flatten them slightly. Boneless steaks or fillets cook more quickly and evenly than those with bones in.

Grilled Garlic-Lime Soft-shell Crabs

SERVES 4

Succulent, fragile soft-shell crabs do not at first seem likely candidates for the grill, but fearless as always, I tried them out one night, and now I rarely ever prepare these crustaceans any other way. Higher heat crisps and cooks them (low heat merely dries them out), while a tart, buttery, and slightly picante marinade complements the sweet meat and keeps them moist. I think buying the crabs already dressed is preferable to killing and cleaning them myself, but note: Dressed crabs should be prepared the same day they are purchased.

INGREDIENTS

½ stick (2 ounces) unsalted butter
¼ cup medium-dry white wine
4 garlic cloves, peeled and crushed through a press
2 tablespoons fresh lime juice

2 tablespoons hot pepper sauce, such as Tabasco
8 large soft-shell crabs, dressed
2 cups wood smoking chips
Salt to taste

Light a charcoal fire and let it burn until the coals are evenly white or preheat a gas grill (medium-high).

Meanwhile, in a small saucepan over low heat, combine the butter, white wine, garlic, lime juice, and hot pepper sauce. Heat, stirring, until the butter is just melted. In a shallow nonreactive dish just large enough to hold them, place the crabs upside down in a single layer. Pour the marinade over them and let stand, turning and working the marinade under the aprons, for 15 minutes.

Wrap the wood chips partially in foil, creating a small packet that is open at the top. Set the packet on the hot coals or hot lava stones; position the grill rack about 6 inches above the heat source.

When the wood chips are smoking heavily, place the crabs, bottoms up, on the grill rack. Spread any remaining marinade or solidified butter from the dish over them. Cover and grill, turning the crabs carefully once (use tongs or a spatula), until they are crisp and lightly colored, about 3 minutes per side.

Remove from the heat immediately, season with salt to taste, and serve hot or warm.

Soft Lobster Tacos

SERVES 4

Chunks of grilled lobster, pulled hot, moist, and smoky from the shell, wrapped into warm corn or flour tortillas, and dolloped with salsa and guacamole, are messy, seductive finger food of the best and most informal kind. For a crowd, double this recipe, prepare both of the suggested salsas, and encourage guests to try first one in a taco and then the other—the contrast between the two is wonderful.

❦

INGREDIENTS

2 live Maine lobsters (about 4 pounds total)
2 cups wood smoking chips, preferably fruitwood
such as apple or cherry
12 6-inch flour tortillas
1 recipe Tomato-Basil Salsa (page 11) or
1 recipe Cactus Salsa (page 12)

1 recipe Guacamole Verde (page 16)
2 cups coarsely diced ripe tomato
2 cups finely shredded romaine

*J*ust before grilling, kill the lobsters by inserting the point of a long knife into the top of the lobster where the head and body shell meet. Turn them over and, using the knife, split the lobsters in half lengthwise. Discard the sac from the head. With the heavy butt of the knife blade, crack the claw shells slightly.

Light a charcoal fire and let it burn until the coals are evenly white or preheat a gas grill (medium-high). Wrap the wood chips partially in foil, creating a small packet that is open at the top. Set the packet on the hot coals or hot lava stones; position the grill rack about 6 inches above the heat source.

When the wood chips are smoking, place the lobsters, cut side up, on the grill. Cover the grill and cook 7 minutes. Turn the lobsters, cover the grill, and cook them another 5 to 7 minutes, or until the meat is just cooked through without being dry.

Transfer the lobsters to 4 plates. Place the tortillas on the grill, turn them after a few seconds, and remove them in another few seconds; they should be warmed, flexible, and just slightly scorched by the grill. Wrap them in a towel to keep them warm and serve them and the lobsters immediately, accompanied by salsa, guacamole, tomatoes, and lettuce.

Skillet-Smoked Shrimp Cakes

SERVES 4

Shrimp, which come rather abundantly (though frozen) to El Paso from both the Gulf of Mexico and the Gulf of California, are a seafood staple here in the high desert. For this dish, I use chopped raw shrimp to create colorful seafood cakes, reminiscent of the currently trendy crab cakes, which are sautéed in butter in a skillet right on the grill. Use a lot of smoking chips and the cakes will pick up just a touch of fragrant flavor. Serve these at supper or brunch, accompanied by Roasted Red Pepper–Mango Salsa (page 10), Tomato-Basil Salsa, or Rosemary Mayonnaise (page 53), or make them into sandwiches served on toasted buns with lettuce, sliced tomato, and a smear of Sweet and Hot Red Chile Mustard (page 23).

INGREDIENTS

5 tablespoons (2½ ounces) unsalted butter

¾ cup kernels and juices cut and scraped from 1 large ear of supersweet or sugar-enhanced fresh corn

½ cup thinly sliced green onions

2 tablespoons finely chopped sweet red pepper

1 teaspoon dried basil, crumbled

1 large egg

1 tablespoon Dijon mustard

¾ teaspoon salt

¾ teaspoon hot pepper sauce, such as Tabasco

1¼ pounds (about 30) medium shrimp, shelled and deveined (about 1 pound after cleaning), coarsely chopped and well chilled

¼ cup fine, dry bread crumbs

3 cups wood smoking chips, preferably hickory

In a small skillet over medium heat, melt 2 tablespoons of the butter. Add the corn, green onions, red pepper, and basil and cook, covered, stirring once or twice, for 5 minutes. Remove from the heat and cool to room temperature.

In a small bowl, whisk together the egg, mustard, salt, and hot pepper sauce.

In a food processor, using short bursts of power and stopping once or twice to scrape down the sides of the work bowl, evenly chop the shrimp (leave some texture). Transfer the shrimp to a bowl. Stir in the corn mixture, the egg mixture and the bread crumbs; combine well. Shape the shrimp mixture into 4 large 1-inch-thick patties, transferring them to a large plate as you do. Cover and chill for 1 hour.

Meanwhile, light a charcoal fire and let it burn until the coals are evenly white or preheat a gas grill (medium). Wrap the wood chips partially in foil, creating a small packet that is open at the top. Place the packet on the hot coals or hot lava stones; position the grill rack about 6 inches above the heat source.

When the wood chips are smoking heavily, set a large heavy skillet on the grill rack. Add the remaining 3 tablespoons of butter and cover the grill. When the butter has melted and is foaming, carefully add the shrimp cakes. Cover the grill and cook the shrimp cakes, turning them once, until they are crisp, golden brown, and just cooked through, about 8 minutes total. Remove the shrimp cakes from the skillet and serve them hot.

Bluefish Grilled in a Coat of Many Spices

SERVES 4

Dark, rich bluefish very successfully holds its own against the flavors of the fire. It's also affordable (even downright cheap).
Regretably, it's also very perishable, and finding it at its freshest anywhere but on the East Coast is not easy. Choose a
fishmonger with high standards and a brisk turnover of product. To further minimize the chances of the fish tasting
gamy, trim away the narrow strip of darker flesh that runs along each fillet. In this dish, bluefish is thickly coated
with spices, which grill into a crisp and flavorful crust. Supply your guests with plenty of fresh lime wedges
for squeezing over their fish.

❧

INGREDIENTS

2 tablespoons plain, unblended chili powder, preferably
from Chimayo, New Mexico
1 tablespoon ground cumin, preferably from
toasted seeds (page 9)
1 tablespoon dried oregano, crumbled
1 tablespoon ground coriander
1 tablespoon ground turmeric

1 teaspoon garlic powder
¾ teaspoon cayenne pepper
¾ teaspoon salt
4 thick, skinless bluefish fillets (about 3 pounds total)
2 cups wood smoking chips
Wedges of fresh lime

In a small bowl mix together the chili powder, cumin, oregano, coriander, turmeric, garlic powder, cayenne pepper, and salt. Rub the spice mixture into both sides of each bluefish fillet, coating them heavily. Cover and let the fillets stand at room temperature while preparing the grill.

Light a charcoal fire and let it burn until the coals are evenly white or preheat a gas grill (medium-high). Wrap the wood chips partially in foil, creating a small packet that is open at the top. Set the packet on the hot coals or hot lava stones; position the grill rack about 6 inches above the heat source.

When the wood chips are smoking heavily, place the bluefish fillets on the grill. Cover and cook for 4 minutes. With a long, wide spatula, carefully turn the fillets. Cover the grill and cook until the fillets are just done and flaking at their thickest, 3 to 4 minutes.

With the spatula, carefully transfer the fillets to plates. Serve hot, accompanied by lime.

Grilled and Marinated Catfish

In this, a favorite hot-weather dish, the fish is grilled and then marinated, letting the grill master (me) cool off before company shows up. Rich but mild, farm-raised catfish benefits from the assertive flavors of the marinade, which is a beautiful gold, flecked with red and green. Use a grill basket for the fillets if you need the reassurance, but a long, wide spatula is just as effective for turning them. When the catfish is almost done it will begin to drip fat onto the fire—stay alert for flare-ups.

INGREDIENTS

1 cup fresh orange juice

⅓ cup olive oil

2 tablespoons fresh lime juice

1 tablespoon minced fresh rosemary

1 chipotle adobado, homemade (page 166) or commercial, minced, plus 2 teaspoons sauce from the chipotles

1 garlic clove, peeled and crushed through a press

¾ teaspoon salt

2 cups wood chips

4 large skinless fillets of farm-raised catfish (about 3 pounds total)

In a bowl, whisk together the orange juice, olive oil, lime juice, rosemary, chipotle with sauce, garlic, and salt.

Light a charcoal fire and let it burn until the coals are evenly white or preheat a gas grill (medium-high). Wrap the wood chips partially in foil, creating a small packet that is open at the top. Set the packet on the hot coals or hot lava stones; position the grill rack about 6 inches above the heat source.

When the wood chips are smoking heavily, place the catfish fillets on the grill rack. Cover and cook 4 minutes. With a long, wide spatula,

carefully turn the fillets. Cover the grill and cook until the fillets are just done through and flaking slightly at their thickest, 3 to 4 minutes.

Carefully transfer the fillets to a shallow serving dish that will just hold them in a single layer. Rewhisk the marinade and pour it over the fillets while they are still warm. Cover and let them stand at room temperature, basting them with the marinade occasionally, for at least 30 minutes or up to 1 hour.

To serve, transfer the fillets to plates and nap them lightly with the marinade.

Fiery Lemon Chicken

SERVES 6

Marinated in lots of lemon juice with plenty of garlic and a generous dose of crushed red pepper, these crispy chickens are smoky, tart, and lusciously moist. Good hot, better at room temperature, they need only a cool green salad and crusty bread by way of accompaniment—perfect summer food. I think tossing the whole lemon peels onto the fire makes for more flavor—it certainly makes things more fragrant—but you may skip that step if you wish.

INGREDIENTS

10 medium lemons, at room temperature
10 garlic cloves, peeled and crushed through a press
1 tablespoon crushed red pepper flakes

2 young chickens (about 3½ pounds each)
Salt to taste

Halve and juice the lemons; there should be about 1 cup juice. Reserve the peels.

In a small bowl, whisk together the lemon juice, garlic, and red pepper flakes.

With a long, sharp knife or poultry shears, cut away the backbones of the chickens. Crack the breastbones and flatten the chickens with the palm of your hand. Remove any visible fat.

Loosen the skin of the chicken breasts and thighs by running your fingers between it and the flesh. Place the chickens, skin side up, in a shallow nonreactive dish just large enough to hold them. Spoon about one fourth of the lemon mixture under the skin of each chicken, then pour the remaining lemon mixture over the chickens. Cover and let stand in the refrigerator, turning once, for 2 hours.

Light a charcoal fire and let it burn until the coals are evenly white or preheat a gas grill (medium). Create a "cool zone" by raking the charcoal to one side of the grill, or if you're using propane, shut off one or two burners. Scatter the reserved lemon peels over the coals or firestones.

Position the grill rack about 6 inches above the heat source. Place the chickens, meaty side up, on the cool zone. Cover and cook, basting the chickens occasionally with the marinade and rearranging their positions on the rack (but not turning them over) until the skin is crisp and brown and the meat is just cooked through while remaining juicy, about 40 minutes.

Remove the chickens from the heat, season them with salt to taste, and serve hot, warm, or cold.

Chicken with Curried Marmalade-Mustard Glaze

SERVES 6 TO 8

This recipe is the textbook example of how to handle sweet glazes on the grill. The chicken skin is removed (less fat to drip and cause flare-ups) and the bird is cooked over indirect heat: On a propane grill, shut off the central burner; with charcoal, rake the coals to one side and grill the chicken on the other. The sweet smoke of fruitwood chips goes well with this deep-flavored glaze.

INGREDIENTS

2 3½- to 4-pound young chickens, quartered and skinned
2 cups Curried Marmalade-Mustard Glaze (page 36)

2 cups wood smoking chips, preferably fruitwood
¾ teaspoon salt

In a shallow nonreactive dish just large enough to hold them, coat the chicken with half the mustard glaze. Cover and let stand in the refrigerator, turning once or twice, for 1 hour.

Meanwhile, light a charcoal fire and let it burn until the coals are evenly white or preheat a gas grill (medium). Wrap the wood chips partially in foil, creating a small packet that is open at the top. To create a "cool zone," rake the charcoal to one side of the grill; if you're using propane, shut off one or two burners. Set the packet on the hot coals or hot lava stones; position the grill rack about 6 inches above the heat source.

When the wood chips are smoking, season the chicken with the salt. Arrange the leg quarters on the rack, meaty side down, on the cool zone of the grill. Cover and cook 15 minutes. Turn the leg quarters and move them to the edges of the cool zone. Arrange the chicken breasts, meaty side down, in the center of the cool zone, cover, and grill for 15 minutes.

Turn the breasts meaty side up. Spread the remaining mustard mixture evenly over all the chicken quarters and continue to grill, covered, rearranging as necessary in order to brown them evenly but continuing to avoid direct heat, until just cooked through but juicy, about 10 minutes.

Remove the chicken from the grill immediately and serve hot or warm.

Cactus Chicken

SERVES 6 TO 8

The time of the prickly pear cactus seems to be at hand. Touted as a drought-resistant crop of the next century (global warming and all that), cactus pads (nopales) are both fed to cattle and grilled as vegetables in trendy restaurants, while its juicy berrylike fruit (tuna) is being touted, for better or worse, as the kiwifruit of the nineties. Studies indicate the juice may lower the level of cholesterol in the blood. There is even a Texas Prickly Pear Council. I have not been invited to join, but I still do my share to promote the spiny treats by serving this crimson, sweet-tart grilled chicken often. I'm lucky enough to be able to buy tunas already peeled (they're a street vendor staple just across the border in Juárez), but sticker-free varieties are being developed. The high season for tunas in El Paso is late summer, but they're available in markets in Latin American neighborhoods most of the year. Once peeled, they can be wrapped and frozen for up to 3 months.

INGREDIENTS

2 pounds (about 16 medium) peeled prickly pear fruit, coarsely chopped
⅓ cup fresh lime juice
¼ cup honey

2 young chickens (about 3½ pounds each), quartered and skinned
2 cups wood smoking chips, preferably fruitwood
Salt to taste
Freshly ground black pepper to taste

In a food processor, purée the cactus fruit. Force the purée through a strainer set over a bowl; discard the seeds. There should be about 2 cups of seedless purée.

In a medium nonreactive pan over medium heat, combine the cactus purée, lime juice, and honey. Bring to a simmer, skimming any scum that

foams to the top, and cook, uncovered, stirring once or twice, until reduced by one fourth, about 15 minutes. Remove from the heat and cool to room temperature.

In a shallow nonreactive dish just large enough to hold them, coat the chicken quarters with the cooled cactus mixture. Cover and marinate in the refrigerator, turning once or twice, for 1 hour.

Light a charcoal fire and let it burn until the coals are evenly white or preheat a gas grill (medium). Wrap the wood chips partially in foil, forming a small packet that is open at the top. To create a "cool zone," rake the charcoal to one side of the grill; if you're using propane, shut off one or two burners. Set the packet on the hot coals or hot lava stones; position the grill rack about 6 inches above the heat source.

When the wood chips are smoking, arrange the leg quarters on the rack, meaty side down, on the cool zone of the grill. Cover and cook 15 minutes. Baste the leg quarters with some of the cactus mixture, then turn them and move them to the edges of the cool zone. Arrange the chicken breasts, meaty side down, in the center of the cool zone, cover, and grill for 15 minutes, basting all of the chicken quarters once or twice with the cactus mixture.

Turn the breasts meaty side up. Continue to grill, covered, basting until the cactus mixture is used up and rearranging the chicken quarters as necessary in order to brown them evenly but continuing to avoid direct heat, until just cooked through but juicy, about 10 minutes.

Remove the chicken from the grill immediately, season with salt and pepper to taste, and serve hot or warm.

Grill-Smoked Salpicón of Chicken

SERVES 2 TO 4 AS A MAIN DISH, 6 TO 8 AS AN APPETIZER

In my first book there is a recipe for salpicón of beef, a unique El Paso specialty and a great dish of food. However, other meats besides beef, and even seafood, can get the salpicón treatment. In this chicken-based variation, modeled after one I enjoy often at Forti's Mexican Elder restaurant, the birds are first grill-smoked, giving them a subtle edge of extra flavor, then the meat is shredded and marinated briefly. Served with warmed corn or flour tortillas into which the picante chicken salad is rolled for eating, it's one of the best, lightest, and most satisfying summer dishes I know.

INGREDIENTS

2 3½-pound young chickens
3 cups wood smoking chips, preferably mesquite
½ cup fresh lime juice
⅓ cup olive oil
2 fresh jalapeño chiles, stemmed and minced
½ teaspoon salt
½ teaspoon freshly ground black pepper

1 medium juicy, ripe tomato (about 6 ounces), cored and cut into ½-inch chunks
1 large ripe California avocado, pitted, peeled, and cut into ½-inch chunks
½ cup whole fresh cilantro leaves
3 tablespoons thinly sliced green onions
Romaine leaves, for garnish
Corn or flour tortillas, warmed

With a long, sharp knife cut away the chickens' backbones. Crack the breastbones slightly and with the palm of your hand flatten the chickens.

Light a charcoal fire and let it burn until the coals are evenly white or preheat a gas grill (medium). To create a "cool zone," rake the charcoal to one side of the grill; if you're using propane, shut off one or two burners. Wrap the

wood chips partially in foil, creating a small packet that is open at the top. Set the packet on the hot coals or hot lava stones; position the grill rack about 6 inches above the heat source.

When the wood chips are smoking, place the chickens, skin side down, on the cool zone of the rack. Cover and grill for 15 minutes. Turn the chickens skin side up and grill for another 15 minutes. Turn the birds skin side down and grill them until just cooked through while remaining juicy, another 12 to 15 minutes. Remove them from the grill and cool to room temperature. Skin the chickens, then remove the meat from the bones and coarsely shred it.

In a medium bowl, stir together the lime juice, olive oil, jalapeños, salt, and pepper and let stand at room temperature for 20 minutes. In a large bowl, toss together the shredded chicken and dressing. *The salad can be prepared to this point up to 1 hour ahead. Cover and refrigerate.*

Just before serving, add the tomato and avocado chunks, cilantro leaves, and green onions to the bowl and toss gently. Adjust the seasoning.

Spoon the salad onto plates that have been lined with romaine leaves and serve immediately, accompanied by warmed tortillas.

HOT TIP You can warm flour tortillas by turning them on the grill for a few seconds per side; they should become flexible and just slightly scorched for maximum texture and flavor. Warm corn tortillas in a steamer over simmering water (right at the grill if yours has a convenient side burner). Heat either kind, tightly wrapped in foil, in a conventional oven. The microwave works only for tortillas that are to be eaten immediately; nuked, they become dry and brittle within minutes.

Chicken Tacos al Carbón

SERVES 6

The differences between tacos al carbón ("charcoaled") and fajitas are negligible. In both, strips of marinated meat are grilled, then rolled into tortillas with mix-or-match embellishments such as salsa, guacamole, and sour cream. The distinctive garnish for tacos al carbón in the El Paso region—a grilled green onion, which is eaten alongside or enfolded in the tortilla along with the other components—is the main clue to the identity of the meal on your plate. Beef is the traditional main ingredient, but chicken is becoming increasingly popular.

INGREDIENTS

2 pounds boneless, skinless chicken breasts, halved and trimmed of cartilage and fat

½ cup fresh lime juice

3 tablespoons olive oil, plus additional oil for grilling the green onions

2 garlic cloves, peeled and crushed through a press

2 cups wood smoking chips, preferably mesquite

18 large green onions, trimmed (leave no more than 3 inches of green top)

Salt to taste

Freshly ground black pepper to taste

18 6-inch flour tortillas

Guacamole Verde (page 16) or sour cream

Salsa Borracho (page 6) or Grilled Pico de Gallo (page 4)

With a meat pounder or the bottom of a small saucepan, flatten the thicker portions of the chicken breast halves slightly. In a small bowl, combine the lime juice, 3 tablespoons olive oil, and garlic. In a shallow nonreactive bowl just large enough to hold them comfortably, pour the lime juice marinade over the chicken breasts. Cover and let stand in the refrigerator for 1 hour.

Meanwhile, light a charcoal fire and let it burn until the coals are evenly white or preheat a gas grill (medium). Wrap the wood chips partially in foil, creating a small packet that is open at the top. Set the packet on the hot coals or hot lava stones; position the grill rack about 6 inches above the heat source.

When the wood chips are smoking heavily, place the chicken breasts on the rack. Cover and cook, basting them with any remaining marinade and turning them once, until just done through while remaining juicy, about 4 minutes total. Transfer the chicken breasts to a cutting board, tent with foil, and let rest for 5 minutes. Brush the green onions with olive oil and place them on the grill rack. Cover and cook, turning them once or twice, until they are lightly browned and limp, 3 to 4 minutes. Transfer them to a plate.

Cut the chicken lengthwise into ½-inch strips. Season lightly with salt and pepper to taste and transfer to a heated platter. Warm the tortillas on the grill, turning them once, until they are flexible, about 30 seconds.

Serve the chicken and tortillas immediately, accompanied by the grilled onions, guacamole, and salsa.

HOT TIP To achieve maximum flavor in foods that are on the grill only a short time—boneless chicken breasts, thin fish steaks or fillets, shrimp, or vegetables, for example—the fragrant wood chips should be smoking heavily before the food hits the grill. Soak them well in water, then drain and scatter them directly on the lava stones or hot coals. (If you're using a foil packet or a metal grill chip box, do not soak the chips, but do be sure they are smoking heavily before you begin to grill.)

HOT MENU

Iced Corona Beer in the Bottle with Wedges of Lime

Chicken Tacos al Carbón (page 92)
Guacamole Verde (page 16)
Salsa Borracho (page 6)

Pink Margarita Sorbet (page 222)
Michael's Spiced Chocolate Shortbreads (page 244)

Mesquite-Grilled Turkey Fajitas Sausages

MAKES ABOUT 2 POUNDS, SERVING 4

Here I've taken the fajitas theme just about as far as it can go. Actually there are no "little sashes" (the literal translation of fajitas) of turkey in this. Instead I've used my basic fajitas marinade as the flavoring agent for sausages that are surprisingly gutsy and succulent, given the all-American bird's current health food status. These are best made with turkey you've boned and chopped yourself—supermarket turkey is too finely ground and contains skin and fat, which I prefer to avoid.

INGREDIENTS

1 tablespoon cider vinegar

5 to 6 feet of pork sausage casing (ordered from a good butcher)

1 medium heavy sweet red pepper, preferably Dutch

1 pound chilled, well-trimmed boneless and skinless turkey white meat, cut into 1-inch chunks

½ pound chilled, well-trimmed boneless and skinless turkey dark meat, cut into 1-inch chunks

⅓ cup fine dry bread crumbs

⅓ cup canned chicken broth

⅓ cup finely chopped cilantro

¼ cup tomato-based commercial hot salsa

1 tablespoon gold tequila

1 tablespoon fresh lime juice

¾ teaspoon salt

1 teaspoon freshly ground black pepper

2 cups wood smoking chips, preferably mesquite

Fill a large bowl with cold water. Stir in the vinegar, add the sausage casing, and soak for 1 hour. Drain the casing. Slip one end of the casing over a sink faucet and run cold water through it. Check for leaks and cut out 4 hole-free sections each about 10 inches long. In a bowl, cover the casings with cold water while preparing the filling.

In the open flame of a gas burner, on a preheated grill (over wood smoking chips if desired), or under a preheated broiler, roast the red pepper, turning it often, until the peel is evenly charred. In a closed paper bag, steam the pepper until cool. Rub off the burned peel, remove the stem, ribs, and seeds, and finely chop the pepper.

In a food processor, working in batches if necessary, using short bursts of power and stopping once or twice to scrape down the sides of the work bowl, chop the turkey. Do not overprocess; some texture, like that of coarsely ground beef, should remain. Transfer the chopped turkey to a bowl.

Stir in the chopped red pepper, bread crumbs, chicken broth, cilantro, salsa, tequila, lime juice, salt, and pepper and mix thoroughly.

Form a small patty of the turkey mixture and in a small skillet over medium heat, sauté it, turning it once or twice, until well browned and cooked through. Cool slightly, then taste. Adjust the seasoning of the remaining sausage meat.

Tie a knot in one end of a section of casing. Insert the open end of a pastry bag fitted with a large plain tip into the open end of the casing, gathering the casing up onto the tip. Fill the pastry bag with one fourth of the turkey mixture. Force the mixture into the casing, sliding the casing off the pastry tip as it fills.

Stop occasionally to shape the sausage. Pierce any air bubbles with a fine needle. Remove the sausage from the pastry tip. Tie a knot in the open end and trim any excess casing. Repeat with the remaining filling and casing. Wrap the sausages well in plastic wrap and refrigerate overnight.

Bring the sausages to room temperature and prick each one twice with the tip of a knife. Light a charcoal fire and let it burn until the coals are evenly white or preheat a gas grill (medium-low). Wrap the wood chips partially in foil, creating a small packet that is open at the top. Set the packet on the hot coals or hot lava stones; position the grill rack about 6 inches above the heat source.

When the wood chips are smoking heavily, place the sausages on the rack. Cover and grill, turning them occasionally, until they are crisp, well browned, and cooked through while remaining juicy, 12 to 15 minutes total. Remove them from the grill and serve hot.

Grilled Red Chile Doves

SERVES 4

Few foods come off the grill looking, smelling, and tasting as enticing as these little birds. Glazed with a tangy, fiery sauce of New Mexico red chiles, dried apricots, and white wine, sweetened slightly with maple syrup, they are crisp, glistening, and very succulent. In Texas, hunters seek doves—turtledoves, actually—but home cooks can buy farm-raised squabs from good butchers, or order them by mail. Just a hint of fresh rosemary really complements this dish—use a big bunch in place of a brush, for mopping the squabs with the sauce, or throw a big handful right onto the fire near the end of grilling. This recipe can also be used for butterflied farm-raised quail: Serve two per person; the cooking time will be 5 to 7 minutes shorter.

INGREDIENTS

1½ cups dry white wine
⅓ cup (about 2 ounces) finely diced dried apricots
4 dried red New Mexico chile pods, stemmed, seeded, and torn into small pieces
2 dried hot red chiles, such as de árbol or japonés, seeded and minced
1 bay leaf

¼ cup maple syrup
1 tablespoon Dijon mustard
½ teaspoon salt
4 farm-raised squabs (about 4½ pounds total), dressed
2 cups wood smoking chips, preferably hickory or a fruitwood such as apple or cherry

In a small nonreactive saucepan, combine the wine, apricots, red chiles, hot chiles, and bay leaf. Set over medium heat and bring to a boil. Partially cover, lower the heat slightly, and simmer, stirring occasionally, until the chiles and apricots are very tender, about 20 minutes. Remove from the heat and cool to room temperature.

Discard the bay leaf. In a food processor, purée the apricot mixture until very smooth. Transfer the mixture to a sieve set over a bowl and with a rubber scraper, force the purée through the sieve; discard any solids. Stir the maple syrup, mustard, and salt into the strained purée. *This glaze can be prepared up to 3 days ahead. Transfer it to a storage container, cover, and refrigerate. Return to room temperature before using.*

Bring the squabs to room temperature. Discard the giblets. With a long, sharp knife or poultry shears, remove the necks and the first wing . segments; cut away the backbones. Crack the breastbones slightly and with the palm of your hand flatten the birds.

Meanwhile, light a charcoal fire and let it burn until the coals are evenly white or preheat a gas grill (medium). Wrap the wood chips partially in foil, creating a small packet that is open at the top. Set the packet on the hot coals or hot lava stones; position the grill rack about 6 inches above the heat source.

When the wood chips are smoking heavily, place the squabs skin side up on the rack. Grill uncovered for 5 minutes. Turn the squabs skin side down and grill uncovered for 5 minutes. Brush the squabs generously with the glaze, turn and grill, uncovered, for 2 minutes. Continue glazing and turning the squabs at 2-minute intervals until the glaze is used up, they are crisply browned and shiny, and their breast meat, at its thickest, is medium-rare, about 25 minutes total cooking time.

Remove the squabs from the grill and serve them hot.

HOT MENU

❧

Cool Red Wine
Grilled Red Chile Doves (page 96)
Grilled Potato Planks (page 192)
Grilled Marinated Mushrooms (page 196)

Grilled Bananas "Foster" (page 234)

Hickory-Grilled T-Bone Steaks with Roasted Garlic—Green and Red Chile Butter

A very large thick (1½ inches) steak with the bone in works especially well on the grill, the bone contributing to the succulence and the thickness making overcooking (and drying out) less likely. If you prefer to serve less than one pound of meat per person (we live in crazy times), don't resort to skinny steaks. Merely grill fewer thick ones and then carve them into slices for serving when done.

INGREDIENTS

2 cups hickory wood smoking chips
4 1½-inch-thick T-bone steaks (about 6 pounds total), at room temperature
Salt to taste

Freshly ground black pepper to taste
1 recipe Roasted Garlic—Green and Red Chile Butter (page 57), softened slightly

Light a charcoal fire and let it burn down until the coals are evenly white or preheat a gas grill (medium-high).

Wrap the wood chips partially in foil, creating a small packet that is open at the top. Set the packet on the hot coals or lava stones. Position the grill rack about 6 inches above the heat source. Pat the steaks dry. When the wood chips are smoking heavily, place the steaks on the rack, spacing them well apart, cover, and grill, turning them once or twice and rearranging their positions on the rack to create attractive markings, until they are done to your liking, about 8 minutes total for medium rare.

Transfer the steaks to heated plates. Season them lightly with salt and pepper to taste. Spread the top of each steak with one quarter of the garlic chile butter and serve immediately.

Grilled Marinated Flank Steak

SERVES 8, WITH LEFTOVERS

This basic flank steak preparation, in which the meat is marinated in a tangy, vinaigrette-like mixture, is good hot and juicy off the grill (roll the thinly sliced meat into tortillas with salsa and sour cream or guacamole for a fajitas-like experience) and excellent cold as well. I always throw an extra flank steak on the fire, knowing there will be steak salad on the menu tomorrow.

❦

INGREDIENTS

2 or 3 small flank steaks (about 3¾ pounds total)
1 recipe Chipotle Marinade (page 45)
2 cups wood smoking chips, preferably hickory

Salt to taste
Freshly ground black pepper to taste

In a shallow nonreactive dish just large enough to hold them comfortably, pour the marinade over the flank steaks. Cover and let stand at room temperature, turning them once or twice, for 2 hours.

Light a charcoal fire and let it burn until the coals are evenly white or preheat a gas grill (high heat). Wrap the wood chips partially in foil, creating a small packet that is open at the top. Set the packet on the hot coals or hot lava stones; position the grill rack about 6 inches above the heat source.

When the wood chips are smoking heavily, place the steaks on the rack. Cover and grill them for

3½ minutes. Turn them and grill for another 3½ minutes. Rake the coals to one side of the grill, or on a gas grill, lower the heat to medium, and continue to grill the steaks, basting them with the marinade, for another 6 minutes for medium rare, or until done to your liking.

Transfer the steaks to a cutting board, tent with foil, and let stand for 10 minutes. Carve the steaks at a slight angle across the grain into very thin slices; serve hot, warm, or cold with salt and pepper to taste.

Black Bean Chili with Hickory-Grilled Steak and Goat Cheese Cream

SERVES 6

This is an ideal dish for a casual party, featuring earthy, informal chili stylishly and festively presented. The notion of topping an all-bean chili with chunks of medium-rare grilled beef was stolen, I freely admit, from Café Terra Cotta, a terrific Tucson, Arizona, restaurant, though the actual formula here is my own. Skirt steak, the fibrous strip of meat that is classically used in fajitas, is particularly good here, but flank steak or even porterhouse can be substituted if you're feeling flush.

INGREDIENTS

THE GOAT CHEESE CREAM

½ pound soft, mild, rindless goat cheese, such as Montrachet, at room temperature

8 ounces sour cream

About ¾ cup cultured buttermilk

THE CHILI

1 pound dried black beans, picked over and well rinsed

2 tablespoons olive oil

2 ounces bacon, preferably mesquite-smoked, coarsely chopped

2 cups finely chopped yellow onions

2 cups diced sweet red pepper

4 garlic cloves, peeled and finely chopped

2 fresh jalapeño chiles, stemmed and finely chopped

⅓ cup mild chili powder blend

1 tablespoon dried oregano, crumbled

2 teaspoons ground cumin, preferably from toasted seeds (page 9)

½ teaspoon dried thyme, crumbled

½ teaspoon dried sage, crumbled

3 cups canned beef or chicken broth

1 12-ounce bottle mellow dark beer, such as Heineken

1 cup canned crushed tomatoes with added purée

2 teaspoons salt

2 cups well-drained canned or defrosted frozen corn kernels

THE STEAK

3 tablespoons olive oil

2 tablespoons fresh lime juice

2 tablespoons Worcestershire sauce

1 tablespoon soy sauce

1 tablespoon packed dark brown sugar

3 garlic cloves, peeled and crushed through a press

2½ pounds skirt steak, trimmed and halved crosswise for easier handling

2 cups wood smoking chips, preferably hickory

Salt and freshly ground black pepper

Diced tomato, diced red onion, slices of California avocado, and sprigs of cilantro, for garnish

FOR THE GOAT CHEESE CREAM

In a medium bowl, mash the goat cheese. Whisk in the sour cream, then whisk in enough buttermilk to make a thin sauce that can be squeezed from a plastic squeeze bottle or drizzled from a spoon. *Cover and refrigerate, returning to room temperature before using.*

FOR THE CHILI

In a large bowl, generously cover the beans with cold water and let soak for 12 hours.

In a heavy nonreactive, 4½- to 5-quart Dutch oven or flameproof casserole over low heat, combine the olive oil and bacon. Cover and cook, stirring once or twice, until the bacon is lightly browned, about 8 minutes. Stir in the onions, red peppers, garlic, jalapeños, chili powder, oregano, cumin, thyme, and sage. Cover and cook over low heat, stirring once or twice, for 10 minutes. Add the beef broth, beer, and tomatoes. Drain the beans and add them. Bring the chili to a simmer and cook uncovered, stirring occasionally, for 1 hour. Stir in the salt and continue to cook, uncovered, stirring often as the chili becomes very thick, until the beans are just tender, about 30 minutes more. Stir in the corn and adjust the seasoning. *The chili can be prepared up to 3 days ahead. Cool completely, cover, and refrigerate. Thin the chili with additional beef broth or water and warm it over low heat, stirring often, before serving.*

GRILLING THE STEAK

In a small bowl, whisk together the olive oil, lime juice, Worcestershire sauce, soy sauce, brown sugar, and garlic. In a shallow nonreactive dish, pour the marinade over the steak. Cover and let stand at room temperature, turning once or twice, for 1 hour.

Meanwhile, light a charcoal fire and let it burn until the coals are evenly white or preheat a gas grill (medium-high). Wrap the wood chips partially in foil, creating a small packet that is open at the top. Set the packet on the hot coals or the lava stones; position the grill rack about 6 inches above the heat source.

When the chips are smoking heavily, place the steak on the grill. Cover and cook, turning it once or twice and basting it with the remaining marinade, until the meat is medium rare at its thickest, about 4 minutes per side. Transfer the steak to a cutting board, tent with foil, and let rest for 10 minutes.

Cut the steak at an angle across the grain into thin slices or, if it is very tender, cut it into ½-inch cubes. Season the steak with salt and pepper to taste. Spoon the chili into wide, deep bowls and arrange the steak over the chili. Drizzle the steak and chili with the goat cheese cream. Garnish each serving with diced tomato and onion, avocado, and cilantro and serve immediately.

Beer-Braised Grill-Finished Beef Short Ribs with Spicy Molasses Mop

SERVES 4 TO 6

Succulent, meaty beef short ribs take a fair amount of oven time to reach optimum tenderness, but that step can be done a day or two ahead. A brief 10-minute turning over a smoky fire then heats and crisps the ribs while the dark, tangy mop glazes them a rich brown. Pass the remaining mop at the table as a dipping sauce.

INGREDIENTS

5 pounds well-trimmed beef short ribs, as much as possible all the same size

3½ cups canned beef broth

1 large yellow onion, peeled and thinly sliced

1 12-ounce bottle mellow dark beer, such as Heineken

3 garlic cloves, peeled and finely chopped

¾ teaspoon dried thyme, crumbled

3¼ teaspoons salt

½ cup plus 1 tablespoon unsulfured molasses

3 tablespoons balsamic vinegar

2½ tablespoons hot pepper sauce, such as Tabasco

2 cups wood smoking chips, preferably hickory

Position a rack in the middle of the oven and preheat the oven to 350°F.

In a heavy 5-quart casserole or Dutch oven, combine the short ribs, beef broth, onions, beer, garlic, thyme, and 1 teaspoon of the salt. Cover, set over medium heat, and bring to a simmer. Set the casserole in the oven and cook the ribs, stirring them once or twice, until they are very tender, about 1¼ hours. Cool the ribs in the braising liquid to room temperature.

Remove the ribs from the broth, scraping off any clinging onions. Strain and degrease the broth. In a medium saucepan over medium heat,

bring the broth to a brisk simmer. Cook, uncovered, skimming occasionally, until reduced to 1½ cups, about 25 minutes. Cool to room temperature. *The recipe can be prepared to this point up to 2 days ahead. Wrap the ribs well, cover the reduced broth, and refrigerate both. Return them to room temperature before proceeding with the recipe.*

In a medium bowl, whisk together the reduced broth, molasses, vinegar, hot pepper sauce, and the remaining 2¼ teaspoons of salt.

Light a charcoal fire and let it burn until the coals are evenly white or preheat a gas grill (medium). Wrap the wood chips partially in foil, creating a small packet that is open at the top. Set the packet on the hot coals or hot lava stones; position the grill rack about 6 inches above the heat source and cover the grill. When the wood chips are smoking heavily, place the short ribs on the rack. Cover and grill them, basting them on all sides with about one third of the molasses mixture and turning them often, until they are crisp, brown, and heated through, 10 to 12 minutes.

Serve the ribs immediately, passing the remaining molasses mop at the table.

Grilled Country Spareribs in Chipotle-Orange Marinade

SERVES 4 TO 6

It takes a lengthy marination, followed by a long, slow grilling, to tenderize country-style pork ribs, but the effort is worth it. Eventually, the rich, well-spiced meat falls from the bone—and makes wonderful, if messy, eating.

INGREDIENTS

⅓ cup finely chopped yellow onions

⅓ cup fresh orange juice

¼ cup packed dark brown sugar

3 tablespoons fresh lime juice

3 chipotles adobado, homemade (page 166) or commercial
plus about 1 tablespoon clinging sauce

3 garlic cloves, peeled and finely chopped

1 tablespoon minced orange zest (colored peel)

1 tablespoon chili powder blend

1½ teaspoons dried oregano, crumbled

4 pounds country-style pork ribs

3 cups wood smoking chips, preferably hickory

In a food processor, combine the onions, orange juice, brown sugar, lime juice, chipotles with their sauce, garlic, orange zest, chili powder, and oregano and process until fairly smooth. In a shallow nonreactive dish just large enough to hold them, pour the marinade over the pork ribs. *Cover and refrigerate, stirring once or twice, for at least 24 hours and up to 48 hours. Return the ribs to room temperature before proceeding with the recipe.*

Light a charcoal fire and let it burn until the coals are evenly white or preheat a gas grill (medium). Rake the coals to one side of the grill or if you're using propane, shut off a burner on one side of the grill. Set a shallow metal drip pan filled with 1 inch of water in the grill on the side away from the heat source. Wrap the wood chips partially in foil, creating a small packet that is open at the top. Set the packet on the hot coals or hot lava stones; position the grill rack about 6 inches above the heat source.

When the wood chips are smoking, place the ribs on the rack above the drip pan. Cover and grill, turning the ribs occasionally, rearranging their position over the drip pan, and basting them with any remaining marinade. Add additional water if the drip pan cooks dry. The ribs are done when they are tender, crisp, and well browned, about 1 hour. Remove them from the heat and serve hot.

Grilled Spareribs with Pineapple-Mustard Glaze

SERVES 4 TO 8

Precooking the ribs to shorten the time the cook spends hovering over a hot grill is a good idea, but boiling them (the usual method) is a bad idea, since rich pork flavor gets thrown out with the water. In this method, in which the ribs are baked instead in foil packets, the rendered sparerib juices are reduced, rescued, and stirred into the tangy glaze, and none of their meaty goodness is lost. This recipe will feed eight if accompanied by hamburgers or chicken, four if served alone.

❧

INGREDIENTS

2 sides (about 5½ pounds) regular
(not baby back) spareribs
¾ teaspoon salt
½ teaspoon freshly ground black pepper

About ½ cup canned chicken broth
1 recipe Pineapple-Mustard Glaze (page 29)
2 cups wood smoking chips, preferably fruitwood or hickory

Preheat the oven to 375°F. Sprinkle the spareribs evenly with the salt and pepper. Wrap each side of ribs tightly in foil. Set the wrapped ribs on a baking sheet and bake about 1 hour, or until tender. Cool the ribs in the foil to room temperature.

Pour off and degrease the rib juices. Add chicken broth to the rib juices if necessary to yield 1⅓ cups. *The recipe can be prepared to this point up to 1 day ahead. Wrap the ribs tightly, cover the rib juices, and refrigerate both. Return them to room temperature before proceeding with the recipe.*

For easier handling, cut each side of ribs in half. In a medium saucepan over medium heat, bring the rib juices to a simmer. Cook, uncovered, stirring once or twice, until the juices are reduced to a few syrupy spoonfuls, 7 to 10 minutes. Scrape these into the pineapple-mustard glaze and stir to combine.

Light a charcoal fire and let it burn until the coals are evenly white or preheat a gas grill (medium-low). Wrap the wood chips partially in foil, creating a small packet that is open at the top. Set the packet on the hot coals or hot lava stones; position the grill rack about 6 inches above the heat source.

continued

When the chips are smoking heavily, place the ribs on the grill (use the cooler edges of the grill if necessary to prevent the glaze from burning) and cook, turning and basting the ribs often

with the glaze, using it all, until they are well coated, shiny, and crisp, about 20 minutes.

Remove the ribs from the heat, cut them apart if desired, and serve hot or warm.

Spicy Pork and Red Wine Sausages

MAKES 2¹/₂ POUNDS, SERVING 6 AS A MAIN COURSE

Chorizo, the finely ground, intensely spiced, and utterly dubious Mexican sausage widely sold in El Paso, is used almost more as a seasoning than as meat. Cooked, it quickly crumbles into tiny bits, perfect for scattering over pizzas and quesadillas or for stirring into scrambled eggs, but not very satisfying to eat on its own. Here is a homemade sausage inspired by chorizo, but coarser and less spicy—definitely intended as the hearty main course of a summertime feast. If you have a stand mixer with a sausage-stuffing attachment, this will go quickly; if you must use a pastry bag as I do, well, consider sausage making a low-tech labor of love.

INGREDIENTS

1 tablespoon cider vinegar

5 to 6 feet of pork sausage casing (ordered from a good butcher)

2 pounds well-trimmed, cubed boneless pork, chilled

¹/₂ pound fresh pork fat, diced and chilled

¹/₂ cup red wine

4 garlic cloves, peeled and crushed through a press

1 tablespoon pure, unblended chili powder, preferably from Chimayo, New Mexico

1¹/₂ teaspoons dried oregano, crumbled

1¹/₂ teaspoons salt

1 teaspoon ground cumin, preferably from toasted seeds (page 9)

2 cups wood smoking chips, preferably hickory

Fill a large bowl with cold water. Stir in the vinegar, add the sausage casing, and soak for

1 hour. Drain the casing. Slip one end of the casing over a sink faucet and run cold water

through it. Check for leaks, and cut out 6 hole-free sections each about 10 inches long. In a bowl, cover the casings with cold water while preparing the filling.

In a food processor, working in batches, using short bursts of power and stopping once or twice to scrape down the sides of the work bowl, coarsely and evenly chop together the pork and pork fat. In a bowl, combine the chopped meat, wine, garlic, chili powder, oregano, salt, and cumin and mix thoroughly.

Form a small patty of the meat mixture and in a small skillet over medium heat, sauté it, turning it once or twice, until well browned and cooked through. Cool slightly, then taste. Adjust the seasoning of the remaining sausage meat.

Tie a knot in one end of a section of casing. Insert the open end of a pastry bag fitted with a large plain tip into the open end of the casing, gathering the casing up onto the tip. Fill the pastry bag with one sixth of the pork mixture. Force the mixture into the casing, sliding the casing off the pastry tip as it fills. Stop occasionally to shape the sausage. Pierce any air bubbles with a fine needle. Remove the sausage from the pastry tip. Tie a knot in the open end and trim any excess casing. Repeat with the remaining filling and casing. Wrap the sausages well in plastic and refrigerate overnight.

Bring the sausages to room temperature and prick each one twice with the tip of a knife. Light a charcoal fire and let it burn until the coals are evenly white or preheat a gas grill (medium-low). Wrap the wood chips partially in foil, creating a small packet that is open at the top. Set the packet on the hot coals or hot lava stones; position the grill rack about 6 inches above the heat source.

When the wood chips are smoking heavily, place the sausages on the rack. Cover and grill, turning them occasionally, until they are crisp and well browned and cooked through while remaining juicy, 12 to 15 minutes total. Remove the sausages from the grill and serve hot.

HOT TIP For extra fragrance and extra flavor, consider soaking wood smoking chips for grilling in something besides water. Bourbon, orange juice (include a couple of cinnamon sticks broken into 1-inch sections and toss them onto the fire along with the chips), or dark beer are all good choices. Use at least 1 cup liquid for each cup of wood chips and soak them for at least 30 minutes. Drain the chips and then scatter them directly onto hot coals or lava stones.

Rosemary Fajitas of Lamb

SERVES 8

Fajitas—marinated, grilled beef, smoky and juicy, sliced thin and rolled into warmed tortillas with lashings of guacamole, sour cream, and salsa—are such brilliant and satisfying finger food it's only logical for cooks to dream up variations on the theme. Pork, chicken, and shellfish fajitas have all been sighted, tasted, and judged delicious by me, and now leg of lamb joins the stampede. Slice the meat, set out tortillas and as many accompaniments as you desire (when it comes to fajitas, abundance is essential), and let guests roll their own informal Southwestern "sandwiches."

INGREDIENTS

1 cup tomato-based commercial hot salsa
1 cup amber beer, such as Dos Equis
¾ cup loosely packed cilantro (stems can be included)
6 garlic cloves, peeled and coarsely chopped
¼ cup finely chopped fresh rosemary
¼ cup gold tequila
¼ cup fresh lime juice
2 tablespoons olive oil

1 6- to 7-pound boneless, butterflied leg of lamb, trimmed of external fat
2 cups mesquite wood smoking chips
Salt to taste
24 6- to 8-inch flour tortillas
Grilled Pico de Gallo (page 4), Guacamole Verde (page 15), Grilled Red Onions (page 195), and sour cream

In a food processor or blender, combine the salsa, beer, cilantro, garlic, rosemary, tequila, lime juice, and olive oil and process until fairly smooth. In a shallow nonreactive dish, pour the marinade over the lamb. Cover and let stand at room temperature, turning once or twice, for 2 hours.

Light a charcoal fire and let it burn until the coals are evenly white or preheat a gas grill (medium). Wrap the wood chips partially in foil, creating a small packet that is open at the top. Set the packet on the hot coals or hot lava stones; position the grill rack about 6 inches above the heat source.

When the chips are smoking, place the lamb on the rack. Pour half the marinade over the lamb (there will be a cloud of steam), lower the cover, and grill for 10 minutes. Turn the lamb, pour the remaining marinade over it (more steam), cover, and grill another 10 minutes. Continue to cook the lamb, covered, turning it occasionally, until it is well browned and medium rare at its thickest, about 40 minutes. Transfer it to a cutting board, tent with foil, and let rest for 10 minutes.

Cut the lamb at an angle across the grain into thin slices. Season it with salt to taste and

transfer it to a heated platter. Working in batches, place the tortillas on the grill, turning them once, until warmed through but still pliable, about 30 seconds total.

Serve the lamb and tortillas, accompanied by salsa, guacamole, grilled red onions, and sour cream.

HOT MENU

Mango-Peach Margaritas (page 217)
Barbecued Tequila Shrimp with Bacon (page 177) with West Texas Red (page 17)

Rosemary Fajitas of Lamb (page 108)
Grilled Pico de Gallo (page 4)
Guacamole Verde (page 16)
Sour Cream
Pinto Bean and Cheese Salad (page 181)
Sliced Tomato Salad with Pesto Ranch Dressing (page 185)

Lime Puddings with Blackberry Sauce (page 235)

Grilled Lamb and Poblano Chile Sausages

MAKES ABOUT 3 POUNDS, SERVING 6

I confess to a lifelong resistance to lamb, one I'm gradually overcoming, thanks mostly to how good the stuff tastes when it's been grilled. (On the related subject of goat cheese, however, I remain unconverted.) The lamb available in markets these days is tender and relatively mild, compared to that I loathed as a child, with just a hint of assertive flavor that works well with the smoke and sizzle of an open fire.

INGREDIENTS

1 tablespoon cider vinegar

5 to 6 feet of pork sausage casing (ordered from a good butcher)

4 medium poblano chiles or 5 long green chiles

2 pounds lean, chilled, well-trimmed lamb, cut into 1-inch chunks

½ pound chilled, firm, white pork fat, cut into 1-inch chunks

¼ cup canned beef broth

¼ cup dry red wine

4 garlic cloves, peeled and crushed through a press

3 tablespoons minced fresh oregano or rosemary, or 1 tablespoon dried oregano or rosemary, well crumbled

1½ teaspoons salt

½ teaspoon freshly ground black pepper

2 cups wood smoking chips, preferably hickory

Fill a large bowl with cold water. Stir in the vinegar, add the sausage casing, and soak for 1 hour. Drain the casing. Slip one end of the casing over a sink faucet and run cold water through it. Check for leaks and cut out 6 hole-free sections each about 10 inches long. In a bowl, cover the casings with cold water while preparing the filling.

In the open flame of a gas burner, on a preheated grill (over wood smoking chips if desired), or under a preheated broiler, roast the chiles, turning them often, until the peels are lightly and evenly charred. In a closed paper bag, steam the chiles until cool. Rub off the burned peels, remove the stems, ribs, and seeds, and finely chop the chiles.

In a food processor, working in batches if necessary, using short bursts of power and stopping once or twice to scrape down the sides of the work bowl, chop the lamb and pork fat together. Do not overprocess; some texture, like that of coarsely ground beef, should remain. Transfer the mixture to a bowl.

Stir in the chiles, beef broth, wine, garlic, oregano, salt, and pepper and mix thoroughly.

Form a small patty of the meat mixture and in a small skillet over medium heat, sauté it, turning it once or twice, until well browned and cooked through. Cool slightly, then taste. Adjust the seasoning of the remaining sausage meat.

Tie a knot in one end of a section of casing. Insert the open end of a pastry bag fitted with a large plain tip into the open end of the casing, gathering the casing up onto the tip. Fill the pastry bag with one sixth of the lamb mixture. Force the mixture into the casing, sliding the casing off the pastry tip as it fills. Stop occasionally to shape the sausage. Pierce any air bubbles with a fine needle. Remove the sausage

from the pastry tip. Tie a knot in the open end and trim any excess casing. Repeat with the remaining filling and casing. Wrap the sausages well in plastic and refrigerate overnight.

Bring the sausages to room temperature and prick each one twice with the tip of a knife. Light a charcoal fire and let it burn until the coals are evenly white or preheat a gas grill (medium-low). Wrap the wood chips partially in foil, creating a small packet that is open at the top. Set the packet on the hot coals or hot lava stones; position the grill rack about 6 inches above the heat source.

When the wood chips are smoking heavily, place the sausages on the rack. Cover and grill, turning them occasionally, until they are crisp and well browned and cooked through while remaining juicy, 12 to 15 minutes total. Remove the sausages from the grill and serve hot.

pizzas on the grill

Like pizza baked in a wood-burning oven, pizza baked on the grill is seductively smoky and extra-delicious. It's also immeasurably easier to achieve, since most home cooks do not own a wood-burning oven. While I do not claim to have invented the process (pizza is grilled in Italy, and Al Forno, a Providence, Rhode Island, restaurant, has featured it for years), I do claim to make the finest grilled pizza west of the Pecos, and my method, fine-tuned over several grill seasons, can earn you a similar ranking in your own area code. (Sometimes these are supper, but more often they're the substantial snack of an extended cocktail hour, paired with guacamole, salsa, and a pitcher of margaritas. It's a relaxed and convivial time, with plenty of opportunity for nibbling, sipping, gossiping, and kibitzing, during which I nearly always find myself giving impromptu pizza-grilling lessons.)

The process is unusual though not tricky, relying on indirect heat, and while it's easier on a gas grill, good results can also be achieved by experienced charcoal users. The dough is placed right on the rack, grilled briefly, removed from the grill, flipped, topped, and then returned to the grill, and it is in the timing of these turnings that success lies. Beginners should expect a failure or two (don't make your debut in front of company is my advice), but the rewards of practice and failure, which include a showy star turn at the grill, incomparable pizza, and generous bravos from the crowd, make it all worth while. Pizza toppings are personal and improvisational and I will be disappointed in you if you don't eventually fly solo, but the following formulas have proven successful enough to record and will help get you started.

Pizza Dough

MAKES FOUR 12-INCH PIZZAS

Unlike many pizza doughs, this one does not require refrigeration for easier handling. I can come home from the office, put this on to rise, prepare the toppings, light the fire, and have grilled pizza on the table before sundown!

꧁

INGREDIENTS

1½ cups warm (105° to 115°F) water
1 package dry yeast
2 teaspoons salt

½ teaspoon garlic powder
¼ cup olive oil, plus oil for the bowl
4 cups unbleached all-purpose flour

In a large bowl, whisk together the water and yeast and let stand for 5 minutes. Whisk in the salt, garlic powder, and olive oil. Stir in about 3½ cups of the flour, or until a soft dough forms. Sprinkle the work surface with the remaining flour, turn out the dough, and knead until smooth, about 5 minutes. Lightly oil a large bowl. Put in the dough, turn it to coat it with oil, and cover with a clean towel. Let the dough rise until it is puffy and light, about 2 hours.

The dough can be prepared to this point up to 3 days in advance. Return it to room temperature before using. The dough can be successfully frozen at this point for up to 2 months.

After kneading, punch it down, divide it into fourths if desired, and wrap it tightly. Thaw it in the refrigerator overnight, then set it out, coated with oil, to rise at room temperature.

HOT TIP In place of homemade pizza dough, even my quick version, try buying uncooked dough from a neighboring pizzeria (independents are better candidates for this than major pizza chains). Many charge only pennies. Frozen supermarket bread doughs can also be used; newly and widely available bread or pizza shells (like Boboli) also work on the grill if time is tight.

Barbecued Chicken Pizza

MAKES 4 PIZZAS, SERVING 8 OR MORE

From trendy Los Angeles to the heart of Brooklyn I have observed barbecued chicken pizzas for sale, but I never actually got around to sampling this inventive combination until the night a cold roast chicken and a half-full jar of my Tequila Barbecue Sauce inspired me to produce one. The chicken can be cooked by almost any method, the sauce can be gourmet, homemade, supermarket, or what-you-will, but I have learned that sharp cheese makes the pie better, and so urge you to act accordingly.

❧

INGREDIENTS

5 cups shredded cooked chicken

1 cup hot and smoky, tomato-based barbecue sauce

3 cups wood smoking chips, preferably hickory or mesquite

Flour for the work surface

1 batch Pizza Dough (page 113), divided into 4 equal pieces and briefly kneaded

1 pound grated sharp Cheddar cheese

¾ cup sliced green onions

In a medium bowl, stir together the chicken and barbecue sauce. Cover and let stand at room temperature for 1 hour.

Meanwhile, light a charcoal fire and let it burn until the coals are evenly white or preheat a gas grill (medium). Wrap the wood chips partially in foil, forming a packet that is open at the top. To create a "cool zone," rake the charcoal to one side of the grill; if you're using propane, shut off one or two burners. Set the packet on the hot coals or hot lava stones; position the grill rack about 6 inches above the heat source.

On a lightly floured work surface, roll or pat one piece of pizza dough out into a rough round (mine always seem to be shaped like Australia) about 12 inches in diameter and no more than ¼ inch thick. Transfer the dough to the grill (a wooden pizza peel works well here), placing it on the cool zone. Cover the grill and cook the dough until the top is puffed and the bottom is lightly marked by the grill but not at all crisp, 4 to 5 minutes.

Using the peel, transfer the crust to a work surface and flip it over. Spread one fourth of the chicken mixture over the crust, leaving a ½-inch border. Sprinkle one fourth of the cheese evenly over the chicken. Scatter one fourth of the green onions over the cheese. Return the pizza to the grill, cover, and bake, rotating it once or twice to ensure even browning, until the cheese is melted, the chicken is heated, and the crust is cooked through and lightly crisped or even charred a bit, 8 to 10 minutes.

Transfer the pizza to a cutting board and let stand for 5 minutes before cutting. Repeat with the remaining ingredients. (Turn up the burners or rake in additional coals if the grill becomes too cool for the third and fourth pizzas.)

Lamb Fajitas and New Potato Pizza

MAKES 4 PIZZAS, SERVING 8 OR MORE

Leftover lamb fajitas and leftover rosemary potatoes are combined for a spectacular effect in these pizzas. While you may not find yourself with the makings for this particular combination in the icebox any time soon, I record the particulars anyway, if only to illustrate that unlikely seeming ingredients can make great pizza.

INGREDIENTS

3 cups wood smoking chips
Flour for the work surface
1 batch Pizza Dough (page 113), divided into 4 pieces and kneaded briefly
¾ cup Chipotle Pesto (page 26), Green Chile Pesto (page 26), or commercial pesto sauce

¾ pound leftover Rosemary Fajitas of Lamb (page 108), thinly sliced
½ pound (4 medium) Rosemary-Grilled New Potatoes (page 190) or plain cooked potatoes, thinly sliced
1 pound grated fontina cheese
¼ cup finely chopped fresh rosemary

Light a charcoal fire and let it burn until the coals are evenly white or preheat a gas grill (medium). Wrap the wood chips partially in foil, forming a packet that is open at the top. To create a "cool zone," rake the charcoal to one side of the grill; if you're using propane,

shut off one or two burners. Set the packet on the hot coals or hot lava stones; position the grill rack about 6 inches above the heat source.

On a lightly floured work surface, roll or pat one piece of pizza dough out into a rough round about 12 inches in diameter and no more than ¼ inch thick. Using a wooden pizza peel, transfer the dough to the grill, placing it on the cool zone. Cover the grill and cook the dough until it is puffed on top and lightly marked by the grill but not at all crisp on the bottom, 4 to 5 minutes.

Using the peel, transfer the crust to a work surface and flip it over. Spread 3 tablespoons of the pesto over the crust, leaving a ½-inch border. Arrange one fourth of the lamb and one fourth of the potatoes slices over the pesto. Sprinkle one fourth of the cheese over the pizza

and scatter about 1 tablespoon of the rosemary over the cheese. Return the pizza to the grill, cover, and bake, rotating it once or twice to ensure even browning, until the cheese is melted and bubbling, the lamb is heated, and the crust is cooked through and lightly crisped or even charred a bit, 8 to 10 minutes.

Transfer the pizza to a cutting board and let stand for 5 minutes before cutting. Repeat with the remaining ingredients. (Turn up the burners or rake in additional coals if the grill becomes too cool for the third and fourth pizzas.)

Eggplant and Roasted Red Pepper Pizza

MAKES 4 PIZZAS, SERVING 8 OR MORE

I like to make more than one type of pizza at a grill party, and frequently serve this lighter, meatless pie as an accompaniment to one of my meatier specialities. It's a more traditional approach to pizza making (the cheese is laid down before the remaining toppings go on), one to use as your model if you want pepperoni, mushrooms, or black olives on your grilled pie.

INGREDIENTS

3 large heavy sweet red peppers, preferably Dutch

3 cups wood smoking chips

2 medium eggplants (about 1¾ pounds total), cut crosswise into ½-inch-thick slices

Olive oil for brushing

Flour for the work surface

1 batch Pizza Dough (page 113), divided into 4 pieces and kneaded briefly

1⅓ cups Smoked Plum Tomato Sauce (page 168), plain tomato sauce, or commercial pizza sauce

1 pound grated jalapeño Jack cheese

In the open flame of a gas burner, on a preheated grill (over some of the wood smoking chips if desired), or under a preheated broiler, roast the red peppers, turning them often, until the peels are evenly charred. In a closed paper bag, steam the peppers until cool. Rub off the burned peels, remove the stems, ribs, and seeds, and cut the peppers into julienne strips.

Brush the eggplant slices generously with olive oil.

Light a charcoal fire and let it burn until the coals are evenly white or preheat a gas grill (medium). Wrap the remaining wood chips partially in foil, creating a small packet that is open at the top. Set the packet on the hot coals or hot lava stones; position the grill rack about 6 inches above the heat source.

When the wood chips are smoking, place the eggplant slices on the grill. Cover and cook, turning them once, until lightly browned, 1 to 2 minutes per side. Transfer the eggplant slices to a plate. To create a "cool zone," rake the charcoal to one side of the grill; if you're using propane, shut off one or two burners.

On a lightly floured work surface, roll or pat one piece of pizza dough out into a rough round about 12 inches in diameter and no more than ¼ inch thick. Using a wooden pizza peel, transfer the dough to the grill, placing it on the cool zone. Cover the grill and cook the dough until it is puffed on top and lightly marked by the grill but not at all crisp on the bottom, 4 to 5 minutes.

Using the peel, transfer the crust to a work surface and flip it over. Spread ⅓ cup of the tomato sauce over the dough, leaving a ½-inch border. Scatter one fourth of the cheese over the tomato sauce. Place about one fourth of the eggplant slices over the cheese. Scatter about one fourth of the julienned red pepper over the eggplant.

Return the pizza to the grill, cover, and bake, rotating it once or twice to ensure even browning, until the cheese is melted and bubbling, the eggplant and peppers are heated, and the crust is cooked through and lightly crisped or even charred a bit, 8 to 10 minutes.

Transfer the pizza to a cutting board and let stand for 5 minutes before cutting. Repeat with the remaining ingredients. (Turn up the burners or rake in additional coals if the grill becomes too cool for the third and fourth pizzas.)

Shrimp, Chorizo, and Green Chile Pizza

MAKES 4 PIZZAS, SERVING 8 OR MORE

I first sampled this particular combination of ingredients on a quesadilla—the very pizzalike flour tortilla–based Southwestern cheese snack—and then promptly adapted it for my next batch of grilled pizzas. I suggest you top slices of this with a dollop of Grilled Pico de Gallo (page 4) or Guacamole Verde (page 15)—the pairing of hot, cheesy pie with cold, fiery condiment is wonderful.

INGREDIENTS

½ pound bulk chorizo (spicy Mexican sausage), Spicy Pork and Red Wine Sausages (page 106), or hot Italian-style pork sausage

3 cups wood smoking chips

5 long green chiles

1 pound (about 24) medium shrimp, shelled and deveined

2 tablespoons fresh lime juice

2 tablespoons olive oil

2 garlic cloves, peeled and crushed through a press

¼ teaspoon freshly ground black pepper

Flour for the work surface

1 batch Pizza Dough (page 113), divided into 4 pieces and kneaded briefly

1⅓ cups Smoked Plum Tomato Sauce (page 168) or commercial pizza sauce

1 pound grated Monterey Jack cheese

Crumble the chorizo into a cold skillet. Set it over medium heat and cook, stirring the chorizo often, until it is lightly browned and has rendered any fat, 8 to 10 minutes. Drain on paper towels. *The chorizo can be refrigerated for up to 3 days or frozen for up to 1 month. Wrap it well and return it to room temperature before using.*

In the open flame of a gas burner, on a preheated grill (over some of the wood smoking chips if desired), or under a preheated broiler, roast the long green chiles, turning them often,

until the peels are evenly charred. In a closed paper bag, steam the chiles until cool. Rub off the burned peels, remove the stems, ribs, and seeds, and cut the chiles into julienne strips. *The chiles can be prepared 1 day ahead. Cover and refrigerate, returning them to room temperature before using them.*

In a shallow nonreactive bowl, combine the shrimp, lime juice, olive oil, garlic, and pepper. Cover and let stand at room temperature, stirring once or twice, for 30 minutes. Slide the shrimp onto 4 or 5 skewers.

Light a charcoal fire and let it burn until the coals are evenly white or preheat a gas grill (medium). Wrap the remaining wood chips partially in foil, creating a small packet that is open at the top. Set the packet on the hot coals or hot lava stones; position the grill rack about 6 inches above the heat source.

When the wood chips are smoking, place the shrimp skewers on the grill. Cover and cook the shrimp, turning them once, until pink and just cooked through, about 2 minutes per side. Transfer the shrimp to a cutting board. Cool slightly and coarsely chop. To create a "cool zone," rake the charcoal to one side of the grill; if you're using propane, shut off one or two burners.

On a lightly floured work surface, roll or pat one piece of pizza dough out into a rough round about 12 inches in diameter and no more than ¼ inch thick. Using a wooden pizza peel, transfer the dough to the grill, placing it on the cool zone. Cover the grill and cook the dough until it is puffed on top and lightly marked by the grill but not at all crisp on the bottom, 4 to 5 minutes.

Using the peel, transfer the crust to a work surface and flip it over. Spread ⅓ cup of the tomato sauce on the dough, leaving a ½-inch border. Scatter one quarter each of the shrimp, chorizo, and green chiles over the sauce. Sprinkle one quarter of the cheese over all.

Using the peel, return the pizza to the grill, cover, and bake the pizza, rotating it once or twice to ensure even browning, until the cheese is melted and bubbling, the toppings are heated, and the crust is cooked through and lightly crisped or even charred a bit, 8 to 10 minutes.

Transfer the pizza to a cutting board and let stand for 5 minutes before cutting. Repeat with the remaining ingredients. (Turn up the burners or rake in additional coals if the grill becomes too cool for the third and fourth pizzas.)

sandwiches on the grill

Don't end up in a rut. Beyond the basic burger lies a wealth of sandwich possibilities which a touch of the grill can transform from ordinary into extraordinarily creative and satisfying eating. From the simplest embellishment—merely toasting the bread on the grill, for example—to a full-scale operation in which every element is blessed by contact with fire and smoke, sandwiches that are grilled are sandwiches that are special.

Grilled Lamb Burgers

SERVES 6

If you require red meat in your burgers, I hear you. As a bold alternative to beef, lamb can't be beat, as this simple variation will prove. Served up on homemade cornmeal Kaiser rolls and dolloped with roasted garlic or rosemary mayonnaise, these burgers will please traditional meat eaters and culinary rebels alike. Consider West Texas Red (page 17), Dark Secrets™ Mole Barbecue Sauce (page 19), or Thick Poblano Table Sauce (page 18) as worthy substitutes for either mayonnaise.

❧

INGREDIENTS

2 pounds lean lamb, finely ground for burgers
2 cups wood smoking chips, preferably hickory or mesquite
Salt to taste
Freshly ground black pepper to taste

6 Cornmeal Kaisers (page 202) or large hamburger buns, split, and toasted if desired
Roasted Garlic Mayonnaise (page 52) or Rosemary Mayonnaise (page 53)
Leaves of romaine or arugula and thick slices of beefsteak tomato

Form the ground lamb into 6 thick patties, cover, and refrigerate until cooking.

Light a charcoal fire and let it burn until the coals are evenly white or preheat a gas grill (medium-high). Wrap the wood chips partially in foil, creating a small packet that is open at the top. Set the packet on the hot coals or hot lava stones; position the grill rack about 6 inches above the heat source.

When the chips are smoking heavily, place the patties on the rack, cover the grill, and cook, turning once or twice, until they are lightly browned, about 7 minutes total for medium rare.

Season the burgers with salt and pepper to taste and transfer them to the buns. Serve them immediately, accompanied by either mayonnaise or the sauce of your choice and by lettuce and tomatoes slices.

Grill-Barbecued Chicken Cheeseburgers

MAKES 12

*In burger matters while I'm not a traditionalist, I am a purist, and so I prefer to chop my own chicken in the
food processor. The texture is better, the burgers are juicier, and the meat is free from fat and other fillers.
Add Orange Barbecue Glaze (page 31) or any sweet-hot bottled sauce of your choice, and stand
back—for mysterious reasons of planetary alignment and other unknowns, these simple sandwiches,
like few others, are wildly popular.*

INGREDIENTS

2 pounds boneless, skinless chicken breasts, well chilled

2 pounds boneless, skinless chicken thighs, well chilled

2 cups wood smoking chips, preferably fruitwood

Vegetable oil for the grill

About 4 cups sweet-hot barbecue sauce, divided in half

Salt to taste

Freshly ground black pepper to taste

12 slices medium-sharp American cheese

12 hamburger buns, toasted if desired

Crisp lettuce leaves and sliced tomatoes (optional)

Trim the chicken breasts and thighs, removing all fat and any remaining cartilage. Cut them into 1-inch chunks. In a food processor, using short bursts of power and stopping once or twice to scrape down the sides of the work bowl, chop together the light and dark meat until the texture is that of ground beef; do not overprocess. Shape the ground meat into 12 thick patties. Place the patties on a plate, cover, and refrigerate until grilling time.

Light a charcoal fire and let it burn until the coals are evenly white or preheat a gas grill (medium). Wrap the wood chips partially in foil, creating a small packet that is open at the top. Set the packet on the hot coals or hot lava stones; position the grill rack about 6 inches above the heat source and cover the grill.

When the wood chips are smoking heavily, rub the grill rack with vegetable oil. Place the chicken patties on the rack and cook, covered, turning often and brushing generously with half the barbecue sauce, until lightly browned and almost done through, about 6 minutes. Season each patty with salt and pepper to taste, then top each with a slice of cheese. Cover the grill until the cheese is melted, about 1 minute.

Place the burgers on the toasted buns and serve, accompanied by the rest of the barbecue sauce, lettuce, and tomatoes.

NOTE: To avoid possible salmonella contamination, do not mix any sauce that has come into contact (through spoon or brush) with the raw chicken with the sauce you are using at the table.

Grill–Scrambled Egg, Chorizo, and Avocado Breakfast Sandwiches

MAKES 4 SANDWICHES

Just because your grill is in the suburbs instead of down a long and winding trail somewhere in the boondocks doesn't mean you can't cook up a campfire breakfast or brunch when you want. The basic idea—scrambled eggs with spicy chorizo sausage and avocado—is a casual, El Paso A.M. favorite; cooking the eggs in a skillet on the grill and serving them over thick slices of grill-toasted bread adds the punch of woodsmoke and makes it company fare. Grated jalapeño Jack cheese can be stirred into the eggs along with (or instead of) the avocado.

INGREDIENTS

½ pound bulk chorizo (spicy Mexican sausage), Spicy Pork and Red Wine Sausages (page 106), or hot Italian-style pork sausage

3 cups wood smoking chips

10 large eggs

1 teaspoon hot pepper sauce, such as Tabasco

½ teaspoon salt

4 1½-inch-thick slices of crusty bread from a large day-old oval loaf

Olive oil for brushing the bread

3 tablespoons (1½ ounces) unsalted butter

1 medium ripe California avocado, pitted, peeled, and cut into ½-inch chunks

¼ cup thinly sliced green onions

About 1⅓ cups Two Tomato–Chipotle Salsa (page 7) or Salsa Borracho (page 6)

Crumble the chorizo into a cold skillet. Set over medium heat and cook the chorizo, stirring it often, until it is lightly browned and has rendered any fat, 8 to 10 minutes. Drain on paper towels. *The chorizo can be cooked and then refrigerated for up to 3 days ahead or frozen for up to 1 month. Return it to room temperature before proceeding with the recipe.*

Light a charcoal fire and let it burn until the coals are evenly white or preheat a gas grill (medium). Wrap the wood chips partially in foil, creating a small packet that is open at the top. Set the packet on the hot coals or hot lava stones; position the grill rack about 6 inches above the heat source.

Meanwhile, in a large bowl, whisk the eggs. Whisk in the hot pepper sauce and salt. Brush the bread slices generously on both sides with olive oil. When the wood chips are smoking heavily, place the bread slices on the rack. Cover and grill, turning them once, until they are crisp and lightly browned, about 2 minutes total. Remove them from the grill.

Immediately set a medium-large heavy skillet on the grill rack. Add the butter and cover the grill.

When the butter has melted and is foaming, add the eggs. Cook, stirring often, until the eggs are done to your liking, about 2 minutes for soft and creamy. Remove the skillet from the heat and stir in the chorizo, avocado, and onions.

Place a slice of grilled bread on each of 4 plates. Spoon the scrambled eggs over the grilled bread, dividing them evenly and using them all. Serve immediately, passing salsa at the table.

Michael's Pork Tenderloin Sandwiches with "Burnt" Edges Slaw

MAKES 6 SANDWICHES

This recipe of Michael's is a wonder, yielding smoky, sweetly glazed lean pork tenderloins which are sliced, stacked onto oversized buns, and then topped with a creamy pink barbecue-flavored coleslaw. The dark, crunchy ends and edges of the tenderloins are chopped and stirred into the slaw, so that every succulent morsel of pork ends up on the sandwich—incredible eating!

❦

INGREDIENTS

1 cup Orange Barbecue Glaze (page 31)
3 tablespoons hot pepper sauce, such as Tabasco
½ cup sweet salad dressing, such as Miracle Whip
3 tablespoons Dijon mustard
4 cups finely shredded white cabbage
(most of a 1-pound head)

3 pork tenderloins (about 3 pounds total)
2 cups wood smoking chips, preferably hickory
6 Cornmeal Kaisers (page 202) or any large, round, sandwich rolls, split, and toasted if desired

In a small bowl, stir together the barbecue glaze and hot pepper sauce. In a large bowl, whisk together the salad dressing, ½ cup of the barbecue glaze mixture, and the mustard. Add the cabbage, stir to combine, and adjust the seasoning (the slaw should be spicy). Cover and refrigerate for up to 1 hour.

Meanwhile trim any tough silvery outer membrane off the pork tenderloins. Light a charcoal fire and let it burn until the coals are

evenly white or preheat a gas grill (medium). Wrap the wood chips partially in foil, creating a small packet that is open at the top. Set the packet on the hot coals or hot lava stones; position the grill rack about 6 inches above the heat source and cover the grill.

When the wood chips are smoking, place the tenderloins on the grill, cover, and cook 4 minutes. Brush the tenderloins generously with some of the remaining barbecue glaze, turn, and grill, covered, for 4 minutes. Continue brushing the tenderloins and turning them every 2 minutes or so until they are well glazed and done (just lightly pink at the thickest part), about 18 minutes.

Transfer the tenderloins to a cutting board. Trim off and chop the "burnt" parts—the crisp, brown edges and the tapering end of each tenderloin—and stir them into the slaw. With a sharp knife, cut the tenderloins at a slight angle across the grain into thin slices. Place the sliced pork on the bottoms of the rolls, dividing it evenly and using it all. Generously top the pork on each bun with a mound of slaw, put the tops of the rolls in place, and serve immediately. Any remaining slaw can be served on the side.

Grilled Chicken, Cheese, and Eggplant Sandwiches

MAKES 4 SANDWICHES

This recipe for open-faced sandwiches is merely the record of a successful improvisation, the kind of effortless-to-assemble, wonderful-to-eat bit of food that having ready access to a grill makes second nature. A few simple ingredients are transformed by the flavorful smoke into a stylish meal. Consider this a blueprint. Among the enticing options: adding strips of roasted red pepper or green chile, or grilled mushrooms, trying another cheese, replacing the chile paint with one of my pestos (page 26), or substituting shrimp for the chicken.

INGREDIENTS

2 whole boneless, skinless chicken breasts (about 1½ pounds)
¾ cup Red Chile Paint (page 43)
2 cups wood smoking chips
4 large thick slices of bread from a country-style oval loaf

4 large, ½-inch-thick oval slices of eggplant
Olive oil for brushing
⅓ pound Monterey Jack or mozzarella cheese, thinly sliced
Rosemary Mayonnaise (page 53), Roasted Garlic Mayonnaise (page 52), or Cactus Salsa (page 12)

Separate the chicken breasts into halves and trim away any remaining cartilage and fat. With a meat pounder or the bottom of a small saucepan, flatten the thicker portions of the breast halves slightly. On a plate, spread the chicken breasts on both sides with ½ cup of the chile paint, cover, and let stand at room temperature for 1 hour.

Meanwhile, light a charcoal fire and let it burn until the coals are evenly white or preheat a gas grill (medium). Wrap the wood chips partially in

foil, creating a small packet that is open at the top. Set the packet on the hot coals or hot lava stones; position the grill rack about 6 inches above the heat source.

Brush one side of the bread slices and both sides of the eggplant slices generously with olive oil.

When the wood chips are smoking heavily, place the bread slices, oiled side down, and the eggplant slices on the rack and cover. Grill the bread slices until lightly browned on the oiled side only, 1½ to 2 minutes. Remove them. Grill the eggplant on both sides, turning the slices once, until lightly browned, 3 to 4 minutes total. Transfer the eggplant to a plate.

Place the chicken breasts on the rack, cover, and grill, turning them once, until just cooked through while remaining juicy, about 4 minutes total. Transfer them to a cutting board and cool slightly. Cut each chicken breast at a slight angle across the grain into 4 slices.

Spread the ungrilled side of each piece of bread with 1 tablespoon of the remaining chile paint.

Place the bread slices, painted side up, in a shallow disposable foil pan. Place the cheese slices over the paint. Place an eggplant slice on top of the cheese on each sandwich. Fan the sliced chicken over the eggplant slices. Place the foil pan on the grill, cover, and bake until the cheese is melted and the sandwiches are heated through, about 5 minutes.

Top each sandwich with a dollop of the mayonnaise or salsa and serve immediately.

Grilled Swordfish Club Sandwiches with Rosemary Mayonnaise

MAKES 4 SANDWICHES

Now that most sandwiches are mass-produced and sold by the billions, so simple a thing as a fresh, homemade club can be a revelation. Substitute grilled swordfish for the traditional chicken, add mesquite-smoked bacon and a fresh rosemary mayonnaise, and you have a startlingly good, though casual meal—which pretty much defines how we entertain here on the border. This makes a fine Saturday lunch (one of my favorite times to have company over), paired with Lemon-Pepper Fries (page 193), Sweet Buttermilk Slaw (page 184), and a cold beer or a tall glass of iced tea.

INGREDIENTS

2 tablespoons fresh lime juice

2 tablespoons olive oil

2 large sprigs fresh rosemary, crushed with the butt of a knife

1 garlic clove, peeled and crushed through a press

8 ½-inch-thick slices of swordfish steak (about 1 pound total)

12 slices (about ½ pound) good-quality bacon, preferably mesquite-smoked

2 cups wood smoking chips, preferably mesquite

Salt to taste

Freshly ground black pepper to taste

8 medium-thick slices of bread from a large country-style oval loaf, toasted on 1 side only

About 1 cup Rosemary Mayonnaise (page 53)

8 thin slices of ripe, juicy tomato

4 crisp medium leaves of romaine

In a shallow nonreactive dish, stir together the lime juice, olive oil, rosemary, and garlic. Add the swordfish steaks, cover them with the marinade, and let stand at room temperature, turning them once or twice, for 1 hour.

Place the bacon in a cold skillet, set it over medium heat, and cook, turning the bacon once or twice, until it is crisp, 8 to 10 minutes. Drain on paper towels. Cut the bacon strips in half crosswise.

Light a charcoal fire and let it burn until the coals are evenly white or preheat a gas grill (medium). Wrap the wood chips partially in foil, creating a small packet that is open at the top. Set the packet on the hot coals or hot lava stones; position the grill rack about 6 inches above the heat source.

When the wood chips are smoking heavily, place the swordfish steaks on the rack, cover, and grill 2 minutes. Turn and grill the swordfish steaks until they are just cooked through, another 1 to 2 minutes. Transfer them to a plate and season lightly with salt and pepper to taste.

Generously spread the untoasted side of each slice of bread with rosemary mayonnaise. Place 2 pieces of swordfish over the mayonnaise on each slice of bread. Top the swordfish with the bacon. Top the bacon with two tomato slices then a leaf of romaine. Put the tops of the sandwiches in place. With a long, sharp knife, cut the sandwiches in half and serve immediately.

salads on the grill

t isn't schizophrenic, just a reflection of the enormous possibilities contained in the word *salad*, that in modern Texas salad can mean everything from a dish made with miniature marshmallows and mandarin orange sections to one boasting Italian porcini mushrooms and balsamic vinegar. I love all salads pretty much equally, but few are more appetite-stirring than those that include grilled ingredients. The automatic boost of flavor and enhancement of texture that grilling brings to other foods also extends to salads. Add crisp greens and a tangy vinaigrette and the eating just doesn't get any better.

The Great Caesar Salad with Grilled Shrimp

SERVES 6

Caesar salad plain is a marvelous first course, and since I know it was invented in Tijuana, Mexico, I don't hesitate to team it with border fare, especially something hot and smoky from the grill. Nowadays, though, Caesar salad often gets gussied up into a light main course, sporting the addition of chicken, or, in this case, grilled jumbo shrimp and croutons made from red chile corn bread. Caesar dressing also serves as the marinade for the shrimp. Leave the romaine leaves whole, for the most dramatic presentation, and encourage guests to pick them up with their fingers.

INGREDIENTS

18 very large shrimp (about 1½ pounds), shelled and deveined

2 cups Great Caesar Dressing (page 51)

2 cups wood smoking chips, preferably mesquite

Tender inner leaves of 3 heads of romaine

Red Chile Corn Croutons (recipe follows)

⅓ cup grated Parmigiano-Reggiano cheese

In a medium nonreactive bowl, combine the shrimp and ¾ cup of the Caesar dressing and let stand at room temperature for 1 hour.

Light a charcoal fire and let it burn until the coals are evenly white or preheat a gas grill (medium). Wrap the wood chips partially in foil, creating a small packet that is open at the top. Set the packet on the hot coals or hot lava stones; position the grill rack about 6 inches above the heat source.

When the wood chips are smoking heavily, place the shrimp on the rack. Cover and grill, turning them once or twice and basting them with any

remaining Caesar dressing, until they are pink, curled, and lightly browned, about 6 minutes total. Transfer the shrimp to a plate and cool slightly.

In a very large bowl, toss together the romaine leaves, the remaining 1¼ cups of Caesar dressing, and the croutons. Arrange the leaves on 6 salad plates. Spoon the croutons and any remaining dressing from the bowl over the leaves. Arrange 3 shrimp on each of the salads. Sprinkle the salads evenly with the cheese and serve immediately, passing the pepper mill at the table.

continued

RED CHILE CORN CROUTONS

Position a rack in the upper third of the oven and preheat the oven to 425°F. Cut half a pan of cold Red Chile Corn Bread (page 201) into ¾- inch cubes. Spread the cubes in a single layer in an ungreased pan and bake them until they are crisp and lightly browned, about 15 minutes. Use warm.

Grilled Pork Tenderloin and Grilled Pineapple–Rice Salad

SERVES 8

This recipe produces a complete one-dish meal, consisting of thin slices of crisp and smoky grilled pork tenderloin arranged around a mound of moist rice salad that is studded with chunks of grilled pineapple, black beans, and colorful vegetables. Pass crusty bread and drink a slightly sweet white or pink wine.

INGREDIENTS

4 pork tenderloins (about 3 pounds total)
Brave Bull Marinade and Mop (page 46)
3 cups water
1½ cups converted rice
½ teaspoon salt
⅓ cup canned pineapple juice
3 tablespoons fresh lemon juice
¼ cup corn oil
1 heavy sweet red pepper, preferably Dutch, stemmed, cored, and diced

1 cup frozen tiny peas, thawed and drained
1 cup cooked black beans
½ cup thinly sliced green onions
½ cup finely chopped cilantro
Freshly ground black pepper to taste
2 cups wood smoking chips, preferably fruitwood
½ a large pineapple, peeled, cored, and halved vertically
⅓ cup Kahlúa
Salsa Borracho (page 6) (optional)

Trim away any tough silvery outer membrane from the tenderloins. In a shallow nonreactive dish, pour the marinade over them, cover, and let stand at room temperature, turning them once or twice, for 1 hour.

In a medium saucepan over high heat, bring the 3 cups water to a boil. Stir in the rice and salt, turn the heat to low, and cover. Cook undisturbed until the rice is tender and has absorbed all the water, about 20 minutes. Remove from the heat and let stand, covered, for 5 minutes.

Transfer the rice to a large bowl. Stir in the pineapple juice, lemon juice, and corn oil; cool to room temperature. Stir in the sweet red pepper, peas, black beans, green onions, and cilantro. Season generously with black pepper. Cover and hold at room temperature.

Light a charcoal fire and let it burn until the coals are evenly white or preheat a gas grill (medium). Wrap the wood chips partially in foil, creating a small packet that is open at the top. Set the packet on the hot coals or hot lava stones; position the grill rack about 6 inches above the heat source.

When the wood chips are smoking, remove the tenderloins from their marinade and place them on the rack. Cover and grill 4 minutes. Turn the tenderloins, baste them with some of the marinade and grill, covered, for 4 minutes. Continue to turn the tenderloins every 2 or 3 minutes, basting them often with the rest of the marinade and moving them to the cooler edges of the grill if they begin to scorch, until they are very crisp and brown and just cooked through while remaining slightly pink and juicy at their thickest, about 18 minutes. Transfer the tenderloins to a cutting board and let them rest for 5 minutes.

Brush the pineapple quarters with some of the Kahlúa. Place them on the rack and grill, turning them once or twice and brushing them with the remaining Kahlúa, until they are lightly browned, about 6 minutes total. Remove them from the heat and cool slightly. Cut the pineapple into ½-inch chunks and stir them into the rice salad.

Using a long, sharp knife, cut the tenderloins at a slight angle across the grain into thin slices. Divide the rice salad among serving plates. Arrange the slices of pork, overlapping slightly, around the rice salad. Serve immediately, accompanied by the salsa if desired.

Chicken Fajitas Salad

SERVES 6

The general idea of fajitas (marinated strips—"little sashes" in the literal translation—of grilled meat) finds expression here as a main course salad. Colorful and crunchy, the warm chicken and cool greens are drizzled with a creamy salsa vinaigrette, then garnished with deep-fried corn tortilla "croutons"— a salad festive enough for a party.

INGREDIENTS

2 pounds boneless, skinless chicken breasts, halved and trimmed of any remaining cartilage and fat

½ cup tomato-based commercial hot salsa

½ cup amber beer, such as Dos Equis

½ cup coarsely chopped cilantro (stems can be included)

3 garlic cloves, peeled and chopped

2 tablespoons gold tequila

2 tablespoons fresh lime juice

2 tablespoons olive oil

4 cups corn oil for frying the tortillas

3 corn tortillas, cut into ½-inch-wide strips, or Red Chile Corn Croutons (page 134)

Salt to taste

2 cups wood smoking chips, preferably mesquite

8 cups bite-sized pieces of sturdy, colorful salad greens

2 ripe tomatoes (about ¾ pound total), trimmed and cut into sixths

1 ripe California avocado, pitted and cut into thin slices (do not peel)

1 small red onion, peeled, thinly sliced, and separated into rings

1 recipe Salsa Dressing (page 49)

With a meat pounder or the bottom of a small heavy saucepan, slightly flatten the thickest portions of the chicken breasts.

In a blender or food processor, combine the salsa, beer, cilantro, garlic, tequila, lime juice, and olive oil and process until fairly smooth. In a shallow nonreactive dish, pour the marinade over the chicken breasts. Cover and let stand at room temperature, turning them once or twice, for 1 hour.

Meanwhile, in a deep fryer or heavy pan fitted with a frying thermometer and set over medium heat, warm the corn oil to between 350° and 375°F. (The deep fryer or pan should be no more than half full of oil.) Carefully add the tortilla strips to the hot oil and cook, stirring them once or twice, until they are crisp, about 2 minutes. Drain on paper towels; sprinkle while hot with salt to taste.

Light a charcoal fire and let it burn until the coals are evenly white or preheat a gas grill (medium). Wrap the wood chips partially in foil, creating a small packet that is open at the top. Set the packet on the hot coals or hot lava stones; position the grill rack about 6 inches above the heat source.

When the wood chips are smoking heavily, place the chicken breasts on the rack. Pour half the marinade over the chicken breasts (there will be a cloud of steam), cover, and grill, turning them once and basting them with the remaining marinade, until just cooked through while remaining juicy, about 4 minutes total. Transfer them to a cutting board and let rest for 5 minutes. Cut the chicken breasts lengthwise into ½-inch strips. Season lightly with salt to taste.

Divide the salad greens among 6 plates. Arrange the chicken strips, tomato wedges, slices of avocado, and onion rings atop the greens. Drizzle generously with the dressing. Scatter the crisp tortilla strips over the salads and serve immediately, passing any remaining dressing at the table.

Laurin's Steak Salad

SERVES 8 AS AN APPETIZER, 4 AS A MAIN COURSE

Laurin Lynch, who assisted in putting this book together, is the chef and a partner at Café Centrál, surely El Paso's best and most sophisticated restaurant. Laurin serves contemporary American food with a stylish, Southwestern twist—which pretty much sums up this colorful and vividly flavored and textured salad, modeled on an appetizer served at the café and one of the best destinations for leftover grilled flank steak I know of. Double the portions, halve the guest list, and it also makes a fine hot-weather main course.

INGREDIENTS

⅔ cup dried black beans, picked over

1½ teaspoons salt

⅓ cup Serrano-Rosemary Vinegar (page 61) or red wine vinegar

½ teaspoon ground cumin, preferably from toasted seeds (page 9)

½ teaspoon dried oregano, crumbled

¼ teaspoon freshly ground black pepper

⅔ cup chile-flavored oil (see the Note)

½ cup sour cream

2 teaspoons fresh lime juice

1 pound Grilled Marinated Flank Steak (page 99), at room temperature

12 cups mixed tender and colorful salad greens

In a medium bowl, soak the beans in cold water to generously cover for 12 hours.

Drain the beans. In a small pan, cover them with fresh cold water, set over medium heat, and bring to a boil. Lower the heat slightly and simmer the beans, stirring them once or twice, for 30 minutes. Stir in 1 teaspoon of the salt and cook them another 10 to 15 minutes or until just tender. Drain and cool to room temperature.

In a small bowl, whisk together the vinegar, cumin, oregano, the remaining ½ teaspoon of salt, and the pepper. Gradually whisk in the oil. Let the dressing stand at room temperature for 30 minutes.

In another small bowl, whisk together the sour cream and lime juice. If you wish, put it in a plastic squeeze bottle (like a diner-style ketchup dispenser) and refrigerate.

At a slight angle across the grain, cut the steak into paper-thin slices. Arrange the slices on 8 small chilled plates.

In a large bowl, toss together the salad greens, beans, and dressing. Arrange the greens on the plates beside the sliced steak. Spoon any dressing and beans remaining in the bowl evenly over the salads. Drizzle the sour cream mixture decoratively over the steak slices. Serve immediately.

NOTE: The spicy oil called for here is not a Chinese oil, but rather one of the new chile-flavored oils that are becoming increasingly available in gourmet shops. They vary in flavor and heat; use what you like, or substitute plain olive oil and add a generous pinch of crushed red pepper flakes to the dressing along with the cumin and oregano.

bbq and beyond

We might as well define our terms. Grilled food is cooked over an open flame. Barbecue is a process of slowly cooking and smoking food over an indirect heat source. It's also the experience of climbing into a van with a lot of people you like but may not know and heading down a dark dirt road to eat several big platefuls of that slow-smoked food, typically prepared by a man named Bubba or Earl, offered for sale under a sign reading ALL YOU CAN EAT. Barbecue is now also the name applied to the astonishing array of bottled sauces meant to be dolloped onto Bubba's cuisine. Finally, if the animal protein in question is anything other than beef brisket, pork shoulder, or spareribs (salmon, tuna, or venison, for example), what you are eating is not barbecue, it's smoked food, and if you didn't smoke it yourself it surely cost you so much money that the offer All You Can Eat cannot possibly apply. Which is why I recommend you learn how to smoke your own. Let us begin.

how to smoke:
one man's guide

if grilling is a knack that can be learned by anyone, smoking is more an art. It's not difficult, in fact it's rather slow and dreamy (though it can be hot and sweaty), but it's not for everyone and success is not necessarily assured. Some folks are born to greatness, others may never come close.

Smoking, both the barbecue/Bubba kind and the Tiffany's/salmon kind, has its roots in an older, simpler need. Originally a method of preserving food before there was refrigeration, it is now something done for its own tasty sake. Smoke is loaded with compounds that both flavor and cure or preserve meats and seafoods, and now that we do it for pleasure, adjusting the flavor balance becomes the main challenge; the icebox, after all, will take care of the preservation part.

As with grilling, specifics are not always possible. There are not as many kinds and brands of smokers as there are of grills, but there are enough, and learning to get good results from what you own will be, ultimately, up to you. I smoke on two pieces of equipment that fall near the bottom and the top of the price and complexity ranges for home smokers. The Brinkmann water smoker resembles *Star Wars*'s stubby robot, R2D2. It uses an electric element to generate low heat, small chunks of various woods to produce smoke, and includes a water pan, the evaporation from which prevents the drying out of the food. It's widely available, fairly affordable (it's been knocked off by several companies), and ideal for those who want to smoke something small, only on occasion. While barbecue from it always *tastes* as kick-ass authentic as one would wish, there's still something vaguely *suburban* about the Brinkmann. Maybe it's that electric cord snaking its way to a socket just inside the garage door.

Then there is the Hondo. This cast-iron behemoth consists of a firebox set next to a large smoking chamber topped by a tall smokestack. This is serious business, since the thing is expensive, and since you are using some variation of an actual wood-burning fire, there are pitfalls aplenty. The upside of it is when you finally learn how to run it, the Hondo (there are several similarly designed brands on the market) will make great smoked food for you.

The Brinkmann comes with good directions and is very reliable. Use only the amount of wood chunks specified (more can make food acrid and inedible) and remember that a cold day or a brisk wind will slow the smoking process considerably. Don't open the cover any more than is necessary for mopping and checking doneness—the Brinkmann doesn't generate a lot of heat and all of it vanishes when the smoker is opened.

To operate the Hondo, it helps to have been a Boy Scout. Starting a proper fire is the most important thing. In my Hondo I burn a mixture of well-aged split white oak and mesquite fireplace logs, about two feet long and of varying thickness, just as delivered to me by my wood guy. Some experts recommend that your wood should have no bark on it (makes the barbecue bitter); all experts agree that resinous softwoods like piñon or cedar must not be used.

I start my fire using Georgia fatwood sticks (quick- and hot-burning natural fire starters readily available from catalog companies like L.L. Bean). Three logs go atop a small pyramid of the fatwood, which is lighted. I achieve a fast, hot fire (all dampers open) to burn off any bark (about twenty minutes), and get a good head of coals going. Close the lid to the firebox, leaving all dampers and lid to the main smoke chamber open. At the beginning there is "bad" smoke, which is thick and yellow, and which would quickly make foods too tongue-numbingly bitter to eat. Eventually there is "good" smoke which is lighter, thinner, and whiter. This appears in about thirty minutes, after which I close down the dampers slightly to maintain a slow, even burn. The foods to be smoked then go on the rack (larger cuts of red meat are positioned with their thicker ends toward the opening from the fire chamber, while poultry, seafood, and vegetables are placed at the other cooler end) and the smoker is closed up.

Nearly all expert advice recommends a smoking temperature of about 230°F, but at that temperature my Hondo produces only bad smoke. Instead, I smoke at 300°F, which I can achieve easily and stabilize almost indefinitely over a long day of smoking, feeding the fire only occasionally with a fresh log. This is probably the result of the interaction between the size of the logs I use and the particular thermostat on my particular Hondo, and other imponderables, but the results are never tough or dry, and so for me this temperature works.

Foods that take no more than three hours or so of smoking to be cooked through can be enjoyed straight from the Hondo. Those that must be cooked further for optimum tenderness (beef brisket and pork shoulder, for example) must be shielded from those extra hours of smoke so they won't be too smoky to enjoy. (Commercial smokers and barbecue joints tend to use natural gas for heat, and only a few chips or chunks of wood for flavor, which lets them smoke brisket for all the many hours needed to be falling-apart luscious.) Some home smoke masters wrap the meat in foil at the halfway point and then return it to the smoker until done. Others use a combination of charcoal (for heat) and a few wood chunks (for flavor).

Both systems work, but I have developed a third method which I think beats them both. At the halfway point, the long-smoking item is transferred to a packet of heavy-duty foil, moistened with a bottle of beer (I tend to moisten myself with a bottle at about the same time), sealed up, and then baked in a 350°F oven until tender. Whatever bitterness the smoke may have imparted to the meat is tamed and dispersed by the steam of the beer and the results are moist, tender, and deliciously smoky. No purist would recommend this, but again, for me, this process results in spectacular barbecue.

For a deeper, slightly salty flavor and a supple texture, some meats and seafoods are brined in a sugar, salt, and water solution. Spice rubs patted onto the exteriors of meats form a tasty crust and seem to help prevent drying out; letting the rub stand on the meat overnight allows it to penetrate but isn't essential if time is short (mine always is). Thinner basting liquids—mops—are basted over some meats while they smoke to help keep them moist and to add flavor (large-scale operations actually use a long-handled cotton household mop, hence the name).

Finally, after all this labor, you will slice into a rubbed, smoked, and beer-steamed brisket or a whole wild turkey or a loin of venison and you'll see the "smoke ring," that telltale reddish-brown crust all around the edge of the slice that is telltale sign of successful barbecue and of the great eating to come.

Smoked Loin of Tuna

SERVES 8 OR MORE, DEPENDING ON USAGE

This was my first success in the smoker (after a couple of disastrous failures), so I'm inclined to make it often. The tuna comes from Seattle by plane into Albuquerque, then overland to El Paso. Nevertheless it is always amazingly fresh. Despite the zesty rub and mop (which combine with the smoke to form a delicious crust), the rich flavor of the tuna dominates. I serve it several ways: sliced on a plate and drizzled with Salsa Dressing (page 49) as a first course; on tiny canapé sandwiches with watercress and Black Olive, Lemon, and Cilantro Butter (page 54); and on heartier sandwiches with lettuce, tomato, and Barbecue Mustard (page 37).

INGREDIENTS

3 pounds fresh loin of tuna, in one piece
Chimayo Chile Rub (page 40)

Chunks or logs of fragrant hardwood, preferably a combination of oak and mesquite
2 cups West Texas Red (page 17)

Coat the tuna on all sides with the rub, patting it in firmly. Wrap and refrigerate overnight. Let the tuna come to room temperature.

Prepare a smoker according to the manufacturer's directions, using the wood chunks and achieving a steady temperature of 275° to 300°F. Place the tuna on the smoker rack in the central part of your smoker. Lower the cover and smoke the tuna, rotating it once or twice on the rack (but not turning it over) to promote even smoking and mopping it regularly with the West Texas Red, until it is just cooked through and beginning to flake, about 1½ hours.

Remove the tuna from the smoker and cool to room temperature. It will be most succulent if never refrigerated, but it can be well wrapped and refrigerated for up to 3 days or frozen for up to 1 month. Return the tuna to room temperature before slicing and serving it.

Smoked Salmon

The process by which salmon is commercially smoked is next to impossible to duplicate at home, and so you must not expect to end up with the resilient, silky texture or transparent slices you get when you buy smoked salmon. What you will get is salmon that is moist, delicately smoky, and just falling into tender flakes—delicious stuff, in other words, when served as an appetizer, with either my mom's or my sauce for salmon (recipes follow), an entrée, in salads, in pastas, or on sandwiches. This recipe makes a generous amount—this is party food, after all—but well wrapped and refrigerated the salmon will be good for four or five days, maybe longer. Trust me: It won't go to waste.

INGREDIENTS

8 cups boiling water
⅔ cup kosher salt
½ cup packed dark brown sugar

2 sides (about 6 pounds total) boneless salmon fillet
Chunks or logs of fragrant hardwood, preferably a combination of oak and mesquite

To make a brine in a medium bowl, stir together the boiling water, salt, and brown sugar. Cool to room temperature.

In a large container (a turkey roaster is ideal), pour the brine over the salmon. Use one or two heavy saucers to weight the salmon fillets and keep them beneath the surface of the brine. Cover and refrigerate, turning the fillets once or twice to promote even exposure to the brine, for at least 8 and no more than 12 hours.

Pour off and discard the brine. Rinse the fillets under cold running water and pat them dry. Bring the fillets to room temperature.

Prepare a smoker according to the manufacturer's directions, using the wood chunks and achieving a steady temperature of 275° to 300°F. Place the salmon fillets, skin side down, on the smoker rack in the coolest part of your smoker (the end away from the firebox, for example, or an upper shelf if it has one). Smoke the fillets until they are just cooked through and beginning to flake at their thinnest, about 1½ hours.

Remove the fillets from the smoker and cool to room temperature. For the moistest texture, serve the salmon immediately, without refrigeration. *Or wrap well it and refrigerate, returning it to room temperature before slicing it.*

Norma's Sauce for Smoked Salmon

MAKES ABOUT 1 1/2 CUPS SAUCE, SERVING 6, DEPENDING ON USAGE

Here are dueling salmon sauces, my mom's and mine. They're very similar (the mayonnaise doesn't fall very far from the tree), both are delicious, and both are utterly easy to stir together. Norma suggests combining any flaked, leftover salmon with leftover sauce and stuffing it into a perfect summer tomato for a wonderful hot-weather lunch or light supper.

INGREDIENTS

½ cup mayonnaise
½ cup sour cream
½ cup minced yellow onions

2 teaspoons minced fresh tarragon or ½ teaspoon dried tarragon, crumbled
¼ teaspoon lemon juice
Pinch of freshly ground white pepper

In a small bowl, whisk together the mayonnaise, sour cream, onions, tarragon, lemon juice, and pepper. *Cover and refrigerate for 30 minutes before using.*

My Sauce for Smoked Salmon

Drizzle this over smoked salmon and accompany each portion with a small green salad for an elegant appetizer, or mix it with flaked, smoked salmon and diced apple and spread it on black bread for wonderful sandwiches.

INGREDIENTS

⅓ cup mayonnaise

⅓ cup sour cream

2 green onions, trimmed and thinly sliced

3 tablespoons Sweet and Hot Red Chile Mustard (page 23) or commercial honey mustard

¼ teaspoon fresh lemon juice

A generous grinding of fresh black pepper

In a small bowl, whisk together the mayonnaise, sour cream, green onions, mustard, lemon juice, and pepper. *Cover and refrigerate for 30 minutes before using.*

Smoked Wild Turkey

SERVES 8 OR MORE, DEPENDING ON USAGE

Wild turkey is a very different bird from the white meat—enhanced hybrids found in the supermarket. There is much less breast meat and the taste is slightly stronger (though not really gamy) and fresher, as if some artificial, turkey-flavored additive is missing. It's the kind of absence of a flavor that you can't really recognize until you taste it (if you know what I mean) and then you'll understand what the fuss is all about. You may be acquainted with some generous someone who hunts (and shares) wild turkey or you may even hunt your own, but free-range members of the breed are available from specialty butchers or by mail order. When you have one, consider smoking it, using this simple formula and taking care not to overcook the bird (wild turkeys are lean and can dry out easily). Serve the whole turkey as the centerpiece of a holiday buffet, and use up the leftovers in sandwiches, salads, pastas, and risotti (try combining slivers of smoked turkey, sautéed wild mushrooms, and tiny sweet peas). Use the carcass in soup. A domestic turkey works equally well here.

INGREDIENTS

Chunks or logs of fragrant hardwood, preferably a combination of oak and a fruitwood, such as cherry or apple
2½ cups dry red wine

1 can (about 14 ounces) reduced-sodium chicken broth
½ cup maple syrup
1 10-pound turkey, brought just to room temperature

Prepare a smoker according to the manufacturer's directions, using the wood chunks and achieving a steady temperature of 275° to 300°F. In a jar or pitcher, combine the wine, broth, and maple syrup. Place the turkey on the smoker rack in the center part of your smoker. Lower the cover and smoke the turkey, rotating it once or twice on the rack (but not turning it over) to promote even smoking, and mopping it occasionally with the wine mixture, for about 2½ hours, or until just cooked

through. A thigh, when pricked at its thickest, will yield juices that are yellow tinged with pink (not red).

Remove the turkey from the smoker. Cool on a rack to room temperature. *The turkey can be prepared up to 3 days in advance. Wrap tightly and refrigerate, returning the turkey to room temperature before serving.* Slice thinly, removing the skin first if desired (it may be too smoky).

Smoked Ducks

PRODUCES 2 LARGE DUCKS, SERVING 6 OR MORE DEPENDING ON USAGE

While smaller supermarket ducks can be used here (shorten the suggested smoking time by about one third), I prefer the results when the specially bred hybrid duck known as the moulard is smoked instead. These oversized birds are the source of the fattened livers known as foie gras. Weighing up to 8 pounds, much of it lean, succulent breast meat, moulards make spectacular eating. The skin does not get crisp and in fact is bitterly smoky (discard it) but underneath, the duck flesh is elegantly touched by the flavor and aroma of the fire. Slice the breast meat for salads, sandwiches, or quesadillas (page 152); simmer the legs in place of ham hocks in bean dishes and soups.

INGREDIENTS

Chunks or logs of fragrant hardwood, preferably a combination of oak and mesquite

2 moulard ducks (about 8 pounds each), at room temperature

Prepare a smoker according to the manufacturer's directions, using the wood chunks and achieving a steady temperature of 275° to 300°F. Place the ducks on the smoker rack in the center part of your smoker. Cover and smoke the ducks, rotating them once or twice on the rack (but not turning them over) to promote even smoking, for about 2 hours. The ducks are done when juices from a thigh, when pricked at its thickest, are yellow tinged with pink (not red).

Remove the ducks from the smoker and cool them to room temperature. Remove and discard the duck skin before using the meat. *The ducks can also be tightly wrapped and refrigerated for up to 5 days or frozen for up to 1 month. (Leave the skin on ducks to be frozen, removing it only when they have thawed.)*

Smoked Duck, Poblano, and Mushroom Quesadilla

SERVES 1 OR MORE, DEPENDING ON USAGE

Quesadillas—cheese and other savory ingredients sandwiched between two flour tortillas and griddled or grilled until molten—can serve as a light meal for one (add a salad) or, cut into wedges, can provide drink-time nibbling for several. Like grilled pizzas, grilled quesadillas pick up extra flavor and crispness from the fire. Like pizzas in general, quesadillas are essentially improvisational; if you have no smoked duck, for example, substitute Black Forest ham or another equally assertive ingredient. And speaking of pizzas, the duck, poblano, mushroom, and Jack cheese quartet does indeed make a spectacular topping for one. Follow the general formula in the recipe for Lamb Fajitas and New Potato Pizza on page 115.

INGREDIENTS

2 cups wood smoking chips
1 large poblano chile
2 10-inch flour tortillas
4 ounces grated Monterey Jack cheese

2 ounces thinly sliced smoked duck breast (page 151)
4 Grilled Marinated Mushrooms (page 196) or any cooked mushrooms, thinly sliced
1 green onion, trimmed and thinly sliced

In the open flame of a gas burner, on a preheated grill (using some of the wood smoking chips if desired) or under a preheated broiler, roast the poblano, turning it often, until the peel is lightly and evenly charred. Transfer the chile to a closed paper bag and let stand until cool. Rub away the burned peel, stem and seed the chile, and cut it into thin strips.

Light a charcoal fire and let it burn until the coals are evenly white or preheat a gas grill (medium-low). Wrap the remaining wood chips partially in foil, creating a small packet that is open at the top. Set the packet on the hot coals or hot lava stones; position the grill rack about 6 inches above the heat source.

Place 1 tortilla on the work surface. Scatter half of the cheese evenly over the tortilla. Scatter the duck breast slices, poblano chile strips, mushroom slices, and green onions evenly over the cheese. Scatter the remaining cheese evenly over all and top with the remaining tortilla.

When the wood chips are smoking heavily, place the quesadilla on the grill rack. Lower the cover and grill the quesadilla, rotating it once on the rack to promote even cooking, for 1½ to 2 minutes. When the bottom tortilla is lightly browned, using a wide spatula, carefully flip the quesadilla. Lower the cover and grill until the bottom tortilla is lightly browned, the cheese is melted, and the ingredients are heated through, 1 to 1½ minutes. With the spatula, carefully transfer the quesadilla to a cutting board. With a long, sharp knife or a pizza wheel, cut the quesadilla into wedges and serve immediately.

HOT MENU

Cold White Wine
Smoked Duck, Poblano, and Mushroom Quesadilla (page 152)
Tostaditas (page 205) with Salsa Borracho (page 6)

Grilled Pork Tenderloin and Grilled Pineapple–Rice Salad (page 134)
Grill-Toasted Garlic Bread (page 200)

Strawberry Shortcakes à la Mode (page 226)

Smoked Beef Brisket

SERVES 12 OR MORE, DEPENDING ON USAGE

In Texas, "barbecue" means "brisket." You can order other smoked things at a barbecue joint (spareribs, pork shoulder, short ribs, hot link sausages, for example) and if the pit master is any good you probably should sample it all, but the brisket is the star. When I started learning to operate my big cast-iron smoker, sublime smoked brisket was what I aspired to. Everything else I smoked—ribs, tuna, tomatoes, salmon—good as they were, were mere training exercises for the ultimate challenge. I ruined more than one brisket and burned up a lot of expensive cord wood, but the work was worth it. I can now say that my barbecued brisket is equal to or better than any other on the planet. Serve it in thin slices, drizzle it with a homemade barbecue sauce of your choice, pile it onto a sandwich (also with plenty of sauce), or roll it into warmed flour tortillas with hot salsa. However you plate it up, this *is what beef is all about.*

INGREDIENTS

1 whole oven-ready brisket of beef (about 10 pounds)
1 recipe Rib Rub (page 41)
Chunks or logs of fragrant hardwood, preferably a
combination of oak and mesquite

1 recipe Moonshine Mop (page 30)
1 12-ounce bottle lager beer, such as Heineken

Coat the brisket on all sides with the rub, patting it firmly into the meat. Wrap well and refrigerate overnight. Bring the brisket to room temperature.

Prepare a smoker according to the manufacturer's directions, using the wood chunks and achieving a steady temperature of 275° to 300°F. Place the brisket on the rack in the center of the smoker. Lower the cover and smoke the meat, rotating it on the rack once or twice (but not turning it over) to promote even smoking and basting it with the mop, for 3 hours. Meanwhile, position a rack in the lower third of the oven and preheat the oven to 350°F.

Remove the brisket from the smoker. Partially enclose it in heavy-duty foil and set it in a shallow roasting pan. Pour the beer over the brisket and seal it tightly in the foil. Bake the brisket for about 3½ hours, or until it is fork-tender. *The meat can be prepared several days in advance. Cool it completely and refrigerate in the foil. Reheat the brisket in the oven, still wrapped in the foil, before serving it.*

Transfer the brisket to a cutting board and tent with foil. Discard the juices. Separate the upper and lower halves of the brisket along the natural dividing line. Remove any excess surface fat. At a slight angle across the grain, cut the brisket into thin slices. Serve hot.

HOT MENU

Smoked Beef Brisket (page 154) on Cornmeal Kaisers (page 202) with Thick Poblano Table Sauce (page 18)

Marinated Pepper Slaw (page 183)
Drunken Beans (page 197)

Chocolate Whiskey Pudding (page 236)

Smoked Beef Brisket Hash

SERVES 4 AS BREAKFAST, 2 AS A HEARTY SUPPER

Few leftovers are more spectacularly satisfying than roast beef cooked up into a classic hash. Substitute home-smoked brisket for that roast beef, and the results surpass spectacular, becoming "company good," as my mom would say. Dreaming of this dish seems to make the hours spent over a red-hot smoker fly by. Top it, if you wish, with poached or fried eggs and serve it with a dollop of fiery Fast and Furious Ketchup or Salsa Borracho.

❦

INGREDIENTS

2 medium poblano chiles

2 medium red-skinned potatoes (about 1 pound), peeled

2¼ teaspoons salt

3 tablespoons (1½ ounces) unsalted butter

½ cup finely chopped yellow onions

4 cups diced, well-trimmed Smoked Beef Brisket (page 154)

¼ teaspoon freshly ground black pepper

¼ cup whipping cream

Poached or fried eggs (optional)

Fast and Furious Ketchup (page 28) or Salsa Borracho (page 6) (optional)

In the open flame of a gas burner, on a preheated grill (over wood smoking chips if desired), or under a preheated broiler, roast the chiles, turning them often, until the peels are evenly charred. In a closed paper bag, steam the chiles until cool. Rub off the burned peels, remove the stems, ribs, and seeds, and finely chop the chiles.

In a medium saucepan, cover the potatoes with cold water. Set over medium heat, stir in 2 teaspoons of the salt, and bring to a boil. Lower the heat slightly and simmer the potatoes briskly

until they are tender, about 20 minutes. Drain and cool. Dice the potatoes.

In a large heavy skillet, preferably nonstick, over low heat, melt the butter. Add the poblanos and onions and cook, covered, stirring once or twice, for 10 minutes.

Stir in the brisket, potatoes, the remaining ¼ teaspoon of salt, and the pepper. Cook, covered, stirring occasionally, for 15 minutes. Uncover, stir in the cream, and shape the hash mixture into a thick cake the size of the bottom of the skillet. Cook, uncovered, gently shaking the pan occasionally to prevent sticking, until the bottom is crisp and brown, 10 to 12 minutes.

Invert a large plate over the skillet. Hold the plate and skillet together and reverse them.

Remove the skillet (the hash should now be crusty bottom upward), top the hash with the eggs if desired and serve immediately, passing ketchup or salsa at the table if desired.

Smoked Fresh Ham

SERVES A CROWD

Locating a fresh ham for smoking can be tricky (most of them are already on the way to a commercial smokehouse), but it's worth the effort—few hunks of meat are so impressively festive. Order the ham well in advance from a good butcher and ask that it be boned and tied, for easier carving. Then invite over a couple dozen of your closest friends (fewer, if you quite sensibly want leftovers) and fire up the smoker.

❧

INGREDIENTS

16 cups boiling water
1⅓ cups kosher salt
1 cup packed dark brown sugar
1 fresh unsmoked ham, boned and tied (about 12 pounds)
5 cups dry red wine
2 14-ounce cans reduced-sodium beef or chicken broth

Chunks or logs of fragrant hardwood, preferably a combination of oak and mesquite
1 cup Red-As-Rubies Pepper Jelly (page 62) or commercial hot pepper jelly
1 cup canned pineapple juice

To make a brine, in a large bowl, stir together the boiling water, salt, and brown sugar. Cool to room temperature.

In a large container (a turkey roaster is ideal), pour the brine over the ham. Use one or two heavy plates to weight the ham and keep it beneath the surface of the brine. Cover and refrigerate for 48 hours.

Pour off and discard the brine. Rinse the ham under cold running water and pat dry. Bring the ham to room temperature. In a jar or pitcher, combine the wine and beef broth.

Prepare a smoker according to the manufacturer's directions, using the wood chunks and achieving a steady temperature of 275° to 300°F. Place the ham on the smoker rack in the center part of your smoker. Smoke the ham, rotating it once or twice on the rack (but not turning it over) to promote even smoking and mopping it regularly with about two thirds of the wine mixture for 3 hours. Shortly before the end of the smoking period, position a rack in the lower third of the oven and preheat the oven to 350°F.

Transfer the ham to a shallow roasting pan and set it in the oven. Bake the ham, basting it with the remaining wine mixture, for 2 hours and 45 minutes.

In a small saucepan over low heat, melt the hot pepper jelly. Pour off and discard any wine mixture from the bottom of the roasting pan and replace it with the pineapple juice. Return the ham to the oven and continue to bake it, basting every 10 minutes, first with the melted hot pepper jelly and then with the accumulated juices from the pan, until it is golden brown and shiny and an instant-reading thermometer inserted into the thickest part of the ham (avoid air pockets) registers between 160° and 170°F, about 40 minutes.

Remove the nam from the oven and let it rest, tented with foil, for at least 15 minutes before carving. Serve warm or cool.

Smoked Pork Loin

SERVES 6 TO 8, DEPENDING ON USAGE

Somewhat less work than fresh ham (also less opportunity for leftovers), this loin is an elegant little piece of smoked meat, perfect for slicing thin and nibbling with drinks (serve with Roasted Red Pepper–Mango Salsa, page 10, or Apricot-Piñon Chutney, page 27, and mini corn muffins), piling onto a sandwich, or fanning over a salad of mixed greens, diced apples, and pecans.

☙

INGREDIENTS

8 cups boiling water
⅔ cup kosher salt
½ cup packed dark brown sugar

1 boneless pork loin roast (about 2 pounds)
Chunks or logs of fragrant hardwood, preferably hickory

To make a brine, in a medium bowl, stir together the water, salt, and brown sugar. Cool to room temperature.

In a large container, pour the brine over the pork. Use one or two heavy plates to weight the pork and keep it beneath the surface of the brine. Cover and refrigerate for 12 hours.

Pour off and discard the brine. Rinse the pork under cold running water and pat dry. Bring the pork to room temperature.

Prepare a smoker according to the manufacturer's directions, using the wood chunks and achieving a steady temperature of 275° to 300°F. Place the pork on the rack in the coolest part of the smoker (at the end farthest from the firebox, for example, or on the upper shelf if your smoker has one). Lower the cover and smoke the pork, rotating it on the rack once or twice (but not turning it over) to promote even smoking, for about 2½ hours, or until it is just fully cooked through and tender without showing any sign of pinkness.

Remove the pork from the smoker and cool to room temperature. The pork will be most succulent if it is never refrigerated. Or wrap it well and refrigerate for up to 3 days, returning it to room temperature before slicing and serving it.

Chopped Smoked Pork on a Bun

MAKES 12 SANDWICHES

Short of heading to the back roads of South Carolina, this is the best way I know of experiencing the classic chopped pork barbecue sandwich. Few fistfuls of food are more satisfying, particularly when the lubrication is supplied by your own handcrafted sauce. Home-baked rolls transform this country meal into something extraordinary, but oversized squishy white burger buns are not only acceptable, they're traditional.

INGREDIENTS

1 pork shoulder roast or Boston butt (about 4½ pounds)
1 recipe Hot and Heavy Rub (page 40)
Chunks or logs of fragrant hardwood, preferably hickory
1 12-ounce bottle lager beer, such as Heineken

12 Cornmeal Kaisers (page 202) or oversized sandwich rolls, split, and toasted if desired
Oink Ointment™ (page 20) or Dark Secrets™ Mole Barbecue Sauce (page 19)

Coat the pork on all sides with the rub, patting it firmly into the meat. Wrap well and refrigerate overnight. Bring the pork to room temperature.

Prepare a smoker according to the manufacturer's directions, using the wood chunks and achieving a steady temperature of 275° to 300°F. Place the pork on the rack in the center of the smoker. Lower the cover and smoke the pork, rotating it on the rack once or twice (but not turning it over) to promote even smoking, for 3 hours. Meanwhile, position a rack in the lower third of the oven and preheat to 350°F.

Remove the pork from the smoker. Partially enclose it in heavy-duty foil and set it in a

shallow roasting pan. Pour the beer over the pork and seal it tightly in the foil. Bake about 3 hours, or until the pork is falling-off-the-bone tender. *The pork can be prepared several days in advance. Cool completely and refrigerate in the foil. Reheat the pork in the oven, still wrapped in the foil, before serving it.*

Transfer the pork to a cutting board and tent with foil. Discard the juices. With a long, sharp knife, coarsely chop the pork, discarding any bones or large pieces of fat.

Mound the pork on the rolls, using about 1 packed cup per sandwich, and serve immediately, accompanied by Oink Ointment™ or Dark Secrets™ Mole Barbecue Sauce.

Grill-Finished Smoked Thick Pork Chops with Apple–Red Chile Compote

SERVES 6

For this cool-weather dish I rub very thick, very tender pork loin chops with fiery-sweet chili powder from Chimayo in northern New Mexico. Smoked over fragrant pecan wood and then finished on the grill, the chops are accompanied by a tart, chunky, and slightly picante compote of apples. Add Grilled New Potatoes with Roquefort Butter (page 189) to the plate for an indelibly autumnal menu. And, come summer, the chops are good without the compote, topped instead with a generous dollop of Sweet and Hot Red Chile Mustard (page 23) and accompanied by corn on the cob and Rio Grande Ratatouille (page 178).

INGREDIENTS

THE PORK CHOPS	THE COMPOTE
6 1½-inch-thick loin pork chops (about 4½ pounds total)	2½ pounds (about 5 large) tart apples, such as Granny Smith, cored, peeled, and cut into ¾-inch chunks
3 tablespoons pure, unblended chili powder, preferably from Chimayo, New Mexico	2 cups medium-dry white wine
Chunks or logs of pecan or other fragrant hardwood	⅓ cup sugar
Salt to taste	¼ cup Dried Red New Mexico Chile Purée (page 44)
	3 tablespoons fresh lemon juice
	1 3-inch cinnamon stick

SMOKING THE PORK CHOPS

Rub the pork chops on both sides with the chili powder. Cover and let stand at room temperature for 1 hour.

Prepare a smoker according to the manufacturer's directions, using the pecan wood and achieving a steady temperature of 275° to 300°F. Place the pork chops on the smoker rack in the central part of the smoker, lower the cover, and smoke for about 1½ hours, or until the pork chops are about half cooked and well impregnated with smoky flavor. Remove them from the smoker and cool to room temperature. *The pork chops can be prepared to this point 1 day in advance. Cover and refrigerate. Return them to room temperature before proceeding with the recipe.*

FOR THE COMPOTE

In a heavy medium nonreactive pan over medium heat, combine the apples, wine, sugar, chile purée, lemon juice, and cinnamon stick. Cover and bring to a boil. Lower the heat slightly, partially cover, and simmer, stirring once or twice, until the apples are just tender while still holding their shape and the sauce has thickened slightly, about 30 minutes. Cool to room temperature and discard the cinnamon stick. *The compote can be prepared up to 1 day ahead; cover and refrigerate, returning it to room temperature before using.*

GRILLING THE PORK CHOPS

Light a charcoal fire and let it burn until the coals are evenly white or preheat a gas grill (medium). Position the grill rack about 6 inches above the heat source. Place the pork chops on the rack, cover the grill, and cook, turning them once or twice, until they are lightly browned and just cooked through while remaining juicy, about 5 minutes per side, depending on how much they have cooked in the smoker.

Season the pork chops lightly with salt to taste and transfer them to plates. Spoon the compote partially over and around them and serve immediately.

HOT MENU

Grilled Pico de Gallo (page 4)
Warm Tostaditas (page 205)

Grill-Finished Smoked Thick Pork Chops with Apple–Red Chile Compote (page 162)
Grilled New Potatoes with Roquefort Butter (page 189)

Vanilla Ice Cream with Quick Mocha Sauce (page 239)
Michael's Spiced Chocolate Shortbreads (page 244)

Smoked Spareribs

SERVES 4 TO 6, DEPENDING ON USAGE

These well-rubbed, well-smoked ribs, finished in the oven by my steamed-in-beer method, will be fragrant and tenderly falling from the bone. Serve them in combination with other smoked and grilled meats (Smoked Beef Brisket, page 154, and Spicy Pork and Red Wine Sausages, page 106, will complete a great trio) or feature them solo. Pass West Texas Red (page 17) or Dark Secrets™ Mole Barbecue Sauce (page 19) for dipping and dunking at the table.

INGREDIENTS

5 pounds (2 full sides) regular, not baby back, spareribs, chine bones cracked by the butcher for easier serving
1 recipe Rib Rub (page 41) or 1 recipe Fresh Herb–Cumin Rub (page 42)

Chunks or logs of fragrant hardwood, preferably a combination of oak and mesquite
2 cups Moonshine Mop (page 30) (optional)
1 12-ounce bottle lager beer, such as Heineken

Coat the ribs on all sides with the rub, patting it firmly into the meat. Wrap well and refrigerate overnight. Bring the ribs to room temperature.

Prepare a smoker according to the manufacturer's directions, using the wood chunks and achieving a steady temperature of 275°F to 300°F. Place the ribs on the rack in the center of the smoker. Lower the cover and smoke the ribs, rotating them on the rack once or twice (but not turning them over) to promote even smoking, and basting them occasionally with the mop, if desired, for 2 hours. Meanwhile, position a rack in the middle of the oven and preheat to 350°F.

Remove the ribs from the smoker. Partially enclose each side of ribs in heavy-duty foil and set in a shallow roasting pan. Pour half of the beer into each packet and seal the foil tightly around the ribs. Bake for 1 to 1½ hours, or until the ribs are very tender and about to fall from the bone. *The ribs can be prepared several days in advance. Cool completely, then refrigerate. Rewarm the ribs in a preheated 350°F oven for about 30 minutes, or until just heated through.* Cut the ribs into smaller sections or separate them individually for serving if desired. Serve them hot.

Smoked Loin of Venison

This is simply wonderful eating, rare (when was the last time you had venison?), deeply flavorful, and very satisfying. Texas is still full of hunters, and it's not out of the question for me to be gifted with a loin of fresh wild venison, but most of the time I just dial up one mail-order source or another and have a piece of mild, flavorful, but not at all gamy farm-raised venison shipped by overnight express. The hearty red wine marinade, with notes of orange, juniper, and bay, also becomes the mop for the loin as it smokes. The last time I made this I served it as part of a New Year's Eve buffet, then used the leftovers in sandwiches the next day.

INGREDIENTS

2 ¾-liter bottles medium-dry red wine, such as zinfandel
Zest (colored peel) of 2 large oranges, removed with a vegetable peeler
6 whole unpeeled garlic cloves
6 bay leaves
6 dried red chiles, such as de árbol or japonés

12 whole allspice berries
¼ cup packed light brown sugar
1 boneless loin of farm-raised venison (about 4½ pounds)
Chunks or logs of fragrant hardwood, preferably a combination of mesquite and oak

In a medium nonreactive pan, combine the wine, orange zest, garlic cloves, bay leaves, chiles, and allspice berries. Set over medium heat and bring to a boil. Lower the heat, partially cover the pan, and simmer for 20 minutes. Remove from the heat, stir in the brown sugar, and cool to room temperature.

In a large nonreactive pan (a turkey roaster is ideal), pour the marinade over the venison. Cover and refrigerate for 24 hours. Remove the venison from the marinade and pat dry. Bring

the venison to room temperature. Strain the marinade and transfer it to a jar or pitcher.

Prepare a smoker according to the manufacturer's directions, using the wood chunks and achieving a steady temperature of 275° to 300°F. Place the venison on the smoker rack in the central part of the smoker, lower the cover, and smoke it for about 2½ hours, rotating it on the rack (but not turning it over) to promote even smoking and mopping it occasionally with the strained marinade, until an instant-reading thermometer inserted into the center of the meat registers 165° to 175°F. Remove the venison from the smoker and cool to room temperature.

The venison can be prepared up to 3 days ahead. Wrap well and refrigerate, returning it to room temperature before using it. Slice it thinly across the grain for serving.

Home-Smoked Chipotles Adobado

MAKES ABOUT 3 CUPS

I repeat this recipe for chipotles, which was given in my first book, because it is so suited to the theme of this one, and because I call for these smoked and marinated jalapeños so often in the sauces and marinades herein. Green jalapeños can be used, but red ones are more beautiful and have a deeper, sweeter flavor. Grow your own, or in the store, select chiles that have begun to turn red; they will eventually ripen. (Those picked without any red at all in their peels will always remain green.) I rarely fire up the smoker just to make chipotles, but I can always find room for them on the rack while I'm smoking something else.

INGREDIENTS

Chunks or logs of fragrant hardwood, preferably a combination of oak and mesquite

1¼ pounds red-ripe jalapeño chiles, with stems

½ cup Dried Red New Mexico Chile Purée (page 44) or commercial chile paste, such as Santa Cruz

⅓ cup water

2 tablespoons tomato paste

2 tablespoons cider vinegar

1 tablespoon packed dark brown sugar

1 garlic clove, peeled and crushed through a press

¼ teaspoon salt

Prepare a smoker according to the manufacturer's directions, using the wood chunks and achieving a steady temperature of 275° to 300°F. Place the chiles directly on the smoker rack (or use a shallow disposable foil pan) at the cooler end of the smoking chamber or on the upper rack if your smoker has one. Lower the cover and smoke the chiles for 2½ hours, or until they are soft, brown, and slightly shriveled.

Remove the chipotles from the smoker. In a medium nonreactive saucepan, combine them with the chile purée, water, tomato paste, vinegar, brown sugar, garlic, and salt. Set over medium heat and bring to a simmer. Cook, stirring once or twice, until the sauce is very thick, about 15 minutes. Cool to room temperature.

Transfer the chipotles to a covered storage container and refrigerate for at least 24 hours before using. They can be refrigerated for up to 2 weeks or frozen for up to 2 months.

Unsauced Dried Chipotles After removing the chiles from the smoker, place them on a rack and leave them, loosely covered, at room temperature, until crisp, light, and dry, 1 to 2 weeks, depending on the humidity. Store airtight at room temperature.

Smoked Plum Tomato Sauce

MAKES ABOUT 6½ CUPS

Fresh plum tomatoes smoked over hickory or sweet fruitwood simmer up into something wonderfully different and pungent. The otherwise traditional sauce made from such smoked tomatoes is also unique, its simple, sweet acidity powerfully augmented by the flavor of the wood. I use it most often as the sauce on grilled pizza (pages 114 to 118), but it's also good on pasta tossed with grilled shrimp, ladled over a big steak pizzaiola style, accompanying grilled sausages (pages 106 and 110), or with Green Chile, Corn, and Cheese Strata (page 170).

INGREDIENTS

THE TOMATOES

5 pounds fresh red-ripe, Italian-style plum tomatoes

Chunks or logs of hickory, cherry, or other fragrant hardwood

THE SAUCE

⅓ cup olive oil

2 cups finely chopped yellow onions

6 garlic cloves, peeled and minced

½ teaspoon dried basil, crumbled

½ teaspoon dried thyme, crumbled

½ teaspoon dried oregano, crumbled

½ teaspoon crushed dried red pepper flakes

⅔ cup medium-dry red wine

1 teaspoon salt

SMOKING THE TOMATOES

Prepare a smoker according to the manufacturer's directions, using the wood chunks and achieving a steady temperature of 275° to 300°F. Working in batches if necessary, arrange the tomatoes in a single layer in one or two disposable foil pans (or for a smokier flavor, place them directly on the smoker rack) at the cooler end of your smoker or on the upper rack if there is one. Smoke the tomatoes until they are lightly colored, slightly shrunken, and well impregnated with smoky flavor, 1½ to 2 hours. Remove the tomatoes from the smoker and cool to room temperature. *The tomatoes*

can be smoked in advance. Wrap tightly and refrigerate for up to 3 days or freeze for up to 1 month. Thaw before proceeding with the recipe.

FOR THE SAUCE

In a 4-quart nonreactive saucepan over low heat, warm the olive oil. Add the onions, garlic, basil, thyme, oregano, and crushed red pepper, cover, and cook, stirring once or twice, until the onions are tender and lightly colored, about 10 minutes.

Coarsely chop the tomatoes. Add them with their skins and juices, the wine, and salt to the pan.

Raise the heat to medium and bring to a boil. Lower the heat, partially cover the pan, and simmer, stirring once or twice, until the sauce has thickened and is reduced by one third, about 40 minutes. Cool slightly.

Force the sauce through the medium blade of a food mill, purée it in a food processor, or force it through a sieve. Adjust the seasoning. *The sauce can be prepared in advance. Cool to room temperature, cover, and refrigerate for up to 3 days or freeze for up to 1 month.*

HOT MENU

Smoky Red Pepper and Sun-dried Tomato Spread (page 175) on Grill-Toasted Garlic Bread (page 200)

Mixed Grill of Skewered Shrimp, Mushrooms, and Hot Sausages (page 76)
Green Chile, Corn, and Cheese Strata with Smoked Plum Tomato Sauce (page 170)

Mexican Chocolate Ice Cream (page 238) with Fresh Strawberries

Green Chile, Corn, and Cheese Strata with Smoked Plum Tomato Sauce

SERVES 6 TO 8

This strata, a kind of savory bread pudding, makes a colorful and deliciously gooey accompaniment to plain grilled meats, chicken, and seafood. It's also a wonderful supper or brunch main course, served with ham steaks and a dollop of Red-As-Rubies Pepper Jelly (page 62). The smoked tomato sauce makes it special (I keep some in the freezer at all times), but plain sauce, homemade or commercial, may be substituted.

❧

INGREDIENTS

6 long green chiles
Butter for the baking dish
6 large eggs
2 cups fresh corn kernels and juice, cut and scraped from 6 to 8 medium ears tender supersweet or sugar-enhanced corn
2 cups half-and-half
2 teaspoons hot pepper sauce, such as Tabasco

1 teaspoon salt
8 ½-inch-thick slices (from a 9 × 5-inch loaf) of firm white sandwich bread, day-old but not dry, with the tough crusts removed
½ pound grated jalapeño Jack cheese
3½ cups Smoked Plum Tomato Sauce (page 168), heated to simmering

n the open flame of a gas burner, on a preheated grill (over wood smoking chips if desired), or under a preheated broiler, roast the chiles, turning them often, until the peels are lightly and evenly charred. In a closed paper bag, steam the chiles until cool. Rub off the burned peels, remove the stems, ribs, and seeds, and chop the chiles.

Lightly butter a 13 × 9-inch shallow oval baking dish. In a large bowl, whisk the eggs.

Whisk in the corn, chiles, half-and-half, hot pepper sauce, and salt. Arrange 4 slices of the bread in a single layer in the prepared dish. Ladle half the corn mixture over the bread. Sprinkle half the cheese over the corn mixture. Repeat with the remaining bread, corn mixture, and cheese. Cover the dish tightly and let stand at room temperature for 1 hour.

Position a rack in the middle of the oven and preheat the oven to 350°F. Uncover the strata, set it in the oven, and bake until it is puffed and firm and the top is lightly browned, about 40 minutes. Let it rest on a rack for 5 minutes. Serve accompanied by the tomato sauce.

HOT TIP The fiery quality of chiles is concentrated in the placental tissue—the white ribs or veins to which the seeds are attached.

The actual heat level of any specimen of a particular type of chile will vary widely, based on assorted growing conditions. The only way to be certain of how *picante* any chile is, is to taste it. To reduce the heat, trim away some or all of the seeds and veins. The resulting chile will still be slightly spicy and will retain all of its delicious flavor.

starters, salads, and starches

Texas appetites are big, so are Texas plates, and there's plenty of room on them for satisfying starters, salads, and starches of all sorts. In fact, though the foods that come from the grill and the smoker (pretty much meat) are definitely the reason for the getting together, it would be a bleak steak or burger, slab of brisket, or pork shoulder sandwich, that was not well accompanied by coleslaw, beans, onion rings, macaroni salad, and plenty more. There can hardly be too many items for diners to choose from on the hot-and-cold self-service side dish counter at the typical barbecue joint, and I advise you to follow a similar philosophy when entertaining, Lone Star style, at home.

Hot Nuts

These chile-seasoned nuts are spicy, also crisp and smoky, thanks to the big cast-iron skillet in which they are grill-baked over an open fire (or you can use a 375°F oven). Most of that heat comes from the chili powder blend, so choose accordingly.

INGREDIENTS

2 cups wood smoking chips, preferably hickory

3 tablespoons chili powder blend

1 teaspoon kosher salt

2 large egg whites

2 teaspoons Worcestershire sauce

1 teaspoon hot pepper sauce, such as Tabasco

½ teaspoon liquid smoke seasoning

1½ cups (about 6 ounces) roasted, unsalted peanuts

1½ cups (about 6 ounces) pepitas (hulled pumpkin seeds, available in health food stores)

Nonstick spray

Light a charcoal fire and let it burn until the coals are evenly white or preheat a gas grill (medium). Wrap the wood chips partially in foil, creating a small packet that is open at the top. Set the packet on the hot coals or hot lava stones; position the grill rack about 6 inches above the heat source.

Meanwhile, in a small bowl, mix together the chili powder and salt. In a medium bowl, whisk together the egg whites, Worcestershire sauce, hot pepper sauce, and liquid smoke. Add the peanuts and *pepitas* and stir to coat. While the egg white mixture is still wet, sprinkle the chili powder mixture over the nuts, stirring constantly to coat them evenly. Lightly coat a 12-inch cast-iron skillet with nonstick spray.

When the wood chips are smoking heavily, place the skillet on the grill rack. Add the nut mixture, lower the cover, and grill, stirring occasionally, until the nuts are crisp and lightly browned and the *pepitas* are popping, 8 to 10 minutes.

Transfer immediately to a plate or bowl and cool to room temperature. *The nuts will keep for a week or more. Store airtight at room temperature.*

Smoky Red Pepper and Sun-dried Tomato Spread

MAKES 1 CUP

This intensely sweet, smoky, and picante spread is easy to make and easy to like. Serve it at drinks time, spread onto crisp slices of toasted baguette (do this ahead of time yourself, in the kitchen, for better portion control), or let guests slather it onto slabs of Grill-Toasted Garlic Bread (page 200) (expect it to vanish quickly when so used). Any unlikely leftovers can be spread on sandwiches, almost like a luscious, ruddy mayonnaise.

✎

INGREDIENTS

2 cups wood smoking chips (optional)

2 large sweet red peppers

10 large whole oil-packed sun-dried tomatoes, drained and coarsely chopped

¼ cup oil from the sun-dried tomato jar or good-quality olive oil

1 chipotle adobado, homemade (page 166) or commercial, plus 2 teaspoons sauce from the chipotles

Salt to taste

On a preheated grill over wood smoking chips if desired, in the open flame of a gas burner, or under the broiler, roast the red peppers, turning them often, until the peels are lightly and evenly charred. In a closed paper bag or in a covered bowl, steam the peppers until cool. Rub off the burned peels, remove the stems, ribs, and seeds, and coarsely chop the peppers.

In a food processor combine the chopped peppers, sun-dried tomatoes, oil, and chipotle and sauce. Process until fairly smooth. Taste and add salt if necessary (sun-dried tomatoes are fairly salty; you may need none). *The spread can be prepared up to 3 days ahead. Transfer to a storage container, cover, and refrigerate. Return to room temperature before using.*

Hot Lips Spiced Shrimp

SERVES 6 TO 8

Tingling lips, fingers worth licking, and plenty of zesty flavor are the main rewards of this easy-to-make but messy-to-eat starter, perfect for passing the time while the grill heats up. Put a big bowl of shrimp in the middle of the table, give everyone (1) permission to slurp, (2) a small dish for discarded tails, (3) a cold beer, and (4) a hot, wet washcloth to clean up with afterward.

INGREDIENTS

2 quarts water

1 12-ounce bottle amber beer, such as Dos Equis

10 small dried red chiles, such as japonés or de árbol

8 whole unpeeled garlic cloves

1 tablespoon yellow mustard seeds

4 bay leaves

¼ cup commercial horseradish

2 tablespoons Worcestershire sauce

2 tablespoons hot pepper sauce, such as Tabasco

⅓ cup olive oil

1½ pounds (about 30) large shrimp, peeled (except for the tails) and deveined

1 large lemon, thinly sliced

1 tablespoon salt

In a large saucepan, combine the water, beer, chiles, garlic, mustard seeds, and bay leaves. Set over medium heat and bring to a brisk simmer. Partially cover and cook for 10 minutes.

Meanwhile, in a small bowl, whisk together the horseradish, Worcestershire sauce, and hot pepper sauce. Whisk in the olive oil.

Add the shrimp, lemon slices, and salt to the simmering beer mixture and cook, stirring once or twice, until the shrimp are pink, curled, and just tender, about 3 minutes. Pour the shrimp mixture through a fine strainer; drain well.

Immediately transfer the contents of the strainer (everything—the shrimp, chiles, lemon slices, bay leaves, mustard seeds, and garlic cloves) to a large bowl. Add the horseradish mixture and toss. Cool to room temperature, stirring once or twice; serve, preferably without resorting to refrigeration.

Barbecued Tequila Shrimp with Bacon

SERVES 4 TO 6

I think my version of grilled, bacon-wrapped shrimp knocks this culinary cliché on its teakettle. Marinated in Coyote, a unique wild herb–flavored golden tequila from Seagram's, then wrapped with mesquite bacon and brushed with fiery barbecue sauce, the shrimp are a cocktail hour knockout. Serve them with one of several entirely unnecessary—but delicious—dips, blend up a batch of margaritas, and folks will holler with pleasure.

INGREDIENTS

1 pound (about 20) large shrimp, peeled and deveined
2 tablespoons Coyote or other gold tequila
1 tablespoon fresh lime juice
¼ teaspoon freshly ground black pepper
6 or 7 strips of bacon, cut crosswise into thirds
2 cups wood smoking chips, preferably mesquite or hickory

⅔ cup West Texas Red (page 17) or another thin, spicy, tomato-based barbecue sauce
Roasted Garlic Mayonnaise (page 52), Rosemary Mayonnaise (page 53), or additional West Texas Red, warmed (optional)

In a medium nonreactive bowl, combine the shrimp, tequila, lime juice, and pepper. Cover and let stand at room temperature, stirring once or twice, for 1 hour.

Wrap each shrimp in a piece of bacon. Slide the shrimp onto 4 or 5 flat metal skewers, positioning them to prevent the ends of the bacon pieces from unwrapping.

Light a charcoal fire and let it burn until the coals are evenly white or preheat a gas grill (medium). Wrap the wood chips partially in foil, creating a small packet that is open at the top.

Set the packet on the hot coals or hot lava stones; position the grill rack about 6 inches above the heat source.

When the wood chips are smoking heavily, place the skewers on the grill, cover, and cook, turning them once or twice and brushing the shrimp with the barbecue sauce, until the shrimp are pink and just cooked through and the bacon is crisp, about 6 minutes total.

Slide the shrimp from the skewers and serve immediately, accompanied by one of the dipping sauces if desired.

Rio Grande Ratatouille

Most of the traditional ingredients—zucchini, eggplant, peppers, onions, garlic—of ratatouille, the Provençal French vegetable ragout, appear in this cool side dish, but I prefer to grill them individually rather than stew them together. The effect is rather more saladlike than the classic, long-simmered original, and it is a great accompaniment for such plain but smoke-grilled meats as chicken, lamb, beef, or robustly flavored seafood. Garnished with pitted chopped, black Greek olives and accompanied by thick slabs of beefsteak tomatoes, slices of fresh mozzarella cheese, and crusty bread, this also makes a spectacular hot-weather main dish for six.

INGREDIENTS

2 cups wood smoking chips
2 pounds (about 6 medium) zucchini, scrubbed and quartered lengthwise
1 large eggplant (about 1 pound), cut lengthwise into ¾-inch-thick slices
Olive oil for grilling the vegetables, plus ⅓ cup olive oil
3 large heavy sweet red peppers, preferably Dutch

4 long green chiles
1 medium onion (about ½ pound) peeled and thinly sliced
6 garlic cloves, peeled and finely chopped
3 tablespoons balsamic vinegar
¾ teaspoon salt
Freshly ground black pepper to taste

Light a charcoal fire and let it burn until the coals are evenly white or preheat a gas grill (medium). Wrap the wood chips partially in foil, creating a small packet that is open at the top. Set the packet on the hot coals or hot lava stones; position the grill rack about 6 inches above the heat source.

Brush the zucchini and eggplant generously with olive oil. When the wood chips are smoking heavily, place the zucchini, eggplant, peppers, and chiles on the rack and cover. Grill the zucchini and eggplant, turning them once or twice, until lightly browned, about 2 minutes per side. Transfer them to a plate and cool to room temperature. Grill the peppers and chiles, turning them often, until the peels are evenly charred. In a closed paper bag, steam the peppers and chiles until cool. Rub off the burned peels, remove the stems, ribs, and seeds, and cut the peppers and chiles into julienne strips. Coarsely chop the zucchini and eggplant. In a large bowl, combine the peppers, chiles, zucchini, and eggplant.

In a medium skillet over medium heat, warm the remaining ⅓ cup olive oil. Add the onions and garlic and cook, stirring once or twice, until they are tender and lightly colored, about 8 minutes. Cool slightly, then add the onion mixture to the bowl of vegetables and chiles.

Stir in the balsamic vinegar, salt, and a generous grinding of pepper. Adjust the seasoning. *The ratatouille can be prepared up to 1 day ahead. Cover and refrigerate, returning it to room temperature before serving.*

HOT MENU

❧

Chilled White Wine
Bluefish Grilled in a Coat of Many Spices (page 84)
Rio Grande Ratatouille (page 178)
Red Chile Corn Bread (page 201)

Strawberries Dipped into Quick Mocha Sauce (page 239)

Newfangled Macaroni Salad

SERVES 12

*A creamy, old-fashioned antidote to fancified modern pasta salads, this picnic side dish still manages to taste fresh
and different. Even without pickle relish and Miracle Whip, it's a natural beside almost any grilled or
barbecued main course. I like a lot of bacon in this salad (it's a family trait), but feel free to adjust
the amount downward according to your conscience and waistline.*

INGREDIENTS

¾ pound thick-sliced bacon, preferably mesquite-smoked

2 teaspoons salt

12 ounces elbow twists, or any other short, thick,
curly dried pasta shape

2 cups mayonnaise, regular or reduced-fat

½ cup cultured buttermilk

3 tablespoons fresh lemon juice

2 tablespoons Dijon mustard

2 tablespoons sugar

1 pound frozen peas, thawed and drained

10 ounces cultivated brown (cremini) or white mushrooms,
trimmed and thickly sliced

Leaves of curly spinach

Place the bacon strips flat in a cold skillet, set over medium heat, and cook, turning them once or twice, until crisp, about 9 minutes. Drain on paper towels. Coarsely chop the bacon.

Fill a large pot with water, set it over high heat, and bring it to a boil. Add the salt and the pasta and cook, partially covered, stirring once or twice, until the pasta is just tender, about 9 minutes, depending on the brand and shape. Drain, rinse with cold water, and drain again.

In a medium bowl, whisk together the mayonnaise, buttermilk, lemon juice, mustard,

and sugar. *The salad can be prepared to this point several hours in advance. Cover all the ingredients and hold them at room temperature.*

In a large bowl, toss together the pasta, bacon, peas, and mushrooms. Add the dressing and mix thoroughly; adjust the seasoning.

Line a serving platter or bowl with the spinach leaves. Mound the pasta salad on the leaves and serve more or less immediately (the pasta absorbs the dressing and quickly becomes dry if it sits around).

Pinto Bean and Cheese Salad

SERVES 6 TO 8

This sturdy, simple little salad goes great alongside any rather plain grilled meats (especially beef) or with chicken. When the tomatoes grown in El Paso's Upper Valley are especially fine (late August), I coarsely chop one or two large ones and stir them into the salad just before I serve it. Store-bought pickled jalapeños are okay in this; home-canned red ones (page 64) are spectacular.

❧

INGREDIENTS

1 pound dried pinto beans, picked over

2 teaspoons salt

3 tablespoons liquid from pickled jalapeños

3 tablespoons sherry vinegar

6 tablespoons olive oil

6 pickled jalapeño chiles, stemmed and thinly sliced

½ cup thinly sliced green onions

½ pound sharp Cheddar cheese, cut into ¼-inch cubes

⅓ cup minced cilantro

In a large bowl, cover the beans generously with cold water and let them soak overnight.

Drain the beans. In a large saucepan, cover them generously with fresh cold water. Set the pan over medium heat and bring the water to a boil. Lower the heat and briskly simmer the beans for 30 minutes. Stir in the salt and cook another 10 to 15 minutes, or until they are just tender.

Drain and immediately transfer the hot beans to a large bowl. Add the pickled jalapeño liquid, vinegar, and olive oil and cool to room temperature, stirring once or twice.

Stir in the jalapeños and green onions. *The salad can be prepared to this point several hours in advance. Cover and refrigerate, returning it to room temperature before proceeding with the recipe.* Stir in the cheese and cilantro, adjust the seasoning, and serve.

Grill-Smoked Red Pepper and Asadero Cheese Salad

SERVES 6

*Asadero is a mild fresh border cheese that is primarily esteemed for the way it melts and strings—
perfect on nachos, quesadillas, and enchiladas or in soups and dips. It's not just for melting, though.
When brought to room temperature, asadero is moist, tender, and sweetly milky, and combines perfectly
with a smoky, zesty salad of marinated sweet red pepper strips. No asadero?
Fresh mozzarella makes a perfect substitution.*

❧

INGREDIENTS

2 cups wood smoking chips, preferably hickory
4 large heavy sweet red peppers, preferably Dutch
3 tablespoons olive oil
2 tablespoons balsamic vinegar

2 garlic cloves, peeled and crushed through a press
½ teaspoon salt
Freshly ground black pepper to taste
1½ pounds asadero or mozzarella cheese, sliced into ½-inch-thick slices, at room temperature

Light a charcoal fire and let it burn until the coals are evenly white or preheat a gas grill (medium). Wrap the wood chips partially in foil, creating a small packet that is open at the top. Set the packet on the hot coals or hot lava stones; position the grill rack about 6 inches above the heat source.

When the wood chips are smoking, place the peppers on the grill. Lower the cover and grill the peppers, turning them often, until they are evenly charred on all sides. In a closed paper bag, steam the peppers until cool. Rub off the burned peels, remove the stems and seeds, and cut the peppers into julienne strips. *The peppers can be prepared up to 3 days ahead. Refrigerate, returning them to room temperature before using.*

In a medium bowl, combine the pepper strips, olive oil, vinegar, garlic, salt, and pepper to taste. Let stand at room temperature, stirring occasionally, for 1 hour.

Line a deep platter with partially overlapping slices of cheese. Spoon the peppers and their juices into the center of the platter and serve immediately.

Marinated Pepper Slaw

SERVES 12

Sweet bell peppers and "spring" onions (as we El Pasoans call green onions) supply the flavor and jalapeños provide the heat in this not-your-momma's coleslaw, the perfect crunchy, fiery accompaniment to many a grilled main course. For slightly less fire, remove the white ribs and seeds from the jalapeños, then cut them into julienne.

INGREDIENTS

3 large heavy sweet red peppers, preferably Dutch, trimmed, seeded, and cut into julienne

3 fresh jalapeño chiles, stemmed and sliced into thin rounds

⅔ cup olive oil

½ cup red wine vinegar

3 tablespoons sugar

12 cups finely shredded white cabbage (most of a 2½-pound head)

½ cup thinly sliced green onions

2 teaspoons salt

In a medium bowl, toss together the red peppers and jalapeños.

In a small nonreactive saucepan, combine the olive oil, vinegar, and sugar. Set over medium heat and bring just to a simmer. Pour the hot dressing over the peppers and let stand, stirring once or twice, until cool. *The marinated peppers can be prepared up to 1 day ahead. Cover and refrigerate, then return to room temperature before proceeding with the recipe.*

In a large bowl, toss together the shredded cabbage, green onions, marinated peppers with their dressing, and the salt. Adjust the seasoning. Serve the slaw within an hour or so if you like it crunchy (I do). *For a more tender slaw, refrigerate it for up to 6 hours, returning it to cool room temperature before serving.*

Sweet Buttermilk Slaw

SERVES 6 TO 8

Simplicity itself, this easy sweet-and-sour slaw goes well beside many grilled summer entrées, and especially spareribs and chicken. I also like it piled onto a sandwich of Smoked Pork Loin (page 160) or Smoked Wild Turkey (page 150). A love of Miracle Whip is one of the seven requirements for genuine Texas citizenship—please don't hold it against me.

INGREDIENTS

1½ cups Miracle Whip
1 cup cultured buttermilk
2 tablespoons sugar
1 tablespoon fresh lemon juice

1 teaspoon hot pepper sauce, such as Tabasco
½ teaspoon salt
10 cups coarsely shredded red cabbage (from a 2-pound head)

In a large bowl, whisk together the Miracle Whip, buttermilk, sugar, lemon juice, hot pepper sauce, and salt. Add the cabbage and mix well. Cover and refrigerate for at least 2 hours or overnight if you like a more tender slaw. Adjust the seasoning, toss well, and serve.

Sliced Tomato Salad with Pesto Ranch Dressing

SERVES 8

It's hard to imagine a more perfect plate of summer food than grilled steak, chicken, or fish, plus this terrific salad. If you find both red and yellow tomatoes, combine them for an especially colorful dish.

INGREDIENTS

8 large perfectly ripe, juicy tomatoes (about 4 pounds total)

1 recipe Pesto Ranch Dressing (page 50)
Sprigs of fresh basil, for garnish (optional)

Just before serving, trim the tomatoes and cut them into thick slices. Arrange the slices on a platter. Adjust the seasoning of the dressing. Drizzle the tomatoes generously with the dressing, garnish the salad with the sprigs of basil if desired, and serve immediately, passing any remaining dressing at the table.

Border Bruschetta Salad

SERVES 8

At my house, a favorite meal is a grilled but otherwise pristine prime porterhouse steak, accompanied by nothing more than a big helping of this chunky, delicious salad. The smoky, oversized croutons of grilled bread absorb the tangy dressing, while the earthy blue cheese and sweet-hot onions provide pleasant shocks of taste and texture; steak juices mingle with everything. For the best results, use perfectly ripe, juicy tomatoes, high-quality cheese (like the Iowa brand, Maytag), and firm peasant-style bread.

❧

INGREDIENTS

⅓ cup plus 3 tablespoons olive oil

6 garlic cloves, peeled and crushed through a press

1 cup wood smoking chips, preferably hickory or mesquite

6 large 1-inch-thick slices of bread from a day-old peasant-style round loaf

2 pounds (about 6 medium) ripe, juicy tomatoes

3 tablespoons sherry vinegar

¾ teaspoon salt

½ teaspoon freshly ground black pepper

1 medium red onion, peeled, thinly sliced, and separated into thin rings

8 ounces blue cheese, crumbled, at room temperature

I n a small bowl, combine the ⅓ cup of the olive oil and half the garlic and let stand at room temperature for 30 minutes.

Light a charcoal fire and let it burn until the coals are evenly white or preheat a gas grill (medium). Wrap the wood chips partially in foil, creating a small packet that is open at the top. Set the packet on the hot coals or hot lava stones; position the grill rack about 6 inches above the heat source.

Brush the slices of bread generously on all sides with the garlic oil. When the wood chips are smoking heavily, place the bread on the grill, cover, and toast, turning the slices once or twice, until they are crisp and golden brown, about 4 minutes. Cool and with a serrated knife, cut the slices into 1-inch cubes.

Meanwhile, trim the tomatoes and cut them into 1-inch chunks. In a large bowl, combine the tomatoes, their juices, the vinegar, the remaining

3 tablespoons of olive oil, the rest of the garlic, the salt, and pepper and let stand for 15 minutes, stirring gently once or twice.

Just before serving, add the bread cubes and onion rings to the tomato mixture and toss gently. Spoon the salad into a wide bowl, sprinkle the blue cheese evenly over all, and serve immediately.

HOT MENU

Guacamole Verde (page 16)
Two Tomato–Chipotle Salsa (page 7)
Tostaditas (page 205)

Grilled Marinated Flank Steak (page 99)
Border Bruschetta Salad (page 186)

Lemon Ice-Cream Pie with Raspberry Sauce (page 224)

Caesar Potato and Tomato Salad

SERVES 6

This is the terrific potato salad without which no book on grilling would be complete; the addition of wedges of juicy, ripe beefsteak tomatoes makes it a complete picnic side dish.

INGREDIENTS

2½ pounds waxy boiling potatoes, peeled and cut into 1½-inch chunks
2 teaspoons salt
1 tablespoon white wine vinegar
1 tablespoon fresh lime juice

1⅓ cups Great Caesar Dressing (page 51) or Red Chile Caesar Dressing (page 51)
½ cup thinly sliced green onions
Freshly ground black pepper to taste
2 large ripe tomatoes (about 1 pound total), trimmed and cut into eighths

In a large saucepan, cover the potatoes generously with cold water. Stir in the salt, set over medium heat, and bring to a boil. Lower the heat and simmer briskly, stirring the potatoes once or twice, until they are just tender, 10 to 12 minutes. Drain immediately and transfer to a large bowl.

Sprinkle the vinegar and lime juice over the hot potatoes; toss and cool them to room temperature. *The salad can be prepared to this point several hours in advance. Cover the potatoes and store at room temperature.*

Pour 1 cup of the Caesar dressing over the potatoes. Add ⅓ cup of the sliced green onions and pepper to taste and toss gently. Transfer the potatoes to a large serving platter. Arrange the tomato wedges around the edge of the platter. Drizzle the tomatoes with the remaining dressing. Scatter the remaining green onions over all and serve immediately.

Grilled New Potatoes with Roquefort Butter

SERVES 6

Tender skins-on new potatoes grill into hot, crisp, and smoky morsels that are irresistible, as this and the following recipe will illustrate. When the menu includes beef, the pungent Roquefort butter makes these spuds an especially perfect complement, but other flavored butters (pages 54 to 57) will work equally well.

INGREDIENTS

2 pounds (about 18) small red-skinned new potatoes, well scrubbed
1 tablespoon salt plus additional salt to taste
Olive oil for grilling the potatoes

2 cups wood smoking chips
Freshly ground black pepper to taste
1 recipe Roquefort Butter (page 56), slightly softened

In a medium saucepan, cover the potatoes generously with cold water. Stir in the 1 tablespoon of salt, set over medium heat, and bring to a boil. Lower the heat slightly and simmer briskly, stirring once or twice, until the potatoes are just tender, about 9 minutes. Drain and cool to room temperature. *The potatoes can be prepared up to 1 day ahead. Wrap them well and refrigerate; return them to room temperature before proceeding with the recipe.*

Brush the potatoes lightly but evenly with olive oil. Light a charcoal fire and let it burn until the coals are evenly white or preheat a gas grill (medium). Wrap the wood chips partially in foil, creating a small packet that is open at the top. Set the packet on the hot coals or hot lava stones; position the grill rack about 6 inches above the heat source.

When the wood chips are smoking heavily, place the potatoes on the rack. Cover and grill, turning them once or twice, until they are crisp and fairly well browned, about 6 minutes. Remove the potatoes from the heat, season with salt and pepper to taste, and serve immediately, accompanied by the Roquefort butter.

Rosemary-Grilled New Potatoes

SERVES 6

Skewered through their middles with a sprig of fragrant rosemary, then grilled, these new potatoes are not only tasty, they're attractive as well. Serve them alongside grilled lamb, pork, or chicken, or offer them as an appetizer, accompanied by Roasted Garlic Mayonnaise (page 52) or even Rosemary Mayonnaise (page 53) for dipping. (This last notion developed during one frustrating evening when I couldn't stop guests from snatching the smoking spuds right off the grill and nibbling them with their margaritas. Warning's fair.)

INGREDIENTS

2 pounds (about 18) small red-skinned new potatoes, well scrubbed

1 tablespoon salt, plus additional salt to taste

⅓ cup olive oil

¼ cup chopped fresh rosemary leaves, plus 18 4-inch woody sprigs of rosemary

3 medium garlic cloves, peeled and minced

2 cups wood smoking chips, preferably mesquite or hickory

Freshly ground black pepper to taste

In a medium saucepan, cover the potatoes with cold water. Set over medium heat, stir in the 1 tablespoon salt, and bring to a boil. Lower the heat slightly and cook the potatoes, stirring them occasionally, until they are just tender, about 9 minutes. Drain immediately and cool to room temperature. *The potatoes can be prepared up to 2 days ahead. Wrap them well and refrigerate, returning them to room temperature before proceeding with the recipe.*

In a mini food processor, combine the olive oil, chopped rosemary, and garlic and process until fairly smooth. With a skewer, carefully poke a hole through the middle of each potato. Insert a rosemary sprig into each hole so that its ends extend evenly on each side of the potato. Brush the potatoes and protruding rosemary sprigs generously with some of the olive oil mixture.

Light a charcoal fire and let it burn until the coals are evenly white or preheat a gas grill (medium). Wrap the wood chips partially in foil, creating a small packet that is open at the top. Set the packet on the hot coals or hot lava stones; position the grill rack about 6 inches above the heat source and cover the grill. When the wood chips are smoking heavily, place the potatoes on the grill rack. Cover and cook, turning the potatoes often and basting them with the remaining olive oil mixture, until they are lightly crisped and heated through, 4 to 5 minutes.

Remove the potatoes from the heat and season them with salt and pepper to taste. Serve immediately.

HOT TIP Extinguish flare-ups of open flame (caused by fat dripping onto coals or firestones) with water squirted from a plastic plant mister. Avoid flare-ups altogether by removing all skin and visible fat from grilled foods, reducing or omitting oil in marinades and bastes, or by cooking over a drip pan or over indirect heat.

Grilled Potato Planks

These thick slabs of potato—I like a combination of Idaho bakers and sweet potatoes—come crisp,
hot, and smoky from the grill, and make an eye-appealing starchy side dish for almost any meal, grilled or not.
If you're deft, the planks can go right on the rack (which makes them extra crisp)
or you can use a flat, hinged grill basket.

INGREDIENTS

2 very large Idaho baking potatoes
(about 1¾ pounds total)
2 very large sweet potatoes (about 1¾ pounds total)
1 tablespoon salt, plus additional salt to taste

2 cups wood smoking chips
Olive oil for grilling the potatoes
Freshly ground black pepper to taste

In a large pan, cover the baking and sweet potatoes generously with cold water. Stir in the 1 tablespoon of salt and set over medium heat. Bring to a boil, then lower the heat slightly and simmer briskly until the potatoes are just tender when pierced by a skewer, about 20 minutes. Drain and cool slightly.

When you can comfortably handle the potatoes, peel them. Cool completely. *The potatoes can be prepared up to 1 day ahead. Wrap and refrigerate, returning the potatoes to room temperature before proceeding with the recipe.*

Light a charcoal fire and let it burn until the coals are evenly white or preheat a gas grill

(medium-high). Wrap the wood chips partially in foil, creating a small packet that is open at the top. Set the packet on the hot coals or hot lava stones; position the grill rack about 6 inches above the heat source, Slice the potatoes on an angle into ¾-inch-thick slices. Brush the potato slices generously on both sides with olive oil.

When the wood chips are smoking heavily, place the potato slices on the rack. Cover and grill, carefully turning the potato slices with tongs or a spatula once or twice, until they are crisp and attractively marked, 4 to 6 minutes.

Transfer the potatoes to a plate, season with salt and ground black pepper to taste, and serve hot.

Lemon-Pepper Fries

SERVES 8

These oversized fried spuds get a generous shower of minced citrus peel and pepper just before they are served.
Team them with grilled burgers, steaks, or seafood and serve Chili Ketchup for dunking.

INGREDIENTS

1 tablespoon freshly ground black pepper
1 tablespoon minced fresh lemon zest (colored peel)
½ teaspoon coarse salt

4 pounds (6 large) Idaho baking potatoes, well scrubbed
About 10 cups corn oil for deep-frying
Chili Ketchup (page 28) (optional)

In a small bowl, stir together the pepper, lemon zest, and salt.

Cut each potato lengthwise into 10 wedges. Pat dry.

In a deep fryer or in a large deep pan fitted with a frying thermometer and set over medium-high heat, warm the corn oil to between 300° and 325°F. (The deep fryer or pan should be no more than half full.) Working in small batches, lower the potatoes into the hot oil. Cook, stirring once or twice to prevent the oil from boiling over, until the potatoes are somewhat crisp but not browned or cooked through, about

4 minutes. Remove the potatoes from the oil with a slotted spoon and transfer to paper towels. *The potatoes can be fried several hours in advance. Cover with plastic wrap and hold at room temperature.*

Rewarm the corn oil to between 375° and 400°F. Working in batches, lower the potatoes into the hot oil and cook, stirring once or twice to prevent the oil from boiling over, until they are crisp and golden brown, about 3 minutes. With a slotted spoon, transfer them to paper towels. Season the potatoes generously with the lemon-pepper mixture and serve them hot, accompanied by chili ketchup if desired.

Corn-Battered Onion Rings

SERVES 8

Splendidly greasy and quite habit-forming, these big, sweet onion rings, with their tender cornmeal coating, are just the ticket beside a juicy, just-grilled steak or burger or an overstuffed smoked pork sandwich. Serve them with Fast and Furious Ketchup (page 28) or Hot and Hasty Barbecue Sauce (page 29) for dunking.

❧

INGREDIENTS

3 very large yellow onions (3 pounds total), peeled, sliced, and separated into rings

1½ cups unbleached all-purpose flour

½ cup yellow cornmeal, preferably stone-ground

1 tablespoon sugar

2 teaspoons freshly ground black pepper

1 teaspoon salt

1 teaspoon baking powder

2 cups flat lager beer, such as Heineken

2 large eggs, well-beaten

10 cups corn oil for deep-frying

In a large bowl, cover the onion rings with cold water and refrigerate for 2 hours.

In a medium bowl, stir together the flour, cornmeal, sugar, pepper, salt, and baking powder. Stir in the beer and eggs.

In a deep fryer or in a deep 5-quart pan fitted with a frying thermometer, heat the corn oil to between 375° and 400°F. (The deep fryer or pan should be no more than half full.)

Position a rack in the middle of the oven and preheat the oven to 275°F. Line a jelly roll sheet pan with several thicknesses of paper towels.

Drain the onion rings and pat them thoroughly dry. A few at a time, dip the onion rings into the batter. Lift them out (a meat fork with long tines works well here), letting excess batter drip back into the bowl, then carefully lower them into the hot oil. Cook the onion rings, stirring them once or twice to promote even cooking, until they are crisp and golden, 3 to 4 minutes. With a slotted spoon, transfer them to the jelly roll pan and keep them warm in the oven. Repeat with the remaining onion rings. Serve the onion rings hot.

Grilled Red Onions

SERVES 8

These smoky sweet onions are good on burgers, or scattered over a big old steak, or they can be eaten alongside either. A flat grill basket will make it easier to turn the onions, but deft maneuvring with one or two long-handled metal spatulas will also do the job—and the onions will be crisper and browner.

INGREDIENTS

4 medium-large red onions (about 2 pounds total)
2 tablespoons Worcestershire sauce
2 tablespoons balsamic vinegar
2 tablespoons soy sauce

2 tablespoons olive oil
2 cups wood smoking chips, preferably fruitwood or hickory
Salt to taste
Freshly ground black pepper to taste

Trim and peel the onions and cut each one horizontally into 2 thick slices. Arrange the onion slices in a single layer in a shallow nonreactive dish. In a small bowl, stir together the Worcestershire sauce, balsamic vinegar, soy sauce, and olive oil. Pour the mixture over the onions and marinate, basting occasionally, for 1 hour.

Meanwhile, light a charcoal fire and let it burn down until the coals are evenly white or preheat a gas grill (medium). Wrap the wood chips partially in foil, creating a small packet that is open at the top. Set the packet on the coals or the lava stones and position the grill about 6 inches above the heat source. When the chips are smoking heavily, carefully place the onion halves on the grill, cover, and cook, basting them with the marinade and turning them once, until they are browned and tender, about 8 minutes total.

Transfer the onions to a serving plate, season them with salt and pepper to taste, and serve them hot or warm.

Grilled Marinated Mushrooms

SERVES 4 AS A SIDE DISH

Serve these smoky, tender mushrooms alongside plain steak or chicken, where their juices will mingle deliciously with those of the meat, or slice them after grilling and toss them into a salad or onto a pizza. Wild or exotic mushrooms, such as porcini, shiitakes, and portobellos, can also be prepared this way.

INGREDIENTS

2 cups wood smoking chips, preferably mesquite
¼ cup soy sauce
¼ cup Worcestershire sauce
¼ cup balsamic vinegar
3 tablespoons olive oil

2 garlic cloves, peeled and crushed through a press
¼ teaspoon freshly ground black pepper
1 pound (about 24) medium brown (cremini) or cultivated white mushrooms, trimmed and wiped with a damp cloth

Light a charcoal fire and let it burn until the coals are evenly white or preheat a gas grill (medium). Wrap the wood chips partially in foil, creating a small packet that is open at the top. Set the packet on the hot coals or hot lava stones; position the grill rack about 6 inches above the heat source.

Meanwhile, in a shallow nonreactive dish, whisk together the soy sauce, Worcestershire sauce, balsamic vinegar, olive oil, garlic, and pepper. Add the mushrooms and marinate for 10 minutes. Remove the mushrooms from the marinade and slide them onto 2 or 3 flat metal skewers.

When the wood chips are smoking, place the skewered mushrooms on the rack and lower the cover. Grill, basting the mushrooms with the marinade and turning them once or twice, until they are lightly browned and tender, 4 to 5 minutes. Remove the skewers from the grill and slide the mushrooms off the skewers. Serve the mushrooms hot or warm.

Drunken Beans

SERVES 6

These "drunken beans" (frijoles borrachos in borderspeak), which are really only a little tipsy, get extra flavor from the addition of a bottle of dark beer. Make them one day ahead to allow the flavors to develop fully, and serve them alongside grilled or smoked beef, pork, lamb, or chicken.

INGREDIENTS

1 pound dried black beans, picked over

5½ cups water

1 12-ounce bottle mellow dark beer, such as Heineken

4 garlic cloves, peeled and minced

1 large smoked ham hock

1½ cups thick, tomato-based commercial hot salsa

1 teaspoon salt

In a large bowl, cover the beans with cold water and let stand 5 minutes. Drain and repeat twice.

In a 4½- to 5-quart heavy nonreactive pan over medium heat, combine the beans, water, beer, garlic, and ham hock and bring to a boil. Lower the heat, partially cover, and simmer, stirring once or twice, for 1 hour.

Stir in the salsa and salt, cover, and cook for 45 minutes, or until the beans are tender and very thick. Remove the pan from the heat. Remove the ham hock from the beans and cool it. Trim off the fat, remove the meat from the bone, and finely chop the meat. Return the meat to the beans. *When the beans are completely cool, cover and refrigerate for at least 24 hours and up to 3 days.*

To serve, set the beans over low heat, thin slightly with water if necessary, and simmer until just heated through, about 15 minutes. Serve hot.

Kahlúa Baked Beans

SERVES 8 TO 12

Good grilled or smoked foods demand great baked beans, the two belonging together like peanut butter and jelly or Rogers and Astaire. Like barbecue sauces themselves, baked bean recipes tend to get tinkered with over the years. A little of this and a little of that having proven to be just the right flavor boosters on past occasions, the current version—this one is mine—can sometimes seem to have too many things in it to be worth the bother. But since most of them are staples from the fridge, pantry, or spice rack, and since the results are wonderful, who cares? I think the real success of these beans comes from using the bacon fat as well as the crisp bacon bits, but you may omit it if you must.

❧

INGREDIENTS

1½ pounds dried navy beans, picked over
½ pound sliced bacon, preferably mesquite-smoked
2 cups finely chopped yellow onions
1 12-ounce bottle chili sauce
½ cup thick, tomato-based bottled barbecue sauce, preferably hot and smoky
½ cup Kahlúa

½ cup strong brewed coffee
¼ cup Dijon mustard
¼ cup unsulfured molasses
2 tablespoons Pickapeppa Sauce, Heinz 57 Sauce, or another thick, spicy steak sauce
2 tablespoons hot pepper sauce, such as Tabasco
1½ teaspoons salt

In a large bowl, cover the beans generously with cold water and soak for 12 hours. Drain the beans. In a large pot, cover them generously with fresh cold water. Set the pot over medium heat and bring the water to a boil, then lower the heat and simmer, uncovered, stirring once or twice, for 1 hour or more (depending on the age of the beans and the altitude at which you cook), or until the beans are very tender (the finished dish won't taste right unless they're on the soft side—not falling apart, but otherwise utterly tender). Drain the beans, reserving 1½ cups of the bean liquid.

Meanwhile, chop the bacon. Scatter it in a cold skillet, set over medium heat, and cook, stirring occasionally, until the bacon has rendered its fat and is crisp, about 8 minutes. Remove from the heat. Reserve the bacon fat if desired.

Position a rack in the lower third of the oven and preheat the oven to 350°F.

In a large bowl, stir together the beans, the reserved bean liquid, the bacon, the bacon fat if you are using it, the onions, chili sauce, barbecue sauce, Kahlúa, coffee, mustard, molasses, Pickapeppa Sauce, hot pepper sauce, and salt.

Transfer to a heavy 4½- to 5-quart nonreactive casserole or Dutch oven with a tight-fitting lid. Bake for 1 hour. At the halfway mark, uncover, stir well, and bake uncovered for the last 30 minutes. Stir one more time, then bake until the beans are very thick, another 30 to 40 minutes. Serve hot or warm.

HOT MENU

❧

Hot Nuts (page 174)
Cold Beer

Michael's Pork Tenderloin Sandwiches with "Burnt" Edges Slaw (page 126)
Corn-Battered Onion Rings (page 194)
Kahlúa Baked Beans (page 198)

Ultimate Banana Pudding (page 232)

Grill-Toasted Garlic Bread

SERVES 8

This recipe produces thick, smoky slabs of garlic bread so good you may never go back to making it under the broiler again (an especially easy resolution to make if you own a quick-heating, ready-in-minutes gas grill, somewhat less so if you grill over charcoal). Other compound butters (pages 54 to 57) can be substituted. This garlic butter is also good spread on grilled fish or steak.

❧

INGREDIENTS

1 stick (4 ounces) unsalted butter, softened
3 garlic cloves, peeled and crushed through a press
1 teaspoon freshly ground black pepper
1 teaspoon fresh lemon juice
Pinch of salt

1 cup wood smoking chips, preferably hickory or mesquite
16 1-inch-thick, bias-cut slices of bread from a day-old baguette-type loaf
⅓ cup olive oil

In a small bowl, cream together the butter, garlic, pepper, lemon juice, and salt. Transfer to a container and cover. *The butter can be prepared 3 days ahead and refrigerated or frozen for up to 1 month. Soften to room temperature before using.*

Light a charcoal fire and let it burn down until the coals are evenly white or preheat a gas grill (medium). Meanwhile, wrap the wood chips partially in foil, creating a small packet that is open at the top. Brush the bread slices on both sides with the olive oil.

Set the packet on the coals or the lava stones and position the grill about 6 inches above the heat source. When the chips are smoking heavily, place the bread slices on the grill and cover. Cook, turning the bread slices once, until they are crisp and lightly browned, about 2 minutes per side.

Spread the hot toasted bread slices evenly on both sides with the garlic butter and serve immediately.

Red Chile Corn Bread

SERVES 6

Guests usually make short work of this wonderful corn bread, so you'll need to be fast on your feet if you want to save some to use for Red Chile Corn Croutons (page 134). (Or do what I do and bake a double batch.) The sweetly fiery and complex-tasting pure chili powder from Chimayo, New Mexico, is my first choice here, but regular chili powder blends also make good corn bread. Serve this as the accompaniment to chili and other spicy Southwestern ragouts, or bake it into muffins and serve it with eggs at brunch, paired with sweet butter and honey or Red-As-Rubies Pepper Jelly (page 62).

INGREDIENTS

Butter for the pan plus 5 tablespoons (2½ ounces) unsalted butter

2 tablespoons chili powder, preferably pure, unblended chili powder from Chimayo, New Mexico

1¼ cups unbleached all-purpose flour

¾ cup yellow cornmeal, preferably stone-ground

2 tablespoons sugar

2 tablespoons baking powder

½ teaspoon salt

1 large egg, beaten

1 cup cultured buttermilk, at room temperature

Position a rack in the middle of the oven and preheat the oven to 400°F. Butter an 8-inch square baking pan.

In a small saucepan over low heat, melt together the 5 tablespoons of butter and chili powder. Stir until smooth, remove from the heat, and cool slightly.

In a medium mixing bowl, stir together the flour, cornmeal, sugar, baking powder, and salt.

Add the egg, buttermilk, and butter mixture and stir until just combined. Transfer the batter to the prepared pan, spreading it to the edges.

Bake until the corn bread is firm, the edges are crisp, and a tester inserted into the center comes out clean, about 25 minutes.

Cool 5 minutes on a rack before cutting. Serve hot or warm.

Cornmeal Kaisers

MAKES 8 LARGE ROLLS

Hot-from-the-grill burgers or smoky chopped pork sandwiches can be served, it is true, on ordinary buns with no real loss of appreciation, but if you want to really impress (yourself, if not your guests), bake a batch of these golden, tender, and corny rolls. It's a simple dough to handle and the rolls freeze well; just defrost them, split them, and toast them, on the grill if you wish—great eating!

INGREDIENTS

2½ cups milk

¼ stick (1 ounce) unsalted butter

4 teaspoons sugar

1 tablespoon salt

1 package dry yeast

⅔ cup yellow cornmeal, preferably stone-ground, plus additional cornmeal for the baking sheet

4 to 5 cups unbleached all-purpose flour

Corn oil for the bowl

1 large egg

1 tablespoon water

n a medium saucepan, combine the milk, butter, sugar, and salt and set over low heat. Warm, stirring once or twice, until the butter has just melted. Remove the pan from the heat, pour the milk mixture into a large bowl, and cool to between 105° and 115°F. Stir in the yeast and let stand 5 minutes. Stir in the cornmeal and then about 4 cups of the flour, or until a soft, sticky dough forms.

Turn the dough out onto a well-floured work surface and knead, incorporating additional flour if necessary, for 5 minutes, or until the dough is smooth and elastic. Shape the dough into a ball. Oil a large bowl. Put in the dough, turn to coat

it with the oil, and cover the bowl with a clean towel. Let rise at room temperature until doubled in bulk, about 2 hours.

Lightly sprinkle a large baking sheet with cornmeal. Punch the dough down, turn it out onto a lightly floured work surface, and knead it for 1 minute. Divide the dough into 8 equal pieces. Shape each piece into a ball and place the balls of dough on the prepared baking sheet, spacing them about 2 inches apart. Cover with a towel and let rise at room temperature until doubled in bulk, about 1½ hours (the rolls may end up touching each other; this is fine).

Position a rack in the middle of the oven and preheat the oven to 425°F.

In a small bowl, beat the egg together with the 1 tablespoon of water until smooth. With a pastry brush, lightly coat the tops of the rolls with the egg mixture. Set the baking sheet in the oven, lower the temperature to 400°F, and bake for 25 minutes, or until the rolls are puffed, golden brown, and sound hollow when the bottoms are thumped. Transfer the rolls to a rack and cool to room temperature. *The rolls can be prepared up to 3 days ahead and refrigerated or frozen for up to 2 months. Return to room temperature and heat or toast if desired before using.*

❦

Pineapple Margaritas (page 216)
Rosemary-Grilled New Potatoes (page 190) with
Roasted Garlic Mayonnaise (page 52)

Spicy Pork and Red Wine Sausages (page 106)
on a bed of Rio Grande Ratatouille (page 178)
Sliced Upper Valley Tomatoes (page 185)
Grill-Toasted Garlic Bread (page 200)

Mandarin-Coconut Yogurt Freeze (page 223)

❦

Potent Pineapple Margaritas (page 216)

Barbecued Tequila Shrimp with Bacon (page 177)
with Rosemary Mayonnaise (page 53)

Black Bean Chili with Hickory-Grilled Steak and
Goat Cheese Cream (page 100)
Red Chile Corn Bread (page 201)

Buñuelos with Spiced Currant Syrup (page 242)

❦

Lonestar Longneck Beers
Hot Lips Spiced Shrimp (page 176)

Hickory-Grilled T-Bone Steaks (page 98) with
Roasted Garlic—Green and Red Chile Butter
(page 57)
Caesar Potato and Tomato Salad (page 188)
Grilled Marinated Mushrooms (page 196)

Chocolate Whiskey Pudding (page 236) with
Francine's Kahlúa Whipped Cream (page 237)

Tostaditas

SERVES 8 OR FEWER

Warm, freshly fried corn tortilla chips are light and utterly addictive, so it's always a good idea to make more than you'll think you'll want. Even the next day they'll still taste better than most of what you can buy in a bag. If the tortillas are very fresh or if they have been frozen and seem icy, spread them on paper towels and let them dry out a bit—there will be less steam to make the hot oil spatter.

INGREDIENTS

24 6-inch yellow or blue corn tortillas
4 cups corn oil for deep-frying
About 2 teaspoons salt to taste

Stack several tortillas together, and with a long, sharp knife cut the stack into 6 equal wedges. Repeat with the remaining tortillas.

In a deep fryer or in a deep heavy pot fitted with a frying thermometer and set over medium-high heat, warm the corn oil to between 375° and 400°F. (The deep fryer or pot should be no more than half full.) Working in batches to avoid crowding the deep fryer, cook the tortilla wedges, stirring them once or twice, until they are crisp but not brown, about 1 minute. With a slotted spoon transfer them to absorbent paper. Sprinkle them lightly with salt to taste. Repeat the frying and salting with the remaining tortilla wedges. Serve immediately. Or *wrap well and store at room temperature for up to 1 day. Reheat the tostaditas, enclosed in a paper bag, in a 200°F oven, for 10 minutes.*

PART THREE

Afterglow

drinks

IMMY BUFFET DIDN'T INVENT MARGARITAVILLE, HE JUST DISCOVERED ITS EXACT location. That laid-back town of easy friendships and tall, cool drinks has surely existed in some form or another forever. Singing being hot and thirsty work (similar to laboring over a hot grill or making your way through a smoky plateful of good barbecue), something wet is definitely called for. At my own personal Margaritaville, the libations are frequently chilled beer and icy white wine, and I confess to a preference for abundance over quality; there *are* Southwestern wineries and microbreweries, but you will not read about them here. Naturally margaritas get stirred up, along with a few other potent coolers, and there are always plenty of teetotal tipples for the ladies and the youngin's.

Pineapple-Lime Agua Fresca

MAKES ABOUT 2 QUARTS, SERVING 6 TO 8

This refreshing drink is good plain or with a measure of gold tequila, shaken with ice, and served margarita style in a salt-rimmed glass.

INGREDIENTS

1 large (about 4½ pounds) very ripe pineapple, trimmed, cored, and cut into ½-inch chunks (about 5½ cups)

¾ cup fresh lime juice

About ½ cup sugar

6 cups chilled water or 3 cups chilled water and 3 cups chilled seltzer water or club soda

In a food processor or blender, working in batches, purée together the pineapple, lime juice, sugar, and 3 cups of the water. Force the purée through a sieve into a container. Cover and refrigerate until very cold, at least 2 hours. Add the remaining water, adjust the seasoning, adding more sugar if desired, and serve immediately over ice in tall glasses.

HOT MENU

Pineapple-Lime Agua Fresca (page 210)

Grill-Scrambled Egg, Chorizo, and Avocado Breakfast Sandwiches (page 124)
Two Tomato–Chipotle Salsa (page 7)

Chilled Fresh Melon

Rick and Deann Bayless's Horchata

MAKES ABOUT 1½ QUARTS, SERVING 6

One of the best books on Mexican cooking is the Baylesses' Authentic Mexican *(William Morrow). This idea-packed volume is also the only place I have ever seen a recipe for* horchata, *a milky (but nondairy) rice-based drink much beloved here on the border. I have a feeling local recipes are not quite as labor-intensive as this one, which comes from a renowned drinks stand in Oaxaca, but neither are they as rich or aromatic. This sweet quaff is delicious on a hot day, wonderful at brunch, and utterly soothing if one is just a little* cruda *("hung over").*

INGREDIENTS

6 tablespoons rice
6 ounces (about 1¼ cups) blanced almonds
1 1-inch cinnamon stick

3 2-inch strips of lime zest (colored peel), about ¾-inch wide
About 5 cups water
About 1 cup sugar

Thoroughly pulverize the rice in a blender or spice grinder. Transfer to a medium bowl and add the almonds, cinnamon stick, and lime zest. Stir in 2¼ cups hot tap water, cover, and let stand at least 6 hours or, preferably, overnight.

Scoop the mixture into a blender and blend for 3 or 4 minutes, or until it no longer feels very gritty. Add 2 cups of water, then blend for a few seconds more. Set a large sieve over a mixing bowl and line it with 3 layers of dampened cheesecloth. Pour in the almond-rice mixture a little at a time, gently stirring to help the liquid pass through. When all has been strained, gather up the corners of the cheesecloth and twist them together to trap the dregs inside. Squeeze the cheesecloth firmly to expel all the remaining liquid.

Add 2 cups of water and stir in enough sugar to sweeten the drink to your taste. If the consistency is too thick, add additional water. Cover and refrigerate until very cold. Stir before pouring; serve the *horchata* without ice, which will dilute its delicate flavor.

''Limonade''

Limones, the hard, tart yellow limes that are so essential in Mexican cooking (they are the same as Florida's legendary Key limes), make a delicious limeade, the perfect quencher with chile-fired grilled or smoked foods, or on any other thirsty occasion, really. Those limes rarely come to middle America (although we're at last allowed to bring them over the border), but the Persian limes that are so widely available can be used in this recipe, just reduce the sugar slightly to taste. The carbonation of the seltzer drives the scent of the limes right up one's nose. If you think you won't want this refreshing but startling effect, use plain water. The mint isn't traditional but it makes a nice addition.

INGREDIENTS

2 cups fresh lime juice, preferably from yellow
Mexican limes

1⅓ cups sugar

1 loosely packed cup fresh mint leaves, lightly crushed

About 7 cups well-chilled seltzer water or club soda

n a jar or other container, combine the lime juice, sugar, and mint and stir to combine. Cover and refrigerate until very cold, at least 2 hours. Strain out and discard the mint; transfer the lime juice to a large pitcher. Add the chilled seltzer to taste and serve immediately over ice in tall glasses.

Blackberry Lemonade

MAKES 1 GALLON, SERVING 8 ON A HOT DAY

Fresh blackberry purée adds a shock of color and a boost of flavor to plain lemonade, even if (especially if!) that lemonade is mixed up from frozen concentrate. Raspberries can be substituted; so can limeade concentrate.

❧

INGREDIENTS

3 ½-pint baskets fresh blackberries, picked over and rinsed only if necessary

2 12-ounce containers frozen lemonade concentrate, thawed

About 3 tablespoons sugar, or to taste

About 11½ cups water

Lemon slices and sprigs of fresh mint, for garnish (optional)

In a food processor, purée the blackberries. Force the blackberries through a sieve or through the fine blade of a food mill. Discard the seeds. There should be about 1½ cups purée.

In a large (at least a 1-gallon) container, stir together the blackberry purée, lemonade concentrate, sugar, and enough water (about 11½ cups) to yield 1 gallon of lemonade.

Refrigerate until very cold. Serve over ice in tall glasses, garnished if desired with slices of lemon and sprigs of fresh mint.

Mixed Fruit Licuado

MAKES ABOUT 2¹/₂ QUARTS, SERVING 8

Licuados—sweetened pastel-colored drinks combining puréed fresh fruit and milk—are sold throughout Mexico. Displayed in large glass jars (usually with a chunk of ice afloat therein), they are typically accompanied by similar crocks of their nondairy-based cousins aguas frescas *(page 210) as well as the rice drink called* horchata *(page 211) and the limeade on page 212. Licuados may not be what you want to drink with smoked brisket or grilled tuna steaks, but they're great at brunch and kids love them almost any time. Combining several kinds of fruit makes for a richer drink.*

INGREDIENTS

6 cups chilled milk
2 cups mango flesh, cut into ¹/₂-inch chunks
(about 2 medium very ripe mangoes)

2 cups cantaloupe flesh, cut into ¹/₂-inch chunks
(half a medium very ripe cantaloupe)
2 cups hulled fresh strawberries, cut into ¹/₂-inch chunks
About ¹/₂ cup sugar

In a food processor or blender, working in batches, purée together the milk and fruit until smooth. Transfer to a large pitcher and stir in ¹/₃ cup of the sugar. Cover and refrigerate until very cold, at least 2 hours. Adjust the seasoning, adding more sugar to taste. Serve well chilled in tall glasses over ice if desired.

Pineapple Tequila

There's always a big jar of this pineapple-flavored tequila working on my kitchen counter. A touch of the raw Mexican sugar known as piloncillo *mellows things further (brown sugar can be substituted), yielding a smooth but potent liquid that makes fantastic margaritas. When it's been topped up with fresh tequila two or three times, the softened pineapple can be finely diced, warmed in butter with additional brown sugar to taste, and served as an ice-cream topping. I stole the basic idea for this from Santa Fe's Mark Miller (he uses rum); the vanilla beans were the suggestion of El Paso restaurateur Mick Lynch.*

INGREDIENTS

2 large just-ripe pineapples, trimmed, peeled, cored, and cut into 2-inch chunks

2 1-liter bottles gold tequila

2 cones (about 5 ounces total) Mexican raw sugar or ⅔ cup packed light brown sugar

2 whole vanilla beans

In a large, decorative jar, combine the pineapple chunks and tequila. Add the sugar and vanilla beans. Cover and let the tequila stand at room temperature, stirring it when you feel like, for at least 1 week.

Pineapple Margaritas

MAKES 12 GENEROUS COCKTAILS

Made with pineapple and piloncillo-sweetened tequila (page 215), these margaritas require no Triple Sec. To make an edible, eye-appealing garnish, cut ½-inch-thick round slices of peeled fresh pineapple into 4 equal wedges. Make a ½-inch cut into the pointed end of each wedge. Dip the curved side of each wedge into kosher salt and slide the wedge onto the rim of the glass.

❧

INGREDIENTS

2¼ cups Pineapple Tequila (page 215)
1 12-ounce container frozen limeade concentrate, thawed
4 chunks of pineapple, from the tequila jar, finely chopped

About 4 trays of ice cubes
Kosher salt, for the glass rims if desired
3 limes, quartered

In the jar of a blender, combine half the tequila, half the limeade concentrate, and half the pineapple. Fill the jar to the top with ice cubes, cover, and blend on high until slushy and thick. Transfer to a pitcher. Repeat with the remaining tequila, limeade concentrate, pineapple, and ice. Stir to blend, pour into glasses that have been salted, if desired. Squeeze a lime quarter into each cocktail and serve immediately.

Mango-Peach Margaritas

MAKES 12 GENEROUS COCKTAILS

These margaritas, with a base of puréed fresh fruit rather than limeade concentrate, have a lighter, fresher taste. Cantaloupe or strawberries can replace either the peaches or mango in the purée, or can supplement them. I serve these elegant margaritas in unsalted, tall, stemmed glasses and garnish each with a fresh strawberry.

INGREDIENTS

1 medium ripe mango, peeled, pitted, and coarsely diced
2 medium ripe peaches, pitted and coarsely diced
¾ cup gold tequila

¾ cup Triple Sec
½ cup fresh lime juice
About 4 trays of ice cubes

In a food processor, purée together the mango and peaches. There should be about 1½ cups of purée. Transfer to a container, cover, and refrigerate until cold, about 1 hour.

In the jar of a blender, combine half the purée, half the tequila, half the Triple Sec, and half the lime juice. Fill the jar to the top with ice cubes, cover, and blend on high until thick and slushy. Transfer to a pitcher. Repeat with the remaining ingredients. Stir to blend, pour into glasses, and serve immediately.

Trader Vic's Mai Tai

MAKES 1 LARGE, STRONG DRINK

Here's Victor ("Trader Vic") Bergeron on the Mai Tai: "We originated this drink; we made the first Mai Tai; we named the drink. A lot of bastards all over the country have copied it and copyrighted it and claimed it for their own. I hope they get the pox." Well, I've been called worse. Here, in T.V.'s own words, is the classic formula—worth a trip to a really good liquor store for the esoteric ingredients. Few potions cool one down on a hot day quite as effectively as this.

INGREDIENTS

2 ounces 17-year-old J. Wray & Nephew Jamaican rum

½ ounce Garnier orgeat (almond syrup)

½ ounce DeKuyper orange curaçao

¼ ounce rock candy syrup

Juice from 1 fresh lime, cut in half, for garnish

Fresh mint, for garnish

Hand-shake all the ingredients and then garnish with half a lime peel inside the drink and a sprig of mint floated on top of the drink. The drink should be chilled nicely with a considerable amount of shaved ice in a 15-ounce glass.

Brandy Milk Punch

Deceptively mild-looking, this concoction is nevertheless for grown-ups only. Serve tall, frosty glasses of it as part of a cool-weather brunch buffet, and you'll get things off to a great start.

❧

INGREDIENTS

2½ cups very cold milk	2 tablespoons vanilla
1 cup brandy	¼ teaspoon freshly grated nutmeg
½ cup Kahlúa	10 ice cubes

In a blender, combine half of each ingredient. Cover and blend on high until the punch is smooth and frothy. Pour the punch into 4 glasses. Repeat with the remaining ingredients. Serve immediately.

cooling desserts

THERE ARE VARIOUS THEORIES AS TO WHY A TEXAS MEAL MUST CONCLUDE with a Texas dessert, but if you've ever hurt yourself badly on a bowl of atomic salsa or a plate of three-alarm enchiladas, and then grabbed instinctively for a piece of bread and the honey pitcher for solace, you'll know the real reason. Nothing soothes a spice-singed tongue like something a little sweet, and thus I rest my case. If that seems to take the romance out of dessert making (and dessert eating), please note that I do not for a minute suggest that a pitcher of honey is in any way an acceptable dessert. The good news about eating food that you're almost sure will be too hot to handle is that ice cream, pie, shortcake, cookies, puddings, and other medications are waiting in the kitchen to help ease the pain.

Pink Margarita Sorbet

MAKES 2 QUARTS

If frozen margaritas have always seemed more like dessert than drinks to you, you'll approve of this icy confection. Whipped up rather quickly from freezer staples, the sorbet contains no alcohol but may be drizzled with tequila and Triple Sec just before it is served—the perfect chilly antidote to a hot and smoky meal. Frozen raspberries and lemonade concentrate can be substituted; drizzle the resulting sorbet with frozen imported vodka.

INGREDIENTS

1½ pounds frozen unsweetened strawberries, partially thawed

1 12-ounce container frozen limeade concentrate, partially thawed

⅔ cup sugar

2 teaspoons gold tequila, for each topping (optional)

1 teaspoon Triple Sec, for each topping (optional)

1 perfect fresh strawberry, for each garnish (optional)

In a food processor, combine the strawberries, limeade concentrate, and sugar and process until fairly smooth. Pour into the canister of an ice-cream maker and churn according to the manufacturer's directions. Transfer to a storage container, cover, and freeze.

Soften slightly in the refrigerator if necessary. Scoop into dessert bowls. Drizzle each serving with about 2 teaspoons tequila and 1 teaspoon Triple Sec (or to taste). Garnish each serving with a perfect strawberry if you wish and serve immediately.

Mandarin-Coconut Yogurt Freeze

MAKES ABOUT 2 QUARTS

Packed with plenty of tropical fruit and touches of rum and vanilla, this easy frozen dessert seems just right after a hot and smoky meal. Offer it on its own, garnished with assorted berries, or serve a scoop of it beside Grilled Bananas "Foster" (page 234).

INGREDIENTS

2 cups plain yogurt, regular or low-fat

¾ cup canned crushed pineapple

¾ cup sugar

½ cup half-and-half

½ cup sweetened flaked coconut

½ cup coconut cream, such as Coco López

2 tablespoons amber (añejo) rum

2 tablespoons vanilla extract

1 11-ounce can mandarin orange sections, drained

Fresh berries, for garnish (optional)

In a large bowl, whisk together the yogurt, pineapple, sugar, half-and-half, coconut, coconut cream, rum, and vanilla until fairly smooth. Stir in the orange sections. Transfer the mixture to the canister of an ice-cream maker and churn according the manufacturer's directions.

Transfer to a storage container, cover, and freeze. *The yogurt can be prepared up to 3 days ahead. Soften it in the refrigerator if necessary before scooping it into dessert bowls.* Garnish each portion with fresh berries if desired and serve immediately.

Lemon Ice-Cream Pie with Raspberry Sauce

SERVES 8

Most ice-cream pies rely on convenient store-bought ice cream, but I wanted a lemony, rich yet somehow refreshing filling (so soothing after a hot and smoky meal), that commercial ice cream failed to yield, and so decided to make my own. It's more work, but it all gets done a day or two in advance and the results are delicious—a trade-off I gladly make. The Quick Mocha Sauce can be used in place of the raspberry (or blackberry) sauce if desired.

❧

INGREDIENTS

3 large egg yolks
1¼ cups sugar
3 cups half-and-half
Pinch of salt
½ cup buttermilk
½ cup fresh lemon juice
1 tablespoon minced lemon zest (colored peel)

¼ teaspoon lemon extract
1 cup graham cracker crumbs
½ stick (2 ounces) unsalted butter, melted
Raspberry Sauce (recipe follows) or Quick Mocha Sauce (page 239)
Thin slices of lemon, for garnish (optional)

In a medium bowl, whisk the egg yolks. Whisk in 1 cup of the sugar. In a medium saucepan over medium heat, combine the half-and-half and salt and bring to a boil. Gradually whisk the hot half-and-half into the egg mixture. Return the mixture to the saucepan, set over low heat, and cook, stirring constantly, until it thickens into a custard that will heavily coat the back of a spoon, about 5 minutes. Immediately remove the saucepan from the heat and pour the custard into the mixing bowl. Cool to room temperature, then stir in the buttermilk, lemon juice, lemon zest, and lemon extract; the custard will thicken slightly. Cover with plastic wrap, pressing the film onto the surface of the custard, and refrigerate until very cold, at least 5 hours.

In a medium bowl, stir together the graham cracker crumbs and remaining ¼ cup of sugar. Stir in the melted butter and mix until the crumbs are evenly moist. Pat the crumb mixture onto the bottom and up the sides of a 10-inch pie plate. Freeze for at least 1 hour.

Pour the chilled lemon custard into the canister of an ice-cream maker and churn according to the manufacturer's directions (see the Note). Spoon the ice cream into the frozen pie shell, spreading it to the edges and mounding it slightly in the center. Freeze until solid, then wrap it tightly in plastic. *The pie can be prepared up to 3 days ahead.* Soften slightly before serving; use a knife dipped into hot water and wiped dry between each cut to slice the pie. Transfer the slices to plates, drizzle each slice generously with

raspberry, blackberry, or mocha sauce, and garnish each with a lemon slice if desired. Serve immediately.

NOTE: Frozen shell-type ice-cream makers, like the Donvier, will probably not yield enough ice cream to adequately fill the pie crust. Use a more conventional ice-cream maker, the kind requiring ice cubes and table salt.

Raspberry Sauce
MAKES ABOUT 2 CUPS

INGREDIENTS

3 ½-pint baskets fresh raspberries, picked over and rinsed only if necessary

2 tablespoons fresh lime juice
About ⅔ cup sugar

In a food processor, combine the raspberries, lime juice, and ½ cup of the sugar. Process until smooth. Force the sauce through a sieve or through the medium blade of a food mill and discard the seeds (this will reduce the yield to about 1¾ cups). Adjust the sweetness of the sauce with additional sugar to taste. Cover and refrigerate until very cold before using.

 Blackberry Sauce Substitute an equal amount of blackberries for the raspberries. You will use all of the sugar, and you will probably want to sieve out the seeds. This yields 1¾ cups.

Strawberry Shortcakes à la Mode

If America were to choose a national dessert, this terrific summertime combination of hot biscuits, cold ice cream, and juicy red fruit (or the peach variation that follows) would surely give the other candidates—apple pie, chocolate chip cookies, tiramisù—a real run for their money. It gets my vote!

INGREDIENTS

3 pints strawberries, rinsed only if necessary, hulled, and thinly sliced
⅓ cup sugar
1 tablespoon fresh lemon juice

8 Cornmeal Shortcakes (page 227), hot from the oven
About 1½ pints premium strawberry ice cream, slightly softened

In a medium bowl, combine the strawberries, sugar, and lemon juice. Let stand at room temperature, stirring once or twice, for 30 minutes.

Split the hot shortcakes horizontally. Place the bottom halves in dessert bowls. Top each shortcake bottom with a medium-sized scoop of ice cream. Spoon the strawberries and their juices evenly over and around, using them all. Place the upper halves of the shortcakes atop the ice cream and strawberries and serve immediately.

Cornmeal Shortcakes

MAKES 8 SHORTCAKES

The inclusion of cornmeal makes these tender shortcakes muffin-crumbly and golden, perfect partners to all sorts of berries and other prime summer fruit. (And when the weather turns cooler, they're good for supper, smothered with chili, creamed chicken, and the like.)

INGREDIENTS

Butter for the baking sheet, plus 6 tablespoons (3 ounces) unsalted butter, well-chilled and cut into small pieces
2¼ cups unbleached all-purpose flour, plus flour for the work surface

¾ cup yellow cornmeal, preferably stone-ground
¼ cup sugar
1 tablespoon baking powder
1 cup chilled buttermilk

Position a rack in the upper third of the oven and preheat the oven to 425°F. Lightly butter a baking sheet.

In a food processor, combine the 2¼ cups of flour, cornmeal, sugar, and baking powder and pulse to blend. Add the 6 tablespoons of butter and process until a coarse meal forms. With the motor running, add the buttermilk through the feed tube until a crumbly dough forms; do not overprocess.

Lightly flour a work surface. Turn the dough out onto the surface and lightly knead and gather it into a soft ball. Roll the dough out into roughly a 12 × 6-inch rectangle. Cut the dough into 8 equal squares. Transfer the squares to the prepared baking sheet, spacing them well apart. Bake until the shortcakes are crisp and golden and a tester inserted into the center of one comes out clean, about 15 minutes. Remove from the pan; use immediately.

Warm Amaretto Peach Shortcake

SERVES 8

Instead of individual shortcakes, here is just one large, eye-catching one, split, filled with warm, buttery sautéed peaches (or nectarines), and then cut into wedges for serving—a spectacular conclusion to a summer grill feast. The appropriate garnish is a dollop of amaretto-sweetened whipped cream and the best accompaniment is a tall glass of iced coffee (into which smart folks will also stir some of that good whipped cream).

INGREDIENTS

1 batch of dough for Cornmeal Shortcakes (page 227)
1 tablespoon sugar
1 cup chilled whipping cream, preferably not ultrapasteurized
7 tablespoons amaretto

½ stick (2 ounces) unsalted butter
2 pounds (about 6 medium) ripe, juicy peaches or nectarines, pitted and cut into eighths (see the Note)
¼ cup packed light brown sugar
2 tablespoons fresh lemon juice

Position a rack in the middle of the oven and preheat the oven to 425°F. Lightly butter a 10-inch glass pie plate.

Transfer the shortcake dough to the prepared pie plate, shaping it into a round about 1 inch thick. Sprinkle the top of the shortcake with the white sugar and bake until puffed and golden brown, about 20 minutes. Let the shortcake cool in the pie plate on a rack for 10 minutes.

Meanwhile, in a chilled bowl, whip the cream until it forms soft peaks. One tablespoon at a time, beat 4 tablespoons of the amaretto into the cream. Cover and refrigerate until ready to use.

In a large skillet over medium-low heat, melt the butter. Stir in the peaches, brown sugar, the remaining 3 tablespoons of amaretto, and the lemon juice and cook, gently stirring once or twice, until the syrup is thick and the peaches are just warmed through, 3 to 5 minutes.

Carefully transfer the shortcake to a cutting board. With a long, sharp knife, cut the shortcake in half horizontally. Carefully transfer the shortcake bottom to a large serving plate. Spoon about three quarters of the peaches and their syrup evenly over the shortcake bottom. Carefully set the shortcake top over the peaches. Spoon the remaining peaches and syrup over the shortcake top. Drizzle the peaches with some of the whipped cream, cut the shortcake into wedges, and serve immediately, passing the remaining cream at the table.

NOTE: If the peaches need peeling, bring a medium pot of water to a boil. Add the peaches a few at a time, turn them in the boiling water for 30 seconds, and transfer them with a slotted spoon to a bowl of cold water. Drain the peaches; the skins will now slip off fairly easily.

HOT MENU

Cold Beer
Grilled Swordfish Club Sandwiches with Rosemary Mayonnaise (page 130)
Lemon-Pepper Fries (page 193)
Sweet Buttermilk Slaw (page 184)

Iced Espresso
Warm Amaretto Peach Shortcake (page 228)

Grilled Peaches with Burnt Sugar Sauce

SERVES 8

Juicy fresh peaches (also nectarines and pineapple sections) grill beautifully, picking up an attractive color and a subtle edge of additional flavor that is accentuated by the dark and slightly bitter burnt sugar sauce. (If you don't like things on the bitter side, substitute a simple purée of lightly sweetened fresh raspberries or blackberries, page 225.) Two tips: Wood chips aren't wanted here—that much smoke would overwhelm the peaches—and the grill rack must be impeccably clean and free of any meat juices or other charred material.

INGREDIENTS

1 cup sugar

2 cups whipping cream

Pinch of freshly grated nutmeg

4 large firm but juicy thin-skinned peaches, halved and pitted

3 tablespoons walnut oil or flavorless vegetable oil

6 thin slices of plain cake, such as pound cake, cut in half diagonally

Sprigs of fresh mint, for garnish (optional)

In a deep heavy saucepan over medium-low heat, stir the sugar until it begins to melt, about 7 minutes. Let the liquid sugar cook, stirring it once or twice, until it turns a rich, dark brown, about 4 minutes. (This is easier to determine if the lining of your pan is lighter rather than darker.)

Meanwhile, in a medium saucepan over medium-high heat, bring the cream to a boil. Lower the heat slightly, stir in the nutmeg, and simmer the cream, uncovered, until it has reduced to 1¾ cups, about 10 minutes.

Remove the pan of burnt sugar from the heat. Immediately begin to stir the hot cream gradually into the burnt sugar, being careful to avoid a boil-over. If any pieces of burnt sugar are unincorporated after all the cream has been added, return the pan to low heat and simmer, stirring and scraping often, until the remaining lumps are dissolved. Transfer immediately to a heat-proof container and cool to room temperature. *The sauce can be prepared up to 3 days ahead. Cover with plastic wrap, pressing the film onto the surface of the sauce, and refrigerate. Return the sauce to room temperature before using.*

Light a charcoal fire and let it burn down until the coals are evenly white or preheat a gas grill (medium-high). Position the rack about 6 inches above the heat source. Brush the cut sides of the peaches with the walnut oil. Place the peaches, cut side down, on the rack and cover the grill. Cook, rotating the position of the peaches on the rack to create an attractive cross-hatching, until they are just heated through and lightly marked, about 4 minutes. Remove the peaches from the grill immediately.

Cut each peach half into 4 slices. Arrange the peach slices and the cake slices on 8 dessert plates. Generously drizzle the peaches and cake with the burnt sugar sauce, garnish with a sprig of mint if desired, and serve immediately.

HOT MENU

Blackberry Lemonade (page 213)

Grill-Barbecued Chicken Cheeseburgers (page 122)
Grilled Red Onions (page 195)
Marinated Pepper Slaw (page 183)
Newfangled Macaroni Salad (page 180)

Grilled Peaches with Burnt Sugar Sauce (page 230)

Ultimate Banana Pudding

SERVES 8 TO 10

The banana pudding you get in barbecue joints throughout the South and West is pretty much the one from the box of Nabisco Nilla Wafers—custard, cookies, and bananas. Soft and sweet, it's easily mixed up, well in advance of serving, in industrial-sized batches, and after all that hot, rich, and smoky meat, it just tastes right. Recently, though, I have been running across upscale versions of the pudding, part of the high-end, back-to-basics movement, I guess, and a good way for white tablecloth chefs and diners alike to stoke up on a little nostalgia. The idea was irresistible, and so here is my contribution to the trend. If you are sharp-eyed you will recognize it as a simple variation on the classic Italian sweet, tiramisù. I use Galiano because, to me, it always tastes like bananas, but you could probably substitute almost any other liqueur you like.

❧

INGREDIENTS

½ cup water

⅔ cup sugar

1⅔ cups heavy cream

1 pound mascarpone (Italian cream cheese), at room temperature

¾ cup strong, brewed coffee, at room temperature

¼ cup Galiano

1 7-ounce package (about 24) crisp ladyfingers (savoiardi)

2 ripe bananas, peeled and thinly sliced

n a small saucepan, stir together the water and ⅓ cup of the sugar. Set over medium heat and bring just to a boil. Remove from the heat and cool to room temperature.

Whip ⅔ cup of the cream to soft peaks. In a medium bowl, whisk together the mascarpone and the remaining ⅓ cup sugar; do not overmix or the cheese may separate. Fold in the whipped cream.

In a wide, shallow dish, combine the cooled sugar syrup, coffee, and Galiano. Working quickly, dip half the ladyfingers, 1 at a time, into the coffee mixture, then transfer carefully to a shallow serving dish, such as a 13 × 9-inch oval gratin, arranging them in a single layer. Spread about half the mascarpone over the ladyfingers. Arrange the banana slices evenly over the mascarpone. Repeat the soaking process with the remaining ladyfingers, arranging them evenly over the bananas. Top the ladyfingers with the remaining mascarpone mixture, spreading it evenly to the edges of the dish. Cover with plastic wrap and refrigerate for 5 hours. Let the pudding stand at room temperature for about 30 minutes.

Whip the remaining I cup heavy cream to soft peaks. Spoon the pudding onto dessert plates, garnish with a dollop of whipped cream, and serve immediately.

HOT MENU

❧

Chilled Beers
"Limonade" (page 212)
Hot Nuts (page 174)

The Great Caesar Salad with Grilled Shrimp (page 133)
Barbecued Chicken Pizza (page 114)
Eggplant and Roasted Red Pepper Pizza (page 116)

Ultimate Banana Pudding (page 232)

Grilled Bananas "Foster"

SERVES 6

In the fabulous fifties, grilled bananas were a kind of barbecue rage. I haven't seen them offered much lately, though, which is too bad; they deserve a renaissance. Inspired by (but not otherwise resembling) the classic New Orleans chafing dish dessert of the same name, my version combines hot, rum-buttery bananas, grilled (and served) in their skins, accompanied by an icy scoop of tropical fruit-flavored frozen yogurt.

INGREDIENTS

½ cup packed light brown sugar
½ stick (2 ounces) unsalted butter
⅓ cup dark rum, preferably Meyers's
½ teaspoon ground cinnamon
¼ teaspoon ground allspice
Pinch of freshly grated nutmeg

1 teaspoon fresh lemon juice
½ teaspoon vanilla extract
6 large fully ripe but not soft bananas
About 2½ cups Mandarin-Coconut Yogurt Freeze
(page 223), softened slightly for scooping

In a small heavy saucepan over low heat, stir together the brown sugar, butter, rum, cinnamon, allspice, and nutmeg. Bring to a simmer and cook, uncovered, stirring occasionally, for 7 minutes, or until slightly thickened. Remove from the heat, stir in the lemon juice and vanilla and cool slightly.

Meanwhile, place the bananas flat on a work surface. With a sharp knife, cut a shallow slit in the peel on the upper side of each banana, following the natural curve of the fruit. Using your fingertips, gently separate the banana skin from the flesh as far down as you can without tearing it.

Meanwhile, light a charcoal fire and let it burn down until the coals are evenly white or preheat a gas grill (low). Position the rack 6 to 8 inches above the heat source. Place the bananas on the grill rack. Using a bulb baster, squeeze about 2 teaspoons of the rum mixture into the slit in each banana, forcing it down along the sides of the banana flesh are far as possible without tearing the skin. Cover and grill for 2 minutes. Repeat every 2 minutes with the remaining rum mixture until gone, the bananas are tender, and the rum mixture is bubbling, 8 to 10 minutes total.

Carefully transfer the bananas to dessert plates. Place a scoop of frozen yogurt beside each banana and serve immediately.

Lime Puddings with Blackberry Sauce

SERVES 8

These cool, creamy little puddings are deliciously tart, especially when served in a puddle of fresh blackberry sauce, and are actually more of a relief to the palate after something hot and smoky than even ice cream or sorbet. For company, make up a batch of Raspberry Sauce (page 225) as well and serve the puddings with a bit of both. Stir the puddings together by hand—an electric mixer overbeats them and they may separate.

INGREDIENTS

Butter for the ramekins, plus 1 stick (4 ounces) unsalted butter, softened

1⅔ cups sugar

3 large eggs

¼ cup unbleached all-purpose flour

1 cup cultured buttermilk, at room temperature

1 tablespoon Triple Sec

1 tablespoon fresh lime juice

1 tablespoon minced lime zest (colored peel)

1 recipe Blackberry Sauce (page 225), chilled

Sprigs of fresh mint, for garnish (optional)

Lightly butter eight 6-ounce ramekins or custard cups. Position a rack in the middle of the oven and preheat the oven to 350°F.

In a large bowl, cream the stick of butter and sugar until fluffy. Whisk in the eggs and flour. Stir in the buttermilk, Triple Sec, lime juice, and lime zest. Divide the mixture among the prepared ramekins. Set the ramekins in a shallow baking pan and add hot tap water to come halfway up the sides.

Bake the puddings until they are puffed, golden, and just set but not firm, about 25 minutes.

Remove the pan from the oven, remove the puddings from the hot water and cool them on a rack to room temperature. Cover and refrigerate until cold and firm, at least 2 hours. *The puddings can be prepared up to 3 days ahead.*

Spoon the blackberry sauce over the puddings in their ramekins and set the ramekins on dessert plates. Or, run a knife around the edge of each pudding, invert each ramekin onto the dessert plate, and rap firmly; the pudding will drop onto the plate. Spoon the blackberry sauce over or around the unmolded puddings. Garnish each pudding with a sprig of mint and serve cold.

Chocolate Whiskey Pudding

SERVES 6

Those pudding cakes that start out with the sauce on top of the batter and then reverse themselves during baking are a homey subset of desserts I love. They're no longer trendy, it seems, except in retro kitchens like mine, where they turn up often, welcomed with equal parts nostalgia and just plain hunger. None of them is quicker or more intensely chocolaty than this one, which is easy enough for a midweek dinner but tasty enough for company. Remodeled for grown-up palates, this recipe includes a more than generous measure of good bourbon (strong brewed coffee can be substituted) and is topped with plenty of Kahlúa-flavored whipped cream.

INGREDIENTS

THE SAUCE

¾ cup packed light brown sugar

¼ cup lightly packed unsweetened cocoa powder

1⅓ cups water

⅓ cup bourbon

1½ teaspoons vanilla extract

⅛ teaspoon salt

THE CAKE

Butter for the pan, plus 3 tablespoons (1½ ounces) unsalted butter, melted

1 cup flour (measure by sifting the flour into a dry measuring cup and sweeping it level)

1 cup coarsely chopped pecans

¾ cup sugar

¼ cup lightly packed unsweetened cocoa powder

2 teaspoons baking powder

½ teaspoon salt

⅓ cup cultured buttermilk

1½ tablespoons bourbon

½ teaspoon vanilla extract

Francine's Kahlúa Whipped Cream (recipe follows)

Position a rack in the middle of the oven and preheat the oven to 325°F.

FOR THE SAUCE

In a small saucepan, stir together the brown sugar and cocoa powder. Whisk in the water, bourbon,

vanilla, and salt. Set over low heat and bring to a simmer. Remove from the heat and keep warm.

FOR THE CAKE

Lightly butter an 8 × 8-inch baking pan.

In a medium bowl, stir together the flour, pecans,

sugar, cocoa powder, baking powder, and salt. Stir in the buttermilk, melted butter, bourbon, and vanilla to form a thick batter. Spread the batter in the prepared pan. Pour the hot sauce mixture over the batter.

Bake until the cake layer has risen to the top of the pan and is firm and the sauce is bubbling up around the sides of the pan, 35 to 40 minutes. Cool on a rack for 10 minutes. Serve hot, warm, or cold, accompanied by the whipped cream.

Francine's Kahlúa Whipped Cream

MAKES ABOUT 2 CUPS

Francine Maroukian, a Manhattan caterer, is an old friend and a great cook. Her trick of adding Kahlúa instead of vanilla to whipped cream is, she insists, the foundation of her business. I just had to borrow the idea.

INGREDIENTS

1 cup heavy cream,
preferably not ultrapasteurized,
well-chilled
¼ cup Kahlúa

In a bowl, using an electric mixer, beat the cream until soft peaks form. Add the Kahlúa, 1 tablespoon at a time, beating briefly after each addition. Use immediately.

Mexican Chocolate Ice Cream

MAKES ABOUT 1 1/2 QUARTS

Mexican chocolate, in thick tablets that are gritty with ground almonds, heavily sweetened and well-flavored with cinnamon, is not meant for eating out of hand. Typically, it gets whipped up in a blender with hot milk to produce a frothy and soothing beverage, but the temperature can also be lowered, yielding this intense and slightly nubbly ice cream. Top scoops of it with a dollop of unsweetened whipped cream and a perfect strawberry and serve it with a big cup of strong black coffee.

INGREDIENTS

12 ounces Mexican chocolate, preferably
Ibarra, coarsely chopped

4 large egg yolks

1/3 cup sugar

1 quart half-and-half

1 tablespoon vanilla extract

In the top of a double boiler over hot, not simmering, water, heat the chocolate, stirring often. It will not completely melt but will soften into a gooey mass.

Meanwhile, in a large bowl, whisk the egg yolks. Gradually whisk in the sugar.

In a medium heavy pan over high heat, bring the half-and-half just to a boil. Whisking constantly, gradually add the hot half-and-half to the egg mixture. Return this mixture to the pan, set the pan over low heat, and cook, stirring often, until the mixture thickens into a custard that will heavily coat the back of a spoon, about 5 minutes. Immediately remove the pan from the heat and return the custard to the bowl. Add the softened chocolate and vanilla and whisk until dissolved (the mixture will appear grainy). Cool to room temperature and cover with plastic wrap, pressing the film onto the surface of the custard. Refrigerate until very cold, at least 5 hours and preferably overnight.

Transfer the custard to the canister of an ice-cream maker and churn according to the manufacturer's directions. Cover the finished ice cream tightly and store it in the freezer. *The ice cream can be prepared up to 3 days ahead.*

Soften the ice cream slightly in the refrigerator if necessary before serving.

Quick Mocha Sauce

If you have some strong coffee on hand (left over, perhaps, from breakfast), this elegant chocolate sauce can be quickly prepared before dinner and will have cooled to exactly the right silky, pourable temperature by dessert time. Try it as a dip for strawberries, drizzle it over Lemon Ice-Cream Pie (page 224), or spoon it around scoops of Mandarin-Coconut Yogurt Freeze (page 223).

INGREDIENTS

¼ pound semisweet chocolate, chopped
⅓ cup strong brewed coffee

3 tablespoons whipping cream
1 tablespoon Kahlúa

n the top of a double boiler over hot, not simmering, water, combine the chocolate, coffee, whipping cream and Kahlúa. Heat, stirring occasionally, until smooth.

Remove from the heat, transfer to a container and cool slightly. The texture of the sauce is best when it is just lukewarm.

The sauce can be prepared up to 10 days ahead. Cover tightly and refrigerate. Reheat the sauce in the top of double boiler over hot, not simmering, water, until it reaches the desired texture.

Strawberry-Chocolate Layer Cake with Buttermilk Fudge Frosting

SERVES 8

It may not be a law, but it certainly is a custom, that if you are going to write a book even remotely to do with Texas cooking you must include at least one big old layer cake, just as moist and sweet as it's possible to be. Here is my contribution to that noble tradition. Certainly this makes a fine dessert after a grilled or smoked something or other, but it can also be enjoyed on its magnificent own, with nothing more than a tall glass of iced tea for accompaniment. That's hospitality, Texas style!

INGREDIENTS

THE CAKE

⅓ cup lightly packed unsweetened cocoa powder

1 teaspoon baking soda

½ cup boiling water

Butter for the cake pans, plus 1 stick (4 ounces) unsalted butter, softened

1 cup packed dark brown sugar

1 cup sugar

THE FILLING

1-pint basket fresh strawberries, washed only if necessary, patted dry, hulled, and sliced

1 cup sour cream

¼ cup confectioners' sugar

2 large egg yolks

1 cup cultured buttermilk, at room temperature

2 teaspoons vanilla extract

2½ cups unbleached all-purpose flour (measure by sifting the flour into dry measuring cups and sweeping it level)

2 large egg whites

THE FROSTING

1 stick (4 ounces) unsalted butter, softened

2 cups confectioners' sugar

½ cup buttermilk, at room temperature

¾ cup lightly packed unsweetened cocoa powder

1 teaspoon vanilla extract

FOR THE CAKE

In a small bowl, stir together the cocoa powder and baking soda. Whisk in the boiling water; the mixture will be foamy. Cool to room temperature. Lightly butter two 9-inch cake pans. Cut two 9-inch rounds of parchment paper and press I into the bottom of each pan. Butter the parchment paper. Position racks in the upper and lower thirds of the oven and preheat the oven to 350°F.

In a large bowl, with an electric mixer, cream the butter. Mix in the brown sugar and then the white sugar (the mixture will be crumbly). Mix in the egg yolks. Add half of the buttermilk and the vanilla and mix until just combined. Mix in half of the flour. Mix in the remaining buttermilk and the cocoa mixture until just combined. Mix in the remaining flour; do not overbeat.

In a medium bowl, beat the egg whites until stiff peaks form. Fold the egg whites into the batter until just combined; do not overmix. Divide the batter evenly between the prepared pans, spreading it to the edges. Bake the cake layers, one on each oven rack, exchanging their positions from top to bottom at the estimated halfway point, until they have just drawn away from the edges of the pans and a tester inserted into the center comes out clean, about 25 minutes.

Cool the layers in the pans on a rack for 5 minutes. Turn the layers out of the pans onto a rack, peel away the parchment paper, and cool completely.

FOR THE FILLING
In a bowl, stir together the strawberries, sour cream, and confectioners' sugar. Cover and refrigerate for at least 1 hour.

FOR THE FROSTING
In a large bowl, with an electric mixer, cream the butter. Mix in about two thirds of the confectioners' sugar. Mix in half the buttermilk. Mix in the remaining confectioners' sugar and the cocoa powder. Mix in the remaining buttermilk and the vanilla and beat until smooth.

TO ASSEMBLE THE CAKE
Set 1 cake layer, bottom up, on a serving plate. Spread the strawberry filling over the top of the layer, leaving a ½-inch border uncovered. Set the second cake layer, bottom up, on top of the first. Spread the frosting over the sides and then the top of the cake, using it all and swirling it decoratively.

The cake can be assembled up to 6 hours ahead. Refrigerate, uncovered, returning it to room temperature before serving it.

Buñuelos with Spiced Currant Syrup

SERVES 6 TO 8

These traditional Southwestern fried pastries are light and flaky, the yeast-risen cousins of the more-familiar sopaipilla. Here they are generously drizzled with a spiced currant syrup, but the more typical approaches—a dredging in cinnamon sugar or a dolloping with honey—also work deliciously well.

INGREDIENTS

⅔ cup milk

½ stick (2 ounces) unsalted butter

1 tablespoon sugar

½ teaspoon salt

1 teaspoon dry yeast

2½ cups unbleached all-purpose flour, plus flour for the work surface

2 large eggs, well-beaten

About 7 cups corn oil for deep-frying

Spiced Currant Syrup (recipe follows)

In a small saucepan, combine the milk, butter, sugar, and salt. Set over medium heat and bring just to a simmer. Remove from the heat and cool to between 105° and 115°F.

In a small bowl, whisk the warm milk mixture into the yeast and let stand for 5 minutes; whisk again to dissolve all the yeast.

In a medium bowl, make a well in the flour. Add the yeast mixture and the eggs and stir to form a soft dough. Lightly flour a work surface and turn out the dough. Knead until smooth and elastic; form into a ball. Coat a medium bowl with 2 teaspoons of the corn oil. Put in the ball of dough and turn to coat with the oil. Cover

the bowl with a clean towel and let stand at room temperature until doubled in bulk, about 2½ hours.

In a deep fryer or in a wide deep skillet fitted with a frying thermometer and set over medium-high heat, warm the remaining corn oil to between 375° and 400°F. (The deep fryer or skillet should be no more than half full of oil.) Preheat the oven to 250°F. Cover a baking sheet with a layer of paper towels.

Meanwhile, lightly flour a work surface. Punch down the dough, turn it out, and divide it into 12 equal pieces. Form each piece into a ball, then with a rolling pin, roll each ball out into a

6-inch round about ¼ inch thick. With a fingertip, tear a hole about the size of a nickel in the center of each round of dough.

Two at a time, fry the buñuelos in the hot oil, turning them once, until they are puffed, crisp, and golden, about 45 seconds total frying time.

With a slotted spoon, transfer them to the prepared baking sheet pan to drain. Keep the buñuelos warm in the oven until all are fried.

Set one or two buñuelos on each dessert plate. Spoon the syrup evenly over the buñuelos, using it all; serve immediately.

Spiced Currant Syrup

MAKES ABOUT 3¹/₂ CUPS, ENOUGH FOR 12 BUÑUELOS

⌾

INGREDIENTS

1¾ cups water
1 3-inch piece of cinnamon stick
12 whole cloves

1¼ cups honey
⅓ cup dried currants
¼ stick (1 ounce) unsalted butter

In a medium saucepan, combine the water, cinnamon stick, and cloves. Set over medium heat and bring to a boil. Lower the heat, partially cover the pan, and simmer for 15 minutes. Strain the mixture into a second saucepan; discard the spices. Stir in the honey and currants and bring just to a boil. Remove from the heat, stir in the butter, cover, and keep warm.

Michael's Spiced Chocolate Shortbreads

MAKES ABOUT 24 COOKIES

These tender, chocolaty shortbreads, spiced with touches of cinnamon and black pepper, originally appeared in Michael's Cooking for the Weekend. *Serve them with fresh fruit desserts, especially ices and sorbets, or just enjoy them as a treat with a big cup of hot chocolate.*

INGREDIENTS

2 cups unbleached all-purpose flour

⅔ cup lightly packed unsweetened cocoa powder

½ teaspoon ground cinnamon

½ teaspoon finely ground fresh black pepper

½ teaspoon salt

2 sticks (8 ounces) unsalted butter, softened, plus additional butter for the baking sheets

½ cup plus 2 tablespoons sugar, plus additional sugar for coating the cookies

2 teaspoons vanilla extract

Sift the flour, cocoa powder, cinnamon, pepper, and salt together twice onto a piece of waxed paper. In a medium bowl, cream together 2 sticks of the butter and the ½ cup plus 2 tablespoons of sugar until light and fluffy. Mix in the vanilla, then stir in the flour mixture. Stir and then knead the dough (it will be dry and crumbly at first) until it is moist, dark, and supple. Between 2 sheets of waxed paper, roll the dough ¼ inch thick and as evenly as possible. Chill for 30 minutes.

Position a rack in the middle of the oven and preheat to 275°F. Lightly butter 2 baking sheets.

Cut out the cookies with a 2-inch round cutter. Pierce each cookie twice with the tines of a fork.

Spread the sugar for coating on a plate. Lightly press the top of each cookie in the sugar so that the sugar clings to the dough. Arrange the cookies, sugar side up, on the prepared baking sheets, spacing them about 1 inch apart.

Bake the cookies until crisp and firm, about 40 minutes, exchanging the baking sheets on the racks from top to bottom and from front to back at the halfway point. Cool the cookies on the baking sheets on a rack for 5 minutes. Remove the cookies from the baking sheets and cool them completely on a rack. Store the cookies in an airtight container at room temperature. *The cookies can be baked up to 1 week ahead.*

AVOCADOS You'll see two kinds of avocados in the market. One, from Florida, is huge, bright green, and nearly always too bland, stringy, and wet to be of much use. The other, widely grown in California and aggressively marketed by an avocado cooperative, is pear-shaped and smaller, and when it's ripe, the bumpy skin is a glossy black. The several related varieties are usually lumped together under the name of the best-known, Hass. The pale-  green-to-yellow flesh has more flavor, more fat, and more calories, which is why it is so seductive. Avocados, once ripe, quickly become rank and inedible, and since greengrocers would rather that happens on your kitchen counter than in their shop, they are usually found three to five days short of perfection, rendering guacamole and other avocado-based preparations unsuitable for spontaneous cooking. Plan ahead, letting the avocados ripen at home at room temperature, then use them immediately once they're ripe (just softly yielding to gentle thumb pressure), without refrigeration.

BEANS Beans are one of the great staples of the Southwest, providing not only nutrition (in a land where animal protein was originally scarce) but great eating as well. Beans are earthy-tasting but otherwise neutral, and they welcome zesty Southwestern seasonings. Pinto beans are seen most often around El Paso, followed distantly by black beans, garbanzo beans, black-eyed peas, and kidney beans. Dried beans are affordable and keep virtually forever; canned beans are a convenience, though brands vary widely in quality—look for those that remain firm and fresh-tasting after the packing liquid is rinsed off. Soaking dried beans in several changes of water for twenty-four hours or so removes some of

the ingredients that cause gas, and also lets the beans cook more quickly and evenly, but some of the most authentic bean preparations call for unsoaked beans that are cooked until they fall apart. The technique of quick soaking can be used if time is short: Cover unsoaked beans with cold water, bring it to a full boil, then cool them to room temperature in the water. Drain them, add fresh water, and again bring it to a boil; the beans will now cook in about the same time as if they had been soaked overnight.

CHEESES Mexican border cheeses are, in general, mild and somewhat bland, occasionally slightly acidic, fresher and milky-tasting rather than aged and sharp. *Asadero*, often sold in stacks of thin round sheets called tortillas, is sometimes made with *trompillas*, small wild berries that cause milk to coagulate just as animal rennet does. Chihuahua, also called *queso menenito* or Mennonite cheese, was first produced by Mennonite farmers who founded an agricultural community in central Chihuahua. Now produced by other cheese makers as well, it is sold in wedges cut from large wheels. Both cheeses melt easily and string attractively—qualities much sought after by Mexicans, and while some El Paso cheese makers (such as Lincon Dairy) make excellent cheeses, I often cross the border to shop at the Cuauhtemoc Market in Juárez. On the U.S. side, less successful American versions of both cheeses can be found in supermarkets, and cooks here have learned to substitute Monterey Jack or mozzarella (or a combination of the two) and medium-sharp cheddar. Feta cheese is often substituted for queso anejo, a sharper dried cheese that does not melt. Though not very tra-ditional, tangy fresh goat cheeses have a wonderful affinity for border food, and I don't hesitate to experiment with them.

CHILES—FRESH, FROZEN, DRIED, AND CANNED Nothing says more about the spreading acceptance of Southwestern food than the growing interest in chiles of all kinds. America can't seem to get enough of the hot stuff, a state of affairs that makes me very happy indeed. El Pasoans in particular like things fiery (practice and training have a lot to do with chile tolerance), though in my recipes I have tried to give a range in order to accommodate palates that are just getting into shape. It is also worth knowing that stresses of weather, soil, and other imponderables can cause wild fluctuations in the heat level of almost any chile type—such unpredictability being part of the general excitement of cooking with these fiery fruits. Whatever the heat level, chiles come fresh, frozen, dried, or in cans or jars, and each form requires different techniques and has different uses.

The Southwestern United States (as opposed to Mexico proper) cooks with a fairly limited larder of chiles. Fresh chiles are perishable and will turn up only where grocers can be certain of selling them fairly quickly. Among them the small, fat, bright green jalapeños are the most widely available. Hot to very hot, they are good raw or cooked and can be flame-roasted ("parched" as local cooks say) to remove the peel and add a smoky richness. Fresh jalapeños (and all fresh chiles) should be stored unwashed and loosely wrapped in the vegetable keeper of your refrigerator.

Yellow wax or banana peppers (*chiles güero*) are slightly larger than jalapeños and at about the same heat level, and local cooks use them interchangeably, especially in the chunky raw salsa called Grilled Pico de Gallo (page 4).

Serranos are smaller and hotter than jalapeños, with an excellent flavor. When I find them in El Paso (and not all that often), I substitute about one and a half serranos for each jalapeño called for.

The hottest new chile, both in terms of heat level and interest generated, is the small, lantern-shaped habanero. Awesomely hot, this chile ripens from green to red or orange, developing a delicious and almost tropical fruitiness. A native of the Caribbean, it is grown extensively on the Yucatán peninsula, and in Belize;

slightly milder American-grown specimens are becoming more common.

Poblanos, dark green, wedge-shaped chiles, ranging from medium to large and from sweetly *picante* to fairly fiery, are among the most complex-tasting and highly regarded chiles in Mexico. I see them occasionally in El Paso markets and use them fire-roasted, stemmed, seeded, and cut into ¼-inch-long strips (*rajas*) that can be used as an ingredient without further embellishment, or marinated with a little olive oil and crushed garlic and used as a garnish in any number of dishes. Though I usually make chiles rellenos with long green chiles, in Mexico poblanos would be used, and they make magnificent rellenos.

"Long green" is the generic expression I have used in this book for a

type of chile pod commonly called anaheim. In El Paso using that name can get your butt kicked, since we don't think a town whose main claim to fame is Disneyland has any business symbolizing a crop we grow better and more abundantly than anywhere else on the planet. Actually, though there is a local chile crop, most of the growing goes on north of here, in New Mexico's Mesilla Valley (the little town of Hatch is virtually the chile-growing capital of the country and the site of an annual chile festival), and even Texans admit that New Mexico's green chiles are superior to all others. They are cousins of the anaheim, but several (Big Jim and New Mexico No. 6–4, for example) have been improved, crossbred, and otherwise genetically tinkered with (sort of like corn has been in Iowa) to maximize commercial potential. Since they are the major cash crop of New Mexico, as well as the source of plenty of good eating, the effort is clearly worth it.

The seasonal harvest begins to show up around Labor Day (in supermarket aisles stacks of boxes of Velveeta and bins of long green chiles announce the local passion for chile con queso and chiles rellenos) and remains more or less constant until frost sets in. Fresh long green New Mexico chiles are available, in season, from a number of mail-order sources.

For most uses, long green chiles must be roasted, preferably in an open flame, to remove the tough peel and partially cook the flesh. With the beginning of the chile harvest, propane-fired rotary chile roasters show up in supermarket parking lots, and savvy cooks stock up on gunny sacks of long greens while the prices are low. (Purists patiently parch their chiles a few at a time at home, often on a grill over mesquite wood chips, but the convenience of bulk roasting can't be denied. There are also proponents of parching by immersion in deep fat. This may be convenient for restaurants with banks of Fry-O-Lators at the ready, but I find it messy and unpleasant work.)

If you have roasted red peppers for Italian and French preparations, you will be familiar with the general technique. With the tip of a knife, a small steam vent is poked in the stem end of chiles to be used whole, to prevent bursting. In the open flame of a gas burner, or under a preheated electric broiler (less successful), the chiles are turned often until the skin is blistered and lightly charred. The chiles are steamed until cool in a closed paper bag or on a plate covered with a bowl.

For immediate use of the chiles, the burned peel is rubbed off and the chiles are cut into rajas or slit partially open and gently deseeded with a fingertip, to be stuffed and served whole. Charred but otherwise left whole and unpeeled, the chiles can be bagged in plastic and frozen for a year's worth of great eating. When needed they are defrosted and peeled, and even in such chile-centric preparations as chiles rellenos they are excellent. Fresh long greens from elsewhere (even, I suppose, Anaheim) can be had at premium prices at other times of the year, for those who crave rellenos and have neglected to stock their freezers.

Frozen whole and chopped, roasted green chiles are also sold commercially, packed in containers ranging from small tubs to five-pound bags, and can be ordered by mail. Of canned green chiles, however—the sort available in most American supermarkets—there is not much except convenience to be said. Usually steamed rather than roasted, they are mere shadows of the real thing.

Near the end of the season the long green chiles ripen on the plant to bright red, when they are at their most perishable, and, maddeningly, at their sweet, hot best. These don't travel well, but I make the most of them while they last, and those that don't get eaten or frozen get dried, to be turned into long ornamental strings (*ristras*) or sold loose in bulk. Dried long red chiles are soaked to be reconstituted and softened, then they are puréed and sieved, to remove any remaining seeds and hard bits of peel. This is the best way for those who live elsewhere than chile country to savor the taste of red New Mexico chiles, and to this end frozen and jarred versions of red chile paste are also marketed and available by mail order. Long red chiles are also ground into powder and cooks can capture much of the same flavor by seeking out a good, fresh product. The Chimayo area, northeast of Santa Fe, produces what is accepted as the finest chiles for chili powder, and when available it is proudly labeled as such.

Aside from the dried long red chiles with which most local cooks content themselves, a few other dried chiles are occasionally used, usually by cooks with strong ties to Mexico or by adventurers in the new South-western cuisine. Dried poblanos are called anchos and have a rich, deep,

almost chocolaty flavor and a per-fectly balanced heat that make them a fine addition to more complex sauces. Dried chipotles (smoked ja-lapeños) are occasionally used in long-simmered preparations, but they are difficult to soften enough to purée into most dishes. For a hot ac-cent (when your dried red chile pods are on the mild side), add a few chiles *de árbol* or *japonés* or chiltepins to the purée or to a simmering pot. Two or three of any of these small-to-tiny dried red chiles will rapidly raise the heat level of whatever dish uses them.

Most canned chiles, as I have men-tioned, have few uses, although there are two exceptions. Pickled jalapeños (*en escabeche*) retain their crunchy tex-ture and fire and acquire a tart tang that is delicious. Canned chipotles, packed in a vinegary tomato-based sauce (adobo), are brick-red, smoky, and quite addicting (also very hot) and I use them as a seasoning in many sauces or dishes and straight from the can as a condiment. Both pickled jalapeños and chipotles adobado (the latter transferred out of their cans to a glass or plastic container) will keep for a month or longer in the refrigerator.

CHILI POWDER BLEND Chili powder blend is a widely available prepared seasoning mix consisting of one or more kinds of ground red chiles, along with such seasonings as paprika, oregano, cumin, and garlic salt, designed to make the preparation of chili con carne easier and more predictable. I manufacture a chili powder blend and use it increasingly in dishes where a convenient, well-rounded, Southwestern flavor is wanted. The best blends are

not too hot, allowing those who like their Southwestern fare flavorful but mild to use the full amount of chili powder blend called for. (Cutting back won't make a dish less spicy— only less tasty.) Jalapeños, cayenne pepper, crushed red pepper, bottled hot sauce or salsa provide additional fire where wanted, and hot heads know this can be added to the pot by the cook at the stove, or to each bowl by the diner at the table.

CHOCOLATE It is understandable, since the use of chocolate originated in ancient Mexico, that much is still made of it there today. Mexican chocolate, or the kind I find the most useful anyway, comes flavored with ground almonds, cinnamon, and vanilla. It makes delicious hot chocolate, and I am continually exploring new ways of substituting it for ordinary sweetened chocolate in traditional America recipes. It can sometimes be replaced with ordinary sweetened chocolate, augmented with ground cinnamon, extra vanilla and almond extracts to taste, but Ibarra brand—one of the best—is widely available by mail order and is found in some gourmet shops. It comes in hexagonal or octagonal disks or tablets, packaged in several weights. The probability of finding the exact size tablet in the market needed for any given recipe is low, and I usually buy whatever I find and weigh the chocolate, at cooking time, on a kitchen scale.

CHORIZO This highly seasoned pork sausage is found in supermarkets and is most useful in bulk form. (The chorizo of El Paso is not the dry-cured, firm link sausage found in Spanish markets.) The texture is fine and rather loose (there

is a lot of water in the mix), and it is always precooked to render out fat and moisture. To do this, the meat is crumbled in a skillet and sautéed over low heat, stirred often, until lightly browned, about 15 minutes. The cooked chorizo is transferred to absorbent paper to drain. I find it easier to cook a pound or more at a time and then freeze the meat in small amounts, to be defrosted whenever I want it for use in quesadillas, breakfast burritos, and so on.

CILANTRO You either love or hate this pungent herb (also known as fresh coriander and Chinese parsley), but its popularity these days is such that you certainly won't be able to avoid it. (I remember well the outrage of a friend, less than fond of cilantro, who found her otherwise impeccable restaurant order of cheese tortellini generously seasoned with the stuff.) For true appreciation, try an extended visit to Mexico, where cilantro's pungent quality seems the very soul of cookery. It is another perishable ingredient that can be difficult to locate. The fragile leaves should be unwilted (the herb is usually sold in bunches with the roots left on) and the bunch stored in the refrigerator upright in a jar of water, like cut flowers. Drape a plastic bag over the bouquet for extra protection and plan to use the cilantro within a couple of days. Some dishes will call for just the leaves, chopped, while others in which the cilantro is puréed can include the stems.

CORN It can hardly be said too often that corn is the great staple of Southwestern cooking. With beans providing protein balance and chiles

adding the savory emphasis, the bare bones of this great cuisine are revealed and completed. Corn is used in several forms.

Mainly the corn staples we eat are produced from tough field corn (though sugary, tender ears of sweet corn are also increasingly enjoyed). Dried, these corn kernels are called chicos. Slaked in a strong solution of lime and water, the chicos' tough outer skins are loosened and the corn acquires a distinctive flavor. These treated kernels are called posole and can be simmered into soups and stews or to be eaten whole. Posole can be purchased in this form in bags in supermarkets and ordered by mail. Posole that is fully husked and cooked until tender is called hominy and can be purchased canned, packed in water, for use as an easy starch for soups, stews, and side dishes. There is both white and yellow hominy—and I discern no flavor difference.

Slaked corn kernels are also ground into the moist, mealy dough—masa—that is used in fresh corn tortillas, gorditas, tamales, and tamale pie. It is considered that tamales and tortillas made from fresh masa are superior, but there is also a dried treated cornmeal—masa harina de maiz—that can be used as an acceptable alternative. Quaker is the most commonly seen brand, and I have used it in preparations calling for masa with good results. (Fine- or coarse-grain masa can be used interchangeably in my recipes.) Good-quality fresh masa can also be purchased by mail and stored in the freezer until use.

Ordinary American cornmeal is also an El Paso staple, without which I couldn't make corn bread, corn waffles, corn crepes, and so on—not to mention polenta, although that is probably another book! Stone-ground cornmeal retains the germ, and while it is more perishable, it has a fuller corn flavor. Buy small amounts and store the meal in the refrigerator or freezer to extend its shelf life. Preferences for white or yellow cornmeal are regional; I have noticed no flavor difference. Generally, since the golden color is more attractive and more "corny," I cook with yellow meal.

Except, of course, when I cook with blue cornmeal. You may be tired of hearing about this Southwestern staple, but don't dismiss it as trendy; Indians have been grinding and cooking with the indigenous blue corn almost as long as there has been cultivation in the Americas.

Not truly blue (more a purple-gray), the corn is not easy to grow, must be hand-cultivated, is more perishable—and yet for all that is gaining popularity for one simple reason: It tastes great. The meal is tricky to make into tortillas (I don't try, preferring to order mine by mail), but it can be used in corn bread and corn cake recipes, and packaged blue corn tostaditas are increasingly available. The dramatic color is just right in Southwestern cookery, and the intense corn flavor, essential.

Sweet corn has been hybridized to retain its tenderness and natural sugars, and the old advice that the water should be boiling before the corn is even picked is no longer sound. Such supersweet hybrids as Kandy Korn and Honey and Cream are sweet days after picking and need only a few minutes of simmering in water or a quick turn over hot coals to be ready to eat, anointed with butter, lime juice, and a generous shake of chili powder.

CUMIN Tex-Mex fever has increased the use of this spice many-fold over the last ten years, and for many if it isn't heavily dosed with cumin it doesn't taste authentic. Mexicans don't apply cumin with the same gusto Americans do, and in El Paso we don't use as much of it as folks in central Texas. Still, it's a staple spice I wouldn't want to cook without. For a nuttier, richer flavor, toast the seeds, stirring them over low heat in a small heavy ungreased skillet for about 7 minutes, or until they are a rich brown. Toast a quantity (small amounts tend to scorch), store them in a tightly covered jar, and grind them with a mortar and pestle or in a spice mill just before you use them.

OREGANO There is a great deal of confusion surrounding the use of the term *Mexican oregano*, although it appears that the one most commonly sold under that name is actually of the verbena family. When I think of Mexican oregano I think of an especially sharp, potent, and slightly resinous flavor, and now that at least one national spice company is packing Mexican oregano for supermarkets, you can experience that taste for yourself. I prefer Mexican oregano for use in all the recipes in this book, although you can substitute ordinary oregano or a combination of oregano and marjoram if you wish. Be sure to finely crumble the dried herb between your fingers to release as much flavor as possible.

SALSA In 1991, sales of bottled salsa in the United States surpassed those of bottled ketchup for the first time, a remarkably significant event. Based upon the easily concocted fresh table sauces of authentic Mexican cooking (see Part One for some typical recipes), these mixtures are simmered prior to canning, are usually tomato-based, and can range from fiery to mild, chunky to thin, excellent to awful. With its victory over ketchup, salsa has become the mustard of the nineties, serving as a convenient, all-purpose flavor-boosting condiment with multiple uses. As a salsa maker I couldn't be happier, and as a cook I've come to rely on the quick and easy bursts of flavor and color that bottled salsas add to even everyday food. One or more jars, of my brand or another, should be in the pantry of every cook interested in Southwestern food. If salsa is to be combined with several ingredients, select the hottest possible one you can find, in order that the fire remain evident in the finished dish.

TOMATILLOS These so-called Mexican green tomatoes are relatives of the ground cherry and the Cape gooseberry. The firm, round, green fruits, about the size of a large cherry tomato, are enclosed in crackly, paperlike husks which are removed before cooking. Commonly used raw or briefly cooked in salsas and sauces, the tomatillo has a tart, sour, berry flavor that does not take well to canning. Fortunately, fresh tomatillos keep well. Buy them, ideally firm and free of mold, and store them on a paper-towel-lined plate, unwrapped, in the refrigerator, where they will last for up to 3 weeks.

TOMATOES The tomatoes of Mexico are wonderful—medium-size, juicy, and sweet/tart, and they make everything prepared with them especially delicious. I supplement the supply that appears in my supermarket by planting a goodly stand of tomatoes in my own garden, just in case. One can never have too many ripe tomatoes, whether cooking Southwestern or another cuisine. Away from the border, you are advised to seek out similar tomatoes (or to put in your own garden), and to spare no expense if you expect your salsas and other Southwestern fare to have authentic flavor and color.

Of course the turns of the seasons sometimes leave me relying on canned tomatoes, which are preferable to bland, mealy, and pale pink winter tomatoes in chili, soups, stews, and so on. I use plum tomatoes, preferably imported from Italy, and canned crushed tomatoes with

added purée, depending on the recipe. Canned tomatoes should not be used in uncooked salsas—they are too sweet and soft.

TORTILLAS Even Diana Kennedy admits to being unable to make fresh corn tortillas by hand, needing a tortilla press to make things turn out right. I take that one step further and say that except for an afternoon spent experiencing the process firsthand in the kitchen of an excellent local cook, I don't make tortillas at all. El Paso (and to some extent the rest of the country) has reasonable—sometimes excellent—corn and flour tortillas in the supermarkets, and rather than cook no Southwestern food, I recommend you use them. Like the difference between good and great bread, the differences between tortillas are apparent but not usually fatal to the enjoyment of the meal.

Tortillas should be warmed, either to make them flexible and easier to handle or just to make them fresher-tasting and more palatable. There are terra-cotta tortilla warmers around, but I prefer to wrap tortillas in foil and heat them until steamy in a 300°F oven, 12 to 15 minutes. Put up several small packets if you will want tortillas throughout the meal and stagger the heating times. A microwave works well initially, but tortillas warmed in one turn almost immediately into stiff cardboard. Flour tortillas can also be warmed (and lightly toasted) on an ungreased griddle or over a charcoal or gas grill. Corn tortillas freeze well; flour tortillas do not.

sources for southwestern ingredients and grilling and smoking equipment and supplies

ingredients

THE EL PASO CHILE COMPANY

909 Texas Avenue

El Paso, TX 79901

800-274-7468 or 915-544-3434

Commercial barbecue sauces, salsas, chili powders, chile ristras, dried chiles, jalapeño jelly, condiments, snacks, gifts, Mexican chocolate, chipotles, moles, basic ingredients, autographed cookbooks

THE CHILE SHOP, INC.

109 East Water Street

Santa Fe, NM 87501

505-983-6080

Commercial barbecue sauces, salsas, Chimayo and Dixon chili powders, chile ristras, dried chiles, jalapeño jelly, condiments, snacks, gifts, chipotles, basic ingredients

D'ARTAGNAN

399-419 St. Paul Avenue

Jersey City, NJ 07306

800-327-8246 or 201-792-0748

Moulard ducks, farm-raised venison, squab, wild turkey, and other game meats

TEXAS WILD GAME COOPERATIVE

P.O. Box 530

Ingram, TX 78025

512-367-5875

Venison and other game meats

MO-HOTTA-MO-BETTA CATALOG

P.O. Box 4136

San Luis Obispo, CA 93403

800-462-3220

805-544-4051 FAX 805-545-8389

Salsas, sauces, spices, dried chiles, seeds, offbeat marinades, barbeue sauces, and hot stuff

THE GOURMET GALLERY CATALOG

320 North Highway 89A

Sedona, AZ 86336

800-888-3484

602-282-2682 FAX 602-282-2682

Chiles, dried peppers, pure ground and blended chile powder, Southwest herbs, spices, seeds, marinades, and spicy condiments

equipment and supplies

BELSON MANUFACTURING CO., INC.

P.O. Box 207

North Aurora, IL 60542

800-323-5664

Commercial-grade portable grilling equipment

BRINKMANN CORPORATION

4215 McEwen Road

Dallas, TX 75244

800-527-0717 or 214-387-4939

Home water smokers and accessories

GRILL LOVER'S CATALOG

P.O. Box 1300

Columbus, GA 31902

800-241-8981

Home grills, smokers, commercial barbecue sauces, salsas, wood chips and chunks, accessories, and cookbooks

NATURE-GLO

P.O. Box 1669

Brentwood, TN 37027

800-251-2076

Deluxe wood-burning grills, smokers, and wood chunks

PITT'S AND SPITT'S, INC.

14221 Eastex Freeway

Houston, TX 77032

800-521-2947 or 713-987-3474

Deluxe outdoor smoking and grilling equipment, accessories, and cookbooks